FINANCING INVESTMENT IN TIMES OF HIGH PUBLIC DEBT

Financing Investment in Times of High Public Debt

2023 European Public Investment Outlook

Edited by Floriana Cerniglia, Francesco Saraceno, and Andrew Watt

OpenBook Publishers

https://www.openbookpublishers.com

ISBN Paperback: 978-1-80511-200-6
ISBN Hardback: 978-1-80511-201-3
ISBN PDF: 978-1-80511-202-0
ISBN ebook (EPUB): 978-1-80511-203-7
ISBN XML: 978-1-80511-204-4
ISBN HTML: 978-1-80511-205-1

DOI: 10.11647/OBP.0386

Cover image: Photo by Mika Baumeister on Unsplash
Cover design: Jeevanjot Kaur Nagpal

Contents

Acknowledgements

The *Outlook* is the result of a joint effort by several economists belonging to a wide range of academic institutions and policy institutes; each writes in his or her personal capacity.

The work was coordinated by Floriana Cerniglia, Francesco Saraceno, and Andrew Watt with logistical and financial support by CRANEC–Centro di ricerche in analisi economica e sviluppo economico internazionale, Università Cattolica del Sacro Cuore–Milano; Fondazione Astrid, Rome; OFCE–SciencesPo, Paris; and IMK–Macroeconomic Policy Institute–Dusseldorf.

The authors are affiliated to the following institutions:

- Austrian Institute of Economic Research–WIFO (Austria)

- Caisse des Dépôts et Consignations–CDC (France)

- CRANEC, Centro di ricerche in analisi economica e sviluppo economico Internazionale, Università Cattolica del Sacro Cuore (Milan, Italy)

- European Commission

- European Investment Bank–EIB (Luxembourg)

- European Long Term Investor Association–ELTIA (Bruxelles, Belgium)

- Fondazione Astrid (Rome, Italy)

- Institute of Economics and EMbeDS, Scuola Superiore Sant'Anna (Pisa, Italy)

- Institute of Economics, Scuola Superiore Sant'Anna in Pisa (Italy)

- Instituto Valenciano de Investigaciones Económicas–IVIE (Spain)

- Luiss Institute for European Analysis and Policy, Università Luiss Guido Carli (Rome, Italy)

- Macroeconomic Policy Institute–IMK (Dusseldorf, Germany)

- Nottingham University Business School, Jubilee Campus (UK)

- Observatoire français des conjonctures économiques, OFCE-SciencesPo (Paris, France)

- SOAS, University of London (UK)

- Tommaso Padoa–Schioppa Chair on economic and monetary integration, European University Institute (Fiesole, Italy)
- Unicredit S.p.A
- University of Greenwich (UK)
- Università Milano Bicocca (Italy)
- Universitat de València (Spain)
- Vienna Institute for International Economic Studies–WIWW (Austria)

As this *European Public Investment Outlook* goes to print, we want to express our gratitude to those who made our work possible: first and foremost, to all the chapter authors who enthusiastically provided this instalment with high-quality contributions; they also simplified our job as editors by (generally!) respecting the deadlines and responding to our queries. The result is a collective volume that has a consistent message throughout.

We also sincerely thank Alberto Quadrio Curzio, President of CRANEC; Franco Bassanini, President of Fondazione Astrid; Xavier Ragot, President of OFCE-Sciences Po; and Sebastian Dullien, Director of IMK, for their constant support and encouragement. Their help was essential in securing financial and logistical support and, even more importantly, in putting the issue of public investment at the centre of their respective institutions' scientific projects.

Our thanks also go to Giovanni Barbieri from CRANEC for his efficient and painstaking and patient editing of this fourth instalment of the *European Public Investment Outlook*. Thanks are also due to Micaela Tavasani from CRANEC for her proofreading. Last but not least, our gratitude goes to Alessandra Tosi, of Open Book Publishers, who smoothly managed the refereeing process and who believed in and supported our project since it began in 2020. The editorial team at Open Book Publishers once again moved swiftly and efficiently to ensure a timely publication of the *Outlook*.

Floriana Cerniglia
Francesco Saraceno
Andrew Watt

Preface

Franco Bassanini, Sebastian Dullien,
Alberto Quadrio Curzio, and Xavier Ragot

Financing Public Investment at Times of High Debt is the fourth volume of the yearly series on European Public Investment that is becoming a reference in the European debate on macroeconomic and structural policies for growth and sustainability. Like the previous instalments, the 2023 *Outlook* brings together an impressive roster of contributors coordinated by Floriana Cerniglia, Francesco Saraceno, and Andrew Watt, consolidating the cooperation of our institutions and continuing in the creation of a network of European researchers working on the topic of public investment.

The macroeconomic and institutional environment are ever changing: the first *European Public Investment Outlook* in 2020 was published while the world economy was in an unprecedented economic and sanitary crisis and in deflation, while the current volume appears at a moment of high inflation and increasing interest rates. Yet, as different as the macroeconomic conditions are, the need for public policies to support growth and structural transformation, notably public-investment and industrial policies, remains. Indeed, it is growing, due to the need to tackle climate change through a rapid and radical transformation of production and consumption models, and put in place the public policies required to mitigate the social impact of these transformations.

We commend the effort by the editors of the *Outlook* to renew every year the collaboration between our institutions and to keep the attention of policymakers and economists on the topic of public investment, especially at a juncture when the temptation of fiscal consolidation is strong.

In this regard, how to reconcile the sustainability of public finances (in a season of high inflation, low growth, and no-longer-accommodating monetary policies) with the enhanced need to finance old and new global and/or European public goods is a crucial question. In many countries, the increase in public debt — due to the measures adopted to deal with the pandemic and with the increase in energy prices and to mitigate their impact on businesses and families — are motivating a pure and simple return to restrictive fiscal policies. But the need to finance the huge investments required to face climate change and to overcome the challenges and seize the opportunities of the environmental transition and of the digital transformation is an imperative that cannot be postponed. So, too, are the financing of the public policies needed to deal with the aging population, of the investments in research and technologies required to ensure international technological competitiveness, and of the investments in defence and security made necessary by the worsening of international relations. Rather than merely returning to restrictive fiscal policies, it is necessary to explore and develop more sophisticated solutions and tools, which this book begins to outline.

The challenge concerns Europe in a special way. Champion in the production of rules (and often of good rules), the European Union must now equip itself with the necessary tools to face the enhanced need to produce essential European public goods (EPGs). The pandemic has served as a stark reminder of the significance of robust and cooperative health systems that transcend national boundaries. Simultaneously, global events such as the Ukraine crisis and the Middle-East conflict have emphasized the urgent need for the development of a unified EU defence policy. In a world characterized by growing interconnectivity, heightened vulnerability, and the prevalence of externalities and spillover effects, there is an escalating demand for EPGs, extending beyond traditional domains like security to encompass research and development, climate-change mitigation, digital infrastructure, the supply of critical raw materials and components, and more.

While the demand for EPGs is evident, their supply and financing continue to be a complex issue. With Next Generation EU and SURE, the European Union has opened, albeit temporarily and exceptionally, the path to financing EPGs through common resources raised on the financial markets through the issuance of European sovereign bonds. However, political resistance to providing the European Union with permanent financing instruments remains strong. But the succession of crises and emergencies cannot fail to produce a weakening of this resistance. Sooner or later (and it would obviously be better sooner than later), the need to face increasingly challenging and dramatic crises, which European states are not able to overcome with national resources, will require a change in the European policy mix with the strengthening of European central fiscal capacity and with new fiscal rules aimed at underpinning investment and the sustainability of national public finances.

Introduction

Floriana Cerniglia, Francesco Saraceno and Andrew Watt

When the first *European Public Investment Outlook* (Cerniglia and Saraceno 2020) was published, in the summer of 2020, the world economy was in the middle of an unprecedented health and ensuing economic crisis. The policy response to the crisis was bold in all EU countries and involved a significant fiscal effort. Central banks accommodated this effort, in EU countries as well as in the USA, with massive purchases of bonds: the EU's 1.8-trillion-euro Pandemic Emergency Purchase Programme (PEPP) ran from 2020 to the spring of 2022. This allowed interest rates to be kept low and shielded EU governments from possible market pressures in the face of a large increase in public debt (see Figure 0.1).

The macroeconomic environment changed drastically in the Summer of 2021, not only with respect to the pandemic, but also with respect to the previous decade. The economy rebounded virtually everywhere, and the disarticulation of the supply side led to inflationary pressures, most notably in the energy and food sectors. This pressure was later compounded by geopolitical tensions and by the invasion of Ukraine. As inflation picked up, the attitude of central banks changed, and the policy stance turned restrictive. Both the US Federal Reserve and the ECB engaged in a long series of rate increases (the end of which is not yet certain at the time of writing in November 2023) and started shrinking their balance sheets. In this new macroeconomic environment — as sovereign interest rates increase, while economic growth slows and the risk of an economic downturn increases — the issue of public-debt sustainability has come to the fore.

https://doi.org/10.11647/OBP.0386.00

Interest as % of GDP

■ 1999-2008 ■ 2009-2014 ■ 2015-2019 ■ 2020-2022 ■ 2023-2024 (F)

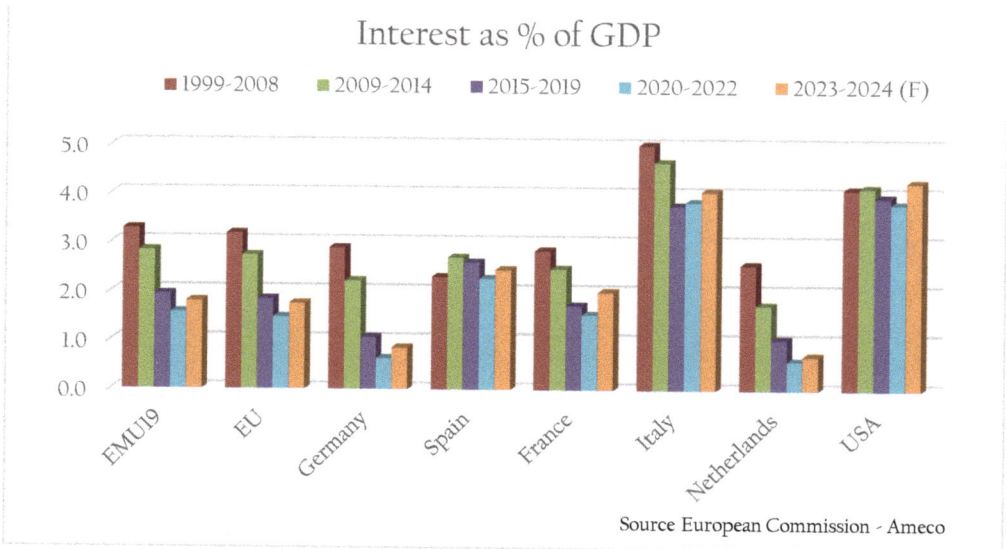

Source European Commission - Ameco

Debt as % of GDP

■ 1999-2008 ■ 2009-2014 ■ 2015-2019 ■ 2020-2022 ■ 2023-2024 (F)

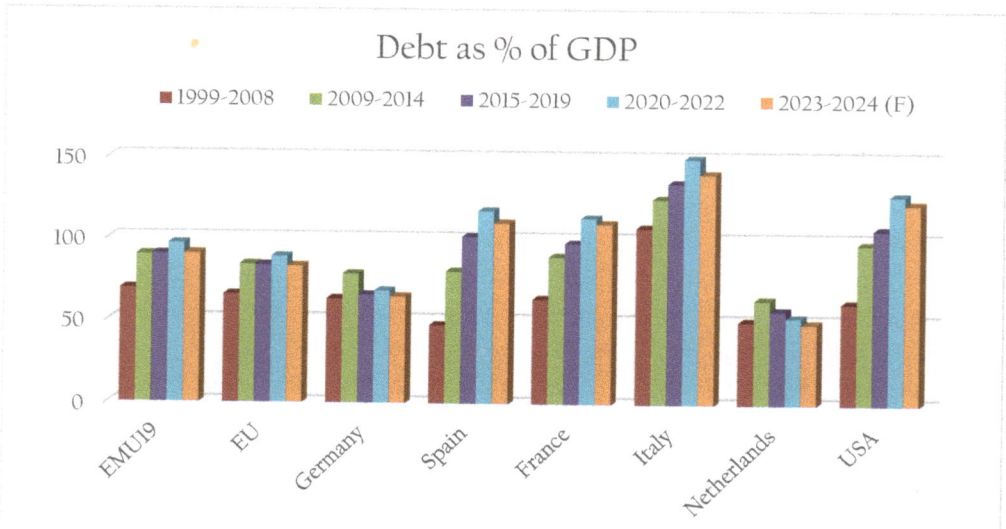

Fig. 0.1 Government Interest Payment and Debt.
Source: European Commission–Ameco.

In the meantime, the legacy of the many crises of the past fifteen years is one of a renewed attention to the role of government. The 'New Consensus' paradigm (Saraceno 2022a) that had dominated since the 1980s was challenged by the Global Financial Crisis of 2007–2009, prompting a wide-ranging process of 'Rethinking macroeconomics' (to cite the title of a series of conferences held at the IMF in the early 2010s and organised by the then Chief economist Olivier Blanchard; see, for example, Blanchard 2016). This process of rethinking is still in progress, and it is quite unclear what will emerge as a new consensus in economics, if one will emerge at all. Nevertheless, whatever the result of the current debate will be, it is highly unlikely that we will return to the pre-2008 consensus of a limited role for public policies in regulating and shaping the economy. The multiple crises that hit the world economy in the past fifteen years were due to a mix of endogenous (the financial crisis), self-inflicted and policy-induced (the sovereign-debt crisis), and exogenous (the pandemic) causes. All highlighted the need for a renewed role of the government in the economy and for a reassessment of the policy mix. Whether that mix calls for a classic Keynesian business-cycle stabilization, as in 2008, for public investment and industrial policies to favour and steer the ecological and digital transitions, for the provision of global public goods such as health and education, or for a coordinated approach by fiscal and monetary policies to fight inflation (or, indeed, secular stagnation) is secondary: few economists today would argue, as many would have done before 2008, that we should constrain public policies and let markets tackle the contingent and structural challenges that our societies repeatedly confront. Thus, advanced economies face a dilemma: how to reconcile the now widely accepted need to finance the public policies that are necessary to manage an increasingly complex environment in which structural, contingent, and geopolitical factors are inextricably linked, with the objective of public-debt sustainability?

After the pandemic, it seemed that policy makers in most European countries had decided on a clear priority in this dilemma: rethink fiscal policies to guarantee the fiscal space necessary to pursue all the pressing policy objectives, while guaranteeing the sustainability of public finances. In other words, sustainability was a constraint on the objective of granting policy-makers the tools to implement proactive policies. The return of inflation in 2021–2022, though, marked a partial revival of the pre-2008 emphasis on limiting the role of government. This was reflected in the return of long-discredited monetarist ideas (Saraceno 2023) but has also resulted in a shift of focus in the debate on policy and sustainability. At least in Europe, against the background of higher interest rates, the main preoccupation in many policy quarters is returning to the question of how to curb public debt. Sustainability, instead of being a constraint in the attempt to create fiscal space, has returned to being the main objective of policy-makers.

This shift of narrative and of priorities can be seen clearly in the discussion on the reform of EU fiscal rules. In November 2022, the European Commission (2022) issued a Communication on the reform of the Stability Pact. This centred around a medium-term perspective in assessing sustainability and on setting out country-specific trajectories that granted some policy space while ensuring that the policies implemented would not threaten sustainable public finances. Most notably, it enabled Member States to argue for fiscal space for specific public investment projects that could convincingly show a positive longer-run impact on debt-servicing capacity. In the few months that passed between the Communication and the actual proposal, that was put on the table in April 2023 (European Commission 2023), the approach changed substantially. Curbing debt was reinstated as a primary objective of the fiscal rules: the amendment to the old Stability Pact originally proposed by the Commission was meant to avoid excessively curbing governments and to limit, at least to some extent, pro-cyclical fiscal policies. The issue of creating the fiscal space, which the current Stability Pact does not provide for, has been downgraded in the latest proposal and is now ancillary with respect to the debt-reduction objective.

This is the background against which this *European Public Investment Outlook*, the fourth of a series, tackles the issue of financing public expenditure and, particularly, public investment in European countries. The authors who contributed to this *Outlook* may differ somewhat on aspects of fiscal policy and on the fiscal rules that the EU should adopt to replace the Stability Pact. Yet, they all share the conviction that, in the coming years, public investment should be not only protected but expanded and deployed, together with other instruments, to facilitate and steer the ecological and digital transition. We hope that this volume of the *European Public Investment Outlook* will contribute to rebalancing the debate on sustainability and fiscal space.

Fiscal sustainability can never be overlooked when designing public policies for the simple reason that the effectiveness of such policies would be hampered if they were to lead to the loss of confidence in the government's credibility and to turbulence in sovereign debt markets. This is especially true in a complex institutional environment like the eurozone, which requires member countries to coordinate twenty fiscal policies among themselves and with the common monetary policy. Yet, we believe that the issue of sustainability should not be dramatized in the current situation and that it should not overshadow the more important issue of how to ensure that fiscal space is created to respond to the challenges of the time. There are, in fact, several reasons why we believe that debt reduction is given too much emphasis in current European debate.

First, although monetary tightening and inflation have caused interest rates to go up quite substantially and caused spreads to reopen between sovereign-debt yields, nominal growth has also increased, because of inflation. The fact that current real interest rates are actually lower than before does not mean much going forward (nominal interest rates will likely not decrease much as inflation returns to normal). Nevertheless, most countries took advantage of low rates in the past few years to increase the average maturity of their debt, and interest payments, as a percentage of GDP, are forecast by the Commission to barely move in the short run, even for more problematic countries like Italy (see Figure 0.1 and Chapter 1). In most of the Eurozone, then, the interest bill will remain smaller, as a percentage of GDP, than had been the case in earlier years and also than in the USA.

Second, while the European Central Bank (ECB) is currently focused on its core business of fighting inflation, it is unlikely to revert to its former non-interventionist attitude regarding spreads and sovereign debt-market instability. Since the 'whatever it takes' speech by then-ECB President Mario Draghi in 2012 and the subsequent launch of the Outright Monetary Transactions (OMT) program, the ECB has implicitly targeted spreads, de facto acting as a lender of last resort. In mid-2022, the Transmission Protection Instrument (TPI) was launched explicitly to permit — in principle, unlimited — purchases of bonds from countries experiencing a deterioration in financing conditions not warranted by country-specific fundamentals. Because turbulent times are (unfortunately) bound to continue, it is inconceivable that the ECB will readopt a non-interventionist stance. Of course, this cannot be taken as a green light to embark on irresponsible fiscal policies: first, the OMT comes with heavy conditionality; second, the TPI, with its caveat about country-specific fundamentals, sends the clear message that only countries with sound fiscal policies can be protected. With these instruments, however, Euro-area member states can now count on a Lender of Last Resort, even if this function is more conditional than in countries such as Japan and the USA. With it in place, they are less likely to face speculative attacks and much better equipped to fight them if they do occur.

Last but not least, high interest rates may not be here to stay, as many currently believe. The forces behind the secular downward trend of neutral interest rates (demographics, inequality, high debt and the ensuing increase in the propensity to save, etc.) have been temporarily muted by the sudden inflation burst that began in 2021. When the certainly-persistent-but-still-temporary drivers of inflation subside, there are reasons to believe that secular stagnation and a chronic tendency to excess savings may start to haunt monetary authorities again (Blanchard 2023; Saraceno 2022b). In any case, the restrictive impact on activity of the interest rate hikes already implemented are still feeding through the economy. A slowing economy will constrain the ability of both price- and wage-setters to seek higher nominal incomes, and policy rates will be cut again.

Previous instalments of this series (Cerniglia et al. 2021; Cerniglia and Saraceno 2020, 2022) highlighted the deterioration of the public capital stock of EU countries, even the richer ones. Many of the dozens of authors involved in the chapters of the previous *Outlook*s emphasized the need, in today's world, to steer away from a purely accounting definition of public investment in favour of a notion encompassing both tangible and intangible capital, such as social capital. These themes emerge in the current *Outlook* as well, in chapters written by academics, policy makers, economists at think tanks and at international organisations, and practitioners. This installment has a specific focus on the issue of financing. Unfortunately, the currently predominant sentiment of EU policy-makers on debt and interest rates is quite unaligned with our assessment: it is likely that debt-reduction will remain one of their primary preoccupations in the near future. How to finance public policies, most notably investment, in an environment of tight budget-constraints, therefore, will be central in the next few years. This question is addressed in the chapters of the first part of this *Outlook* that take into account selected countries' particular challenges and options. The chapters of the second part, taken together, evoke multiple sources of financing of public investment, including the mobilizing of national public resources but also public investment banks, European agencies, monetary policies, financial markets, the EU budget, and so on. It is vital that the European policy and institutional framework both permit and encourage national-level public investment and make adequate provisions for financing European public goods at EU level. Decisive for the former is an investment-friendly reform of the fiscal rules. At the European level, a robust, substantial, and permanent investment facility is needed in view of the urgent challenges relating to decarbonization and of the imminent end to the Next Generation EU's Recovery and Resilience Facility (RRF; Watt 2022).

Financing Investment in Times of High Public Debt, like its predecessors, is divided in two parts. Part I offers an analysis of the state of the art of public investment in Europe (Chapter 1) followed by individual country reports on the European Union's four largest economies: France in Chapter 2, Germany in Chapter 3, Italy in Chapter 4, and Spain in Chapter 5. These chapters share a common focus on comprehending the scope for maintaining and expanding public investment in the coming years while considering the difficulty of financing it at a time when debt-to-GDP ratios are increasing in some countries due to higher interest rates and low growth, and, in some cases, the foreseeable end of finance through the RRF. As in the preceding *Outlook* reports, the country-specific chapters, when relevant, update the information presented in earlier instalments. Additionally, some chapters discuss impact and policy responses related to the economic-recovery plans deployed to address challenges stemming from the COVID-19 pandemic and further compounded by geopolitical tensions, low growth, high inflation, and high interest rates.

Chapter 1, by A. Brasili, A. Kolev, D. Revoltella, J. Schanz, and A. Tueske, assesses the role of public investment within the EU's response to both short-term and long-term challenges such as managing inflation, ensuring financial stability, effecting fiscal consolidation, coping with energy- and food-price shocks, and transitioning towards climate neutrality while maintaining energy security. It provides a comprehensive depiction of the dynamics of public investment in Europe in 2022, encompassing planned investment for the current fiscal year and the ongoing implementation efforts of the RRF along with the associated emerging challenges and hurdles. The analysis draws on data from a multitude of sources, including Eurostat, the *Stability and Convergence Programmes* of Member States, the implementation progress of the RRF, and data from the TED-procurement database.[1]

In Chapter 2, M. Plane and F. Saraceno provide a historical overview and describe the different phases, from the 1940s until today, of public investment in France. An assessment is made of the pace of public-capital accumulation since the COVID-19 pandemic (it is increasing slowly). Two main findings emerge from an analysis of stocks

---

1   TED (Tenders Electronic Daily) is the online version of the 'Supplement to the Official Journal of the EU', dedicated to European public procurement.

and flows: first, public investment and the stock of capital have been largely affected by the macroeconomic cycle; second, the capital stock is still significant (and larger than in other countries). General government net wealth remains positive, although it has decreased significantly since 2008. A large gap exists between the central government and local authorities in terms of savings and investment financing. The authors also discuss how public investment is financed in France and whether the current level of public debt is sustainable.

Chapter 3, by K. Rietzler, A. Watt, and E. Juergens, assesses public investment in Germany. After more than a decade of weak public investment, Germany has accumulated a significant backlog. The additional public investment required over the next decade is estimated to be in the range of €600–800bn, equivalent to 1.6–2.1% of GDP. The current fiscal situation had appeared as relatively favourable from a financing perspective. However the ruling by the constitutional court, just as the publication was going to press, that government plans to finance investment through borrowing, evading the debt brake, are unconstitutional has cast this into serious doubt. There is a serious risk that policy, far from expanding investment, will begin to tighten as early as 2024. Germany lacks the political will to remedy the situation which the debt brake and the court ruling have created and provide the needed boost in public investment, whether through higher borrowing or by raising taxes.

Chapter 4, by G. Barbieri, F. Cerniglia, and E. Dia, provides the country report on Italy with an analysis of the role of the Italian National Recovery and Resilience Plan (NRRP) in boosting public investment up to and beyond 2026. Italy's NRRP, with more than €235bn available for investments and reforms makes it one of the most remarkable modernization initiatives in the last seventy years. The impact of the NRRP is assessed and specific implementation challenges are highlighted, some of which have been caused by factors such as fragmented governance, a lack of effective monitoring, and compliance issues. Overcoming these difficulties is crucial for continuing to receive disbursements from the Commission. The effectiveness of its governance is also examined. Moreover, the authors note that the question remains of how to ensure a positive capital spending trajectory (especially after 2026) in compliance with the new rules set out in the Stability and Growth Pact; only by increasing public investment can the debt-to-GDP ratio decrease at a faster pace.

Chapter 5, by F. Pérez and E. Benages, looks into public investment, the deficit and public debt in Spain from 1995 to 2022. Spain's public investment during that time has had a very erratic trajectory, with some years seeing large capital accumulation and others with negative net investment The sustainability of the pace of investment has been challenged by expenditure policies that are procyclical rather than having a stabilizing effect.

These and other lessons learned should be incorporated into the revision of the EU's economic governance framework to improve the compatibility between the fiscal rules and the increased investment envisaged by the Recovery and Resilience Facility.

Part II of the *2023 European Public Investment Outlook* covers several themes that together address the European Union's available policy options and the toolkit of resources and instruments at its disposal to raise its game as regards public investment. EU policies and investment financing are analysed from the perspective of fragmentation and secular stagnation (Chapter 6), tools to help foster stability, like national promotional banks (Chapter 7), upgrading EU public goods by also introducing a permanent central fiscal capacity (Chapter 11), and options for a permanent EU sovereign fund (Chapter 12). Three chapters have a green focus, acting as natural bridges to the 2022 instalment of *The European Public Investment Outlook — Greening Europe*. These chapters focus on including green public expenditures in the EU budget and fiscal framework (Chapter 8), the role of monetary and financial policies in financing climate investments in the EU (Chapter 9), and a set of measures to deal with the crisis of climate change and restore fiscal progressivity (Chapter 10).

In Chapter 6, P. C. Padoan makes the case that the EU has been impacted by multiple crises due to economic and geopolitical factors. The crises have left scarring effects and may lead to fragmentation with serious and permanent consequences. The author analyses the EU's primary response strategy: Next Generation EU and the associated Recovery and Resilience Facility. This recovery instrument, based on public investment and structural reforms, can be an effective policy tool, provided it combines public investment and structural reforms and allows for adequate time to complete the reform cycle. Its efficacy must be evaluated in the context of a new policy mix designed to solve the multiple crises plaguing the EU's institutional structure.

The role of National Promotional Banks and Institutions (NPBIs) is addressed in Chapter 7, by L. Zylberberg, who specifically studies their impact within the EU context. NPBIs experienced a paradigm shift with the great financial crisis of 2008–2009, which was further reinforced by the COVID-19 pandemic and the Ukraine crisis. The Juncker Plan shed light on the existing investment gaps across Europe and demonstrated that a dynamic European policy was possible. Thanks to the InvestEU programme, European actors such as the EIB Group or national actors via NPBIs and Financial Institutions have thrived in their specific role of fostering essential long-term investments. The author underlines the necessity of developing practical accounting rules that integrate both positive and negative externalities.

A. Pekanov and M. Schratzenstaller, in Chapter 8, discuss two paths to foster increased green public investment in the EU: through possible amendments to the current EU fiscal framework and through funding from the EU budget. Since the Commission's proposal (November 2022) regarding orientations for a reform of the

EU governance framework widens the leeway for debt-financed public investment but does not sufficiently consider existing green public investment needs, several options are considered to ensure a level of green public investment which—together with private resources—could close the existing gaps in green investment. To this end, the EU budget needs to be reoriented towards measures that are effective in achieving decarbonisation and which cannot sensibly be performed at national level, such as the Connecting Europe Facility.

Chapter 9, by Y. Dafermos and M. Nikolaidi, delves into the unprecedented transformation of the EU fiscal, industrial, trade, and regulatory policy frameworks that are necessary to address the climate crisis. The authors advocate that this transformation requires the alignment of EU monetary and financial policies with environmentally sustainable practices. A set of tools are presented that central banks, financial regulators, and financial supervisors can employ to advance the EU decarbonisation and climate-resilience targets.

Fiscal reform is the focus of Chapter 10, by D. Guzzardi, E. Palagi, T. Faccio, and A. Roventini, who probe how to formulate an adequate policy response to restore fiscal progressivity, which is seen as fundamental in addressing the current climate challenge. They advocate closing the tax-rate gaps between income levels to ensure that the green transition, which demands significant financial resources, occurs in a more equitable manner. The authors thus propose a mix of EU fiscal policies, from which the resulting additional resources can be used to promote climate mitigation and adaptation policies. This approach will lower inequality and help move EU economies toward inclusive and sustainable growth.

The importance of including European Public Goods (EPGs) in the ongoing debate on EU reforms is emphasized in Chapter 11, written by M. Buti, A. Coloccia, and M. Messori. They argue that EPGs are a promising step toward a more effective economic union, which needs a permanent fiscal capacity. The discussion of EPGs, they believe, should take into account a number of factors, including the convergence of economic, institutional, and political coherence on the green, digital, and social transition. It should also address the supply of critical raw materials, health, security, and defence.

Another tool that can be used to address the climate challenge and promote economic stability is proposed in Chapter 12. P. Heimberger and A. Lichtenberger argue in favour of a new, permanent EU fiscal capacity using the Recovery and Resilience Fund (RRF) as an operational blueprint. They suggest that, overall, the current tools available to the EU as well as the new ones proposed fall short of providing a realistic vision of financing the required public investment.

Overall, the contributions in *Financing Investment in Times of High Public Debt* focus, from different angles, on the urgent need for a coherent EU framework and fiscal capacity that better facilitates the huge investment needed to ensure macroeconomic growth while addressing the implementation challenges of the green transition. The EU has been slow to establish an appropriate response through its frameworks and existing tool kit and offer only piecemeal solutions. Once again, 'political' reticence toward greater joint-public investment is a theme running through this *Outlook*, bringing to the fore the need for more resources to finance public investments as well as governance reforms that are necessary to make progress.

We hope that *Financing Investment in Times of High Public Debt*, like its previous instalments, will continue to serve as a contribution to the ongoing public policy debate, a discourse that, as clearly stated in all the volume's chapters, is destined to continue to play a pivotal role beyond the end of *Next Generation EU*, in 2026.

References

Blanchard, O. J. (2016) 'Rethinking Macro Policy: Progress or Confusion?', in Blanchard, O. J., et al. (eds), *Progress and Confusion: The State of Macroeconomic Policy*. MIT Press: 287–90, http://www.jstor.org/stable/j.ctt1c2crr6.30

—— (2023) 'Secular Stagnation Is Not Over', *PIIE Realtime Economics Blog*. January 24, https://www.piie.com/blogs/realtime-economics/secular-stagnation-not-over

Cerniglia, F. and F. Saraceno (eds) (2020) *A European Public Investment Outlook*. Cambridge: Open Book Publishers, https://doi.org/10.11647/OBP.0222

—— (eds) (2022) *Greening Europe. 2022 European Public Investment Outlook*. Cambridge, UK: Open Book Publishers, https://doi.org/10.11647/OBP.0328

—— and A. Watt (eds) (2021) *The Great Reset: 2021 European Public Investment Outlook*. Cambridge, UK: Open Book Publishers, https://doi.org/10.11647/OBP.0280

Draghi, M. (2012) 'Speech at the Global Investment Conference in London'. ECB (26 July)

European Commission (2022) 'Communication on Orientations for a Reform of the EU Economic Governance Framework', 9 November

—— (2023) 'Legislative Proposals on New Economic Governance Rules. Fit for the Future', 26 April

Saraceno, F. (2022a) 'The Return of Fiscal Policy. The New EU Macroeconomic Activism and Lessons for Future', *ILO Working Paper* 59 (April): 1–31

—— (2022b) 'Inflazione e Crescita: Verso Una Nuova "Stagnazione Secolare"?', *Commenti ISPI* (29 September) https://www.ispionline.it/it/pubblicazione/inflazione-e-crescita-verso-una-nuova-stagnazione-secolare-36296

—— (2023) 'Taming Inflation Through Global Policy Mix Strategies', *ISPI Commentary* (1 August) https://www.ispionline.it/en/publication/taming-inflation-through-global-policy-mix-strategies-137166

Watt, A. (2022) 'Recovery and Resilience: Stop-gap or Sea-change?', *Social Europe*, 30 May

PART I. STATE OF THE ART

1. Europe

Andrea Brasili, Atanas Kolev, Debora Revoltella, Jochen Schanz, and Annamaria Tueske

This chapter describes the dynamics of public investment over the review period and its likely path ahead. In 2022, public investment growth largely exceeded total expenditures growth, and it is set to increase further. The reinstatement of fiscal rules (after the deactivation of the General Escape Clause) would not necessarily lead to a decline in public investment thanks to the financial resources provided by the RRF. Meanwhile, there is some tentative evidence that high inflation and capacity constraints in the public administration are slowing the implementation of the RRF. Improving implementation capacity is key for the success of the existing plans and preserving absorption capacity for future investments is crucial for Europe to maintain a leading role in the needed digital, green, and energy transitions.

1.1. Public Investment, Current Dynamics, and Plans

Over the review period, the EU has had to respond simultaneously both to imminent and to long-term challenges: to lower inflation while preserving financial stability, to consolidate fiscal budgets while softening the effect of the energy and food price shocks, and to preserve energy security while accelerating the transition to climate neutrality.[1] In its response to the last challenge, support for public investment plays a key role. Combining information from Eurostat, the Member States' Stability and Convergence Programmes, the Recovery and Resilience Facility implementation, and the TED procurement database, this chapter provides an overview of public investment from various perspectives. The first section of this chapter describes the dynamics of public investment in Europe in 2022. In the last three years, public investment as a ratio of GDP increased to levels close to the pre-Great Financial Crisis average. In 2022, public investment growth largely exceeded total expenditures growth. According to Member States' plans, the ratio will increase further, particularly in Southern

---

1   The authors would like to thank Katelijne Klaassen for her precious research work.

    https://doi.org/10.11647/OBP.0386.01

European countries, with a large role played by the RRF. The second section looks at the dynamics of planned investment from the perspective of the available fiscal space. Until 2026, the reinstatement of fiscal rules (after the deactivation of the General Escape Clause) would not necessarily lead to a decline in public investment thanks to the financial resources provided by the RRF, but what will happen in the long run is less clear. The third section describes the ongoing RRF implementation efforts one and a half years after the start of the implementation period and its emerging challenges and difficulties. Small, but rising gaps are observable between planned and realised implementation of the RRF measures as well as between planned and actual disbursements, pointing to capacity constraints and implementation bottlenecks. These findings are corroborated by evidence from the publication of procurement notices as well. Finally, the concluding remarks add a broader context to the above-mentioned sections as well as an outlook regarding the main challenges facing public investment.

1.2 Public Investment in Europe: The Most Recent Data

In 2022, government investment rates in the EU remained high, despite a small decline relative to 2021 (see Figure 1.1). Aggregate investment of the general government in the EU was 3.2% of GDP. This is practically equal to its historical average and somewhat higher than the average since the end of the global financial crisis. Investment rates in Southern Europe are still below their historical average, despite significant progress over the past 4 years. In the rest of the EU, investment rates were mostly above historical averages. The observed modest decline is a consequence of slower growth in nominal investment, compared to nominal GDP (see Table 1.1).

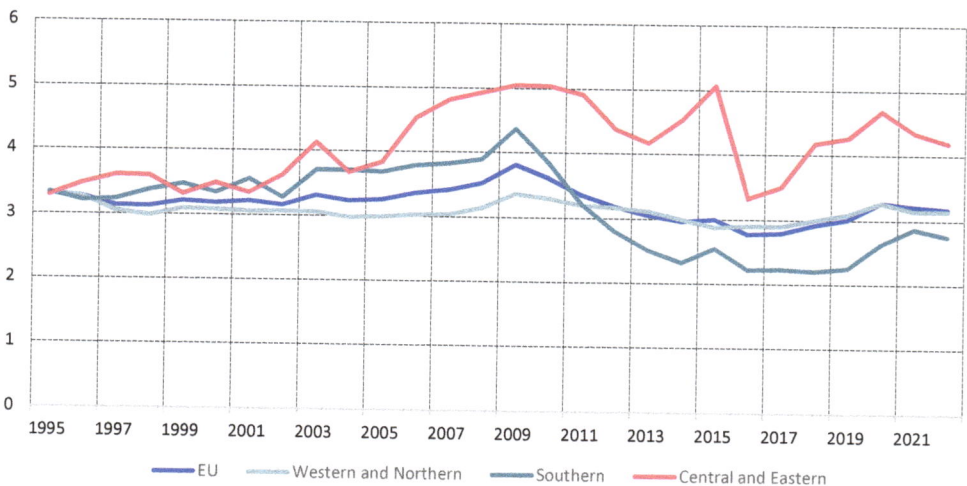

Fig. 1.1 Gross Fixed Capital Formation of the General Government (% GDP).
Source: Authors' calculations based on AMECO.

Government investment grew faster than total government expenditure in the EU. Total expenditures of the general government in the European Union grew by 4.8% in 2022, relative to 2021. This was 3 p.p. slower than expenditure on gross fixed capital formation and shows that EU governments have continued to prioritise investment. Total expenditure grew even slower in Western and Northern EU in 2022, by 3.8%. Only in Central and Eastern Europe did the growth rate of total expenditures exceed the growth rate of investment: by about 1 p.p. The rate of growth of government investment exceeded the increase of government debt by 3.5 p.p. in the EU on aggregate. In Q1 2023, nominal gross fixed capital formation grew by 7.4% YoY, keeping pace with the previous year.

Table 1.1 Investment and GDP (annual % change)

	European Union	Western and Northern	Southern	Central and Eastern
Investment	7.1	7.3	4.1	10.5
GDP	9.3	8.3	9.0	16.0

Source: Authors' calculations based on AMECO

Real government investment remained broadly stable in 2022 (see Figure 1.2). Despite the high growth of nominal investment, real government investment did not change much. The high rate of inflation in 2022 meant that real government investment remained just below its 2021 levels. Real investment in Northern and Western Europe was practically unchanged, while in Southern Europe it was about 1% lower. In Central and Eastern Europe real government investment was about 2% lower than in 2021.

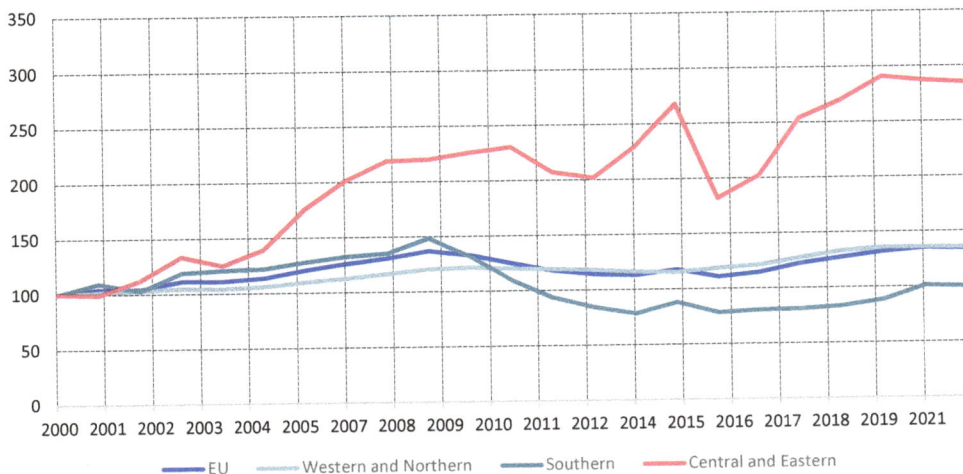

Fig. 1.2 Real Gross Fixed Capital Formation of the General Government (index 2000=100).
Source: Authors' calculations based on AMECO.

Real investment of local governments was more resilient than that of central and regional governments. Overall in the EU, real investment of local governments increased by 1.3% in 2022 relative to 2021. The highest increase was in Southern Europe, where real investment grew by 3.1%, followed by an increase of 2.7% in Central and Eastern Europe. This growth was offset by declines in central and regional government real investment. Real investment of the central government in the EU declined by 1.4%, while regional government investment declined by 4.4%.

EU nominal spending on investment grants and other capital transfers in the EU increased by 14% in 2022. The highest increase in such expenditure was in Western and Northern Europe, where it grew by 22%. In Southern Europe, investment grants and other capital transfers increased by 13%, while they grew 7% in Central and Eastern Europe.

1.3 Projections of Public Investment and Capital Transfers in Member States' Stability and Convergence Programmes

At the end of April 2023, European Union (EU) Member States released their Stability and Convergence Programmes and delivered them to the European Commission (EC). According to the Fiscal Framework Revision proposal, these documents will be merged with the National Reform Plans starting from the European semester of 2024. In this way, a joint assessment can be made of each country's adherence to the fiscal trajectory and to the planned structural reforms and investments. As usual, the plans include multi-years' budgetary evolution according to the envisaged fiscal plans and macroeconomic projections. It must be considered that at the time these plans were released, the European Central Bank (ECB) had already raised interest rates six times in a row (there was a total increase of 350 basis points from July 2022 to March 2023), and market expectations were suggesting a further 75 basis-point increase in the policy rate (with a final rate of 3.75% for the deposit rate and 4.25% for the refinancing rate). At the same time, in the Economic Policy Recommendations, the EC highlighted that 'in the medium term, fiscal policies should ensure fiscal sustainability and prioritise investment to support the twin transition and social and economic resilience'. An emphasis on keeping the bar high on public investment was clear in all the preparatory work and in the proposal of the EU fiscal framework reform (see below and other chapters of this *Outlook*). The salient motivation behind it is the acknowledgement of the increased role of public actions in fields like energy security, the climate transition, digital transition, and the consequent increased opportunity and needs of providing European Public Goods. An important reference on this topic is Fuest and Pisani-Ferry (2019), which highlights the need for the EU to specifically target the production of public goods that are more efficiently provided at EU than at national level. Buti, et al. put this issue in a different perspective in various contributions (see Chapter 11 in this *Outlook*), highlighting the opportunity of supplying European Public Goods as the most palatable way of creating a Central Fiscal Capacity. According to the Stability and Convergence Programmes released in late April, Member States followed the suggestions of the EC and kept the rising trend in the ratio of public investment/GDP intact for the next years.

1.3.1 Projections of Public Investment in Member States' Stability and Convergence Programmes

The Stability and Convergence Programmes that were released in April indicate that the Member States complied with the European Commission's plea for continued high standards for public investment, keeping intact the upward trend in the public investment-to-GDP ratio.

The graph below (Figure 1.3) projects the planned evolution of public investment as a ratio of GDP for the whole European Union and for the macro-regions.[2] This graph shows a continuation of the recent upward trend at the EU level. The public investment-to-GDP ratio is projected to go from 3.2% in 2022 to a peak of 3.6% in 2024–2025 and is expected to fall only slightly, to 3.5%, in 2026. This would be significantly higher than the average over the decade after the GFC (2011–2020) that was 2.8% but also with respect to the average in the decade before the GFC (3.3%), in line with the above-mentioned idea of an increased role for public investment. This movement is a mix of slightly different macro regional evolutions.

According to the projections, there will be a sharp increase in the ratio for Southern EU countries. Southern EU (SE) countries are expected to reach the EU average of 3.6% in 2024 (while they have been well below the EU average throughout the period from 2012 to 2022). Public investments in Central and Eastern European (CE) countries are estimated to stabilize at a high level (at 4.6% of GDP) for the period of 2024 to 2026 after reaching an earlier peak (relative to the EU) of 4.8% in 2023.

In the Northern and Western European (NW) countries, the ratio will move less than in other areas: it will reach 3.4% in 2025–2026 a marginally higher level than the long-term average (at 3.3%).

---

2   Data for EU and for macro-regions are obtained aggregating the numbers suggested by each Member States in their multi-year plans.

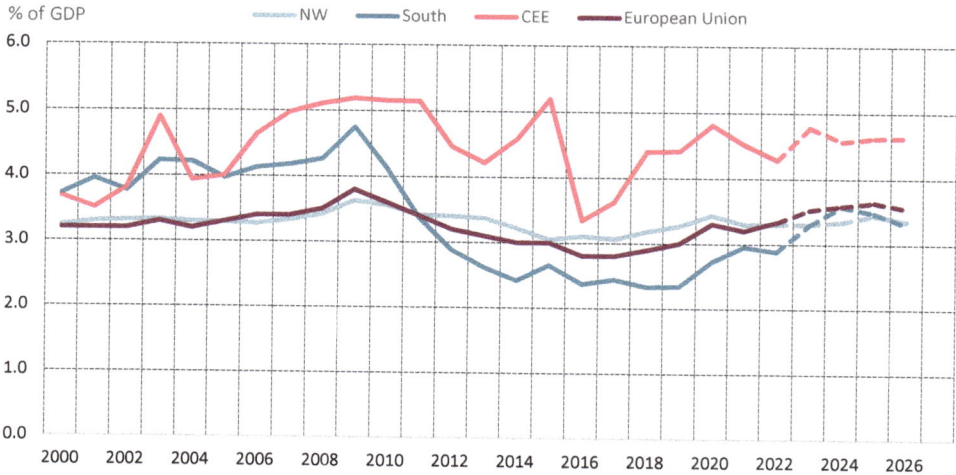

Fig. 1.3 Gross Fixed Capital Formation, as a Ratio of GDP.
Source: Authors' calculations based on AMECO data (2000–2022) and on Member States' Stability and Convergence Programmes.

1.3.2 The Role of Capital Transfers and Investment Grants

Public investments' main motivation is always creating or improving the framework conditions in which private investment may find a more fertile territory to flourish. However, public investment is not the only option to facilitate private investment, capital transfers and, in particular, investment grants can also be used for this purpose.

While capital transfers are sketched in the Stability and Convergence Programmes,[3] investment grants (that are a portion of capital transfers) are not. Figure 1.4 shows the massive use of capital transfers during and after the Great Financial Crisis (to support the financial sector) and during the COVID-19 crisis (to support the non-financial business sector).

Excluding these two episodes, the ratio of investment grants to total capital transfers has been almost stable at an average of 0.65% (that is, investment grants represented on average 65% of capital transfers). It is useful to refer to the whole aggregate for two reasons. Firstly, because investment grants are not reported in plans; secondly, it may represent a useful policy tool (outside of crises episodes when the public sector might respond to specific needs by buying into the equity of private companies).

---

3   But not for example in the EC forecasts nor in AMECO.

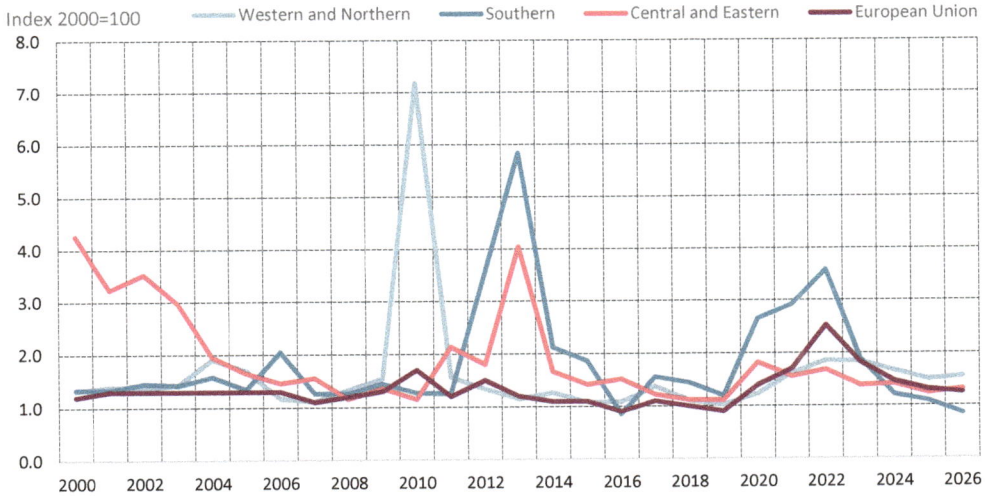

Fig. 1.4 Capital Transfers Before, During, and After Recent Crises.
Source: Authors' calculations based on AMECO data (2000–2022) and on Member States' Stability and Convergence Programmes.

Figure 1.4 also shows that the last period may have structural implications. Countries in NW Europe project a use of capital transfers proportionally larger than that of CE and SE countries. This may reflect a conscious choice: as noted above, the weight of investment grants increased notably in NW countries already in 2021–2022. Capital transfers for NW European countries are projected to represent about 1.6% of GDP from 2023 to 2026 (compared to an average of 1.2% from 2011 to 2019).

1.4 The Role of the Recovery and Resilience Facility (RRF)

This year, the Convergence and Stability programmes mandatorily include a table that shows the role of the RRF on both the revenues and on the expenditures side. On the expenditures side, RRF resources are split into current and capital expenditures. In turn, capital expenditures are split in capital transfers and public investment. In addition, we also include what is reported in the summary RRF table by some countries as 'financial transactions'. This is because the category includes planned participations in start-ups or similar initiatives by some of the Member States, which can be considered as having a similar role as capital transfer. The countries that are making use of these expenditures are Greece, Croatia, Portugal, and Romania. However, current expenditures financed through RRF grants or loans are excluded.

Figure 1.5 shows the contribution of the RRF to support public investment. The average weight of the RRF relative to GDP (shown by dark blue bars) is quite high in the following CE countries: Bulgaria, Croatia, Hungary, and Romania. It is also quite high in the following SE countries: Greece, Italy, and Portugal. Figure 1.6 provides more information about the dynamics and shows the contribution of the RRF to the change in government gross fixed capital formation (GFCF) in the period 2023–2026 compared to their level (as a ratio of GDP) in 2011–2019. For many countries, RRF allows for the acceleration of capital spending in the period considered. The dark and light blue bars almost coincide for Italy, Croatia, Latvia, and Czechia; RRF is a bit lower but gives a very large contribution for Romania and Greece, and it is larger than the acceleration in public investments for Bulgaria, Lithuania, Slovakia, and France. Estonia, Cyprus, Poland, and, particularly, Hungary project a lower level of public investment in the period 2023–2026 than the one they experienced in 2011–2019, but the difference would be much higher without the RRF contribution.

The RRF's role is also large when it comes to capital transfers. Figure 1.7 illustrates the average planned capital transfer as a ratio to GDP for the period 2023–2026 and the average of the expenses that are financed through RRF funds as a ratio to GDP for the same period. It is very clear from this figure that the use of capital transfers is more concentrated in a few countries (in Estonia, Greece, Croatia, Italy, Cyprus, and Portugal).

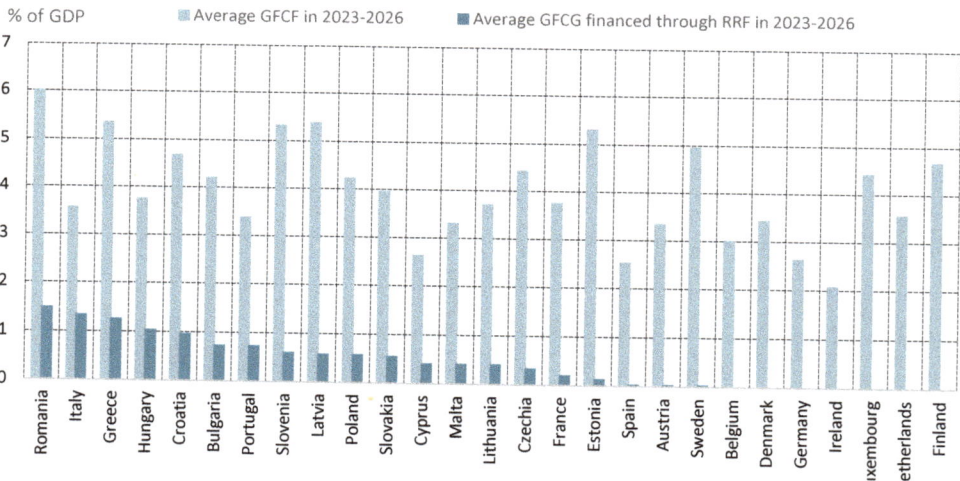

Fig. 1.5 The Role of RRF in Supporting Public Investment, 2023–2026.
Source: Authors' calculations based on Member States' Stability and Convergence Programmes.

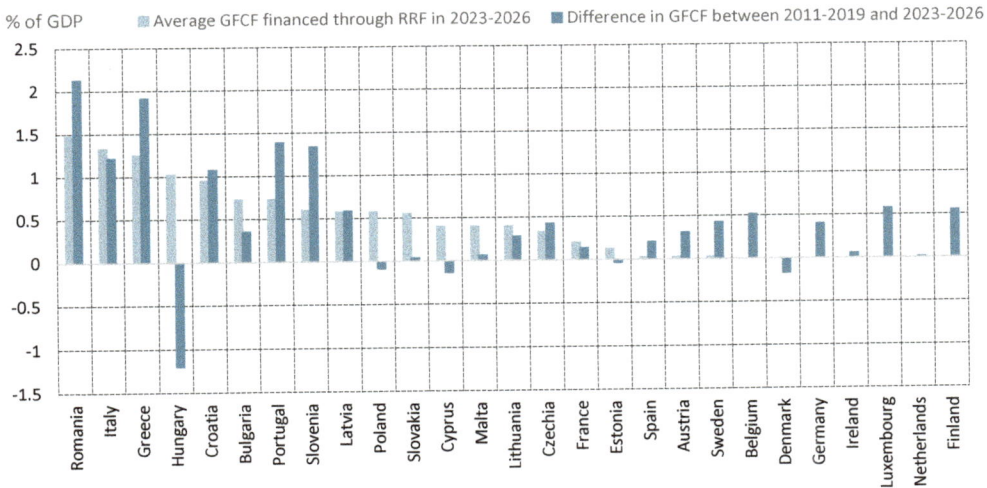

Fig. 1.6 The Role of RRF in Supporting the Acceleration of Public Investment, 2023–2026.
Difference in GFCF between 2011–2019 and 2023–2026

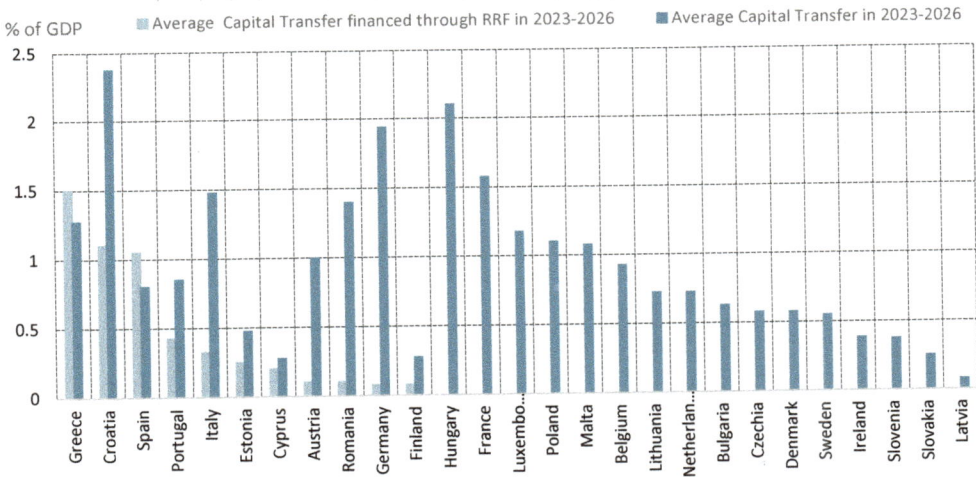

Fig. 1.7 The Role of RRF in Supporting Capital Transfers, 2023–2026.
Note: Spain's average RRF is based on the 2021–2024 period. Greece's average includes financial
transactions, that are sizeable. Financial transactions are also included for Croatia, Portugal
and Romania. For France, the Stability Programme (SP) does not distinguish between capital
transfers and gross fixed capital formation. Both are described as capital expenditures. These
capital expenditures are included here as gross fixed capital formation. As for Italy, the latest plan
includes only the sum for the period 2020–2026 (for both GFCF and capital transfers), while the SP
for 2022 detailed RRF-funded expenditures by year. These amounts have been divided by the total
number of years so that the 2022 target profile has been maintained as much as possible.
Source: Authors' calculations based on Member States' Stability and Convergence Programmes.

In summary: first, Member States have endorsed the EC recommendation to keep the bar high for public investment in their fiscal plans; second, the RRF contributes significantly to this effort, especially in the SE and CE countries.

1.5 Is the Old Framework 'Biting' with Respect to Plans? Will Member States Diminish their Investment Attitude?

As discussed above, the Stability and Convergence Programmes were drafted in a situation where the General Escape Clause was still valid (even though its deactivation had already been decided for 2024), debates around the proposal for a new fiscal framework were also ongoing, and the ECB had not yet completed its tightening cycle. The ambition of this section is to show how these elements combine to shape Member States' policy choices on investment. The EU Commission assessed the evolution of fiscal stance in Member States according to the reference indicator that was proposed in the new fiscal framework (under discussion). In particular, the 'Fiscal Statistical Tables providing background data relevant for the assessment of the 2023 Stability or Convergence Programmes' make reference to the fact that fiscal stance should be judged net of the expenditures financed by RRF grants. This suggestion is also taken into account here.

1.5.1 Interest Expenditures are Projected to Rise Slightly

In their plans, Member States projected that interest expenditures will gradually increase from the current 1.62 to 2.03 as a percentage of GDP. Table 1.2 shows the disaggregation in EU macro regions. While there is a large gap in levels of interest expenditures that is explained by the dimension of the debt (that is much larger for SE countries than for the other areas), the projected increase over the projection horizon is not particularly different. This is likely due to the longer maturity of the underlying portfolios of highly indebted countries.

Table 1.2 Interest Expenditures/GDP

	2022	2023	2024	2025	2026
EU	1.62	1.59	1.80	1.86	2.03
NW	1.02	1.02	1.22	1.28	1.45
SE	3.39	3.08	3.38	3.47	3.68
CEESE	1.38	1.75	1.87	1.82	1.88

Source: Authors' calculations based on Member States' Stability and Convergence Programmes.

The dynamics of interest rates (after the draft of the Stability and Convergence Programmes) can cause some further increase in interest expenditures, but this should not alter this picture dramatically.[4]

1.5.2 General Government Deficits are Projected to Decline

Regarding the deficit, the gradual phasing out of the measures that were introduced to support households and businesses after the Russian invasion of Ukraine, and an improving economic cycle from 2024 on, should favour a decline in deficit. Table 1.3 shows the deficit declining from above 3% in the EU and in all macro regions in 2023 to below that threshold, although by not a huge margin, by 2026.

Table 1.3 General Government Net Lending

	2022	2023	2024	2025	2026
EU	-3.4	-3.7	-2.6	-2.0	-1.7
NW	-2.4	-3.5	-2.3	-1.6	-1.4
SE	-6.0	-3.8	-3.0	-2.5	-2.2
CEESE	-3.9	-4.3	-3.2	-2.8	-2.7

Source: Authors' calculations based on Member States' Stability and Convergence Programmes.

It is important to understand that in case of any slippage in public accounts, public investment, an easy-to-cut item from a (national) politics point of view, may come under pressure.

1.5.3 The evolution of fiscal stance: changes in the structural primary balance

Having a look at the change in structural primary balance can be useful as a way to assess the change in fiscal stance, particularly as the old framework included the assessment of the path and speed of movements towards the Medium-Term Objective. It is important to understand the effect of worsening public finances on public investment. Therefore, it is useful to look at changes in the structural primary balance to determine changes in fiscal policy. Table 1.4 clearly shows that fiscal policy becomes more restrictive after 2023 and that there is a marked decline in the deficit. This decline in the deficit is also clearly smaller after 2024.

---

4   At the moment of finalizing this chapter, while short-term rates are slightly higher with respect to market expectations back in late April, long term rates have declined more than previously thought partially compensating the first effect.

Table 1.4 The Change in Structural Primary Balance as a Simple Indicator of Fiscal Stance

	2023	2024	2025	2026
EU	0.0	1.0	0.5	0.4
NW	-0.8	1.1	0.6	0.3
SE	1.7	0.9	0.3	0.5
CEESE	0.6	0.8	0.1	0.1

Source: Authors' calculations based on Member States' Stability and Convergence Programmes.

It is important to know that, if the RRF grants (shown in Table 1.5) were taken out of the picture, the improvements in the structural primary balances for SE and CEESE countries would disappear.

Table 1.5 The Share of Expenditures that are Financed Through RRF Grants

	2022	2023	2024	2025	2026
EU	0.41	0.44	0.31	0.25	0.17
NW	0.22	0.14	0.12	0.06	0.00
SE	1.08	1.14	0.54	0.51	0.49
CEESE	0.10	0.66	0.86	0.82	0.45

Source: Authors' calculations based on Member States' Stability and Convergence Programmes.

In conclusion, according to the Stability and Convergence Programmes released by the Member States, it appears that the deactivation of the General Escape Clause would not necessarily lead to a decline in public investment, provided that RRF-related grants are excluded from the calculation of the fiscal stance. However, once the RRF ends, the constraints might very well bind, given that the grants exceed the projected improvements in the structural primary balance for SE and also CEESE. Without a substitute for the RRF after 2026, public investment might come under renewed pressure.

1.6 Congestions and Bottlenecks in Public Investment in EU

One key element at the current juncture is the existence of potential limits in the capacity to implement this enhanced public-capital-spending effort supported by the RRF. As demonstrated by the tables and graphs above, the RRF is very large for some countries. Hence, it is not certain that all government agencies involved will succeed in the big effort of implementing the measures of the Recovery and Resilience Plans in time. The RRF governance design is performance-based, implying that each Member State, before asking for a payment, must prove the successful realisation of pre-agreed steps (milestones and targets) of the various measures. Payments are semi-annual and follow documented requests of Member States. In addition, for each country, it is mandatory to provide a semi-annual analysis of how the implementation of the plan is going. This section provides a preliminary overview of this self-reported monitoring exercise and takes a look at delays in RRF-related public procurement.

In April 2023, for the fourth time since the RRF began, Member States uploaded a dataset containing the results of their monitoring to the EC. They also provided evidence of this (summarized) information in their National Reform Plans (along with the Stability and Convergence programmes). Summing up for the EU until the end of 2023, there are about 3195 measures reported upon. The overview of this section will focus on these measures. Looking backward on milestones and targets (that is, those planned to be achieved up to Q1 2023), 32% are marked as fulfilled and 49.4% as completed (but not yet assessed), while 18.6% (that is, less than 1 in 5) were not completed. This represents a 1.1 p.p. increase of not-completed projects compared to the previous reporting round. On the other hand, looking ahead at milestones and targets with target dates in 2023, the vast majority were reported as being either on track (78.6%) or completed (7.4%), with 14% being delayed (a 5 p.p. increase of the latter compared to the previous reporting round).

As demonstrated by Panel A of Figure 1.8, a gap started to open in Q4 of 2021 between the planned-versus-realised number of milestones and targets. The opening became gradually larger over time up to Q1 2023, and it is foreseen to grow further in the remaining quarters of 2023. Requests by Member States for RRF disbursements are sent to the EC once the related package of measures have been implemented (with the exception of pre-financing payments that are not conditional on implementation of milestones or targets). The first payments based on the operational agreements between Member States and the EC were foreseen for Q4 2021. Panel B of Figure 1.8 show that a gap between planned and realised disbursements appeared already in the very first quarter of the foreseen timeline. This gap has further widened from €39bn in Q4 2021 to €113bn in Q2 2023.

Panel A. Increasing gap in planned vs realised number of measures

Panel B. Widening gap between planned and realised disbursements

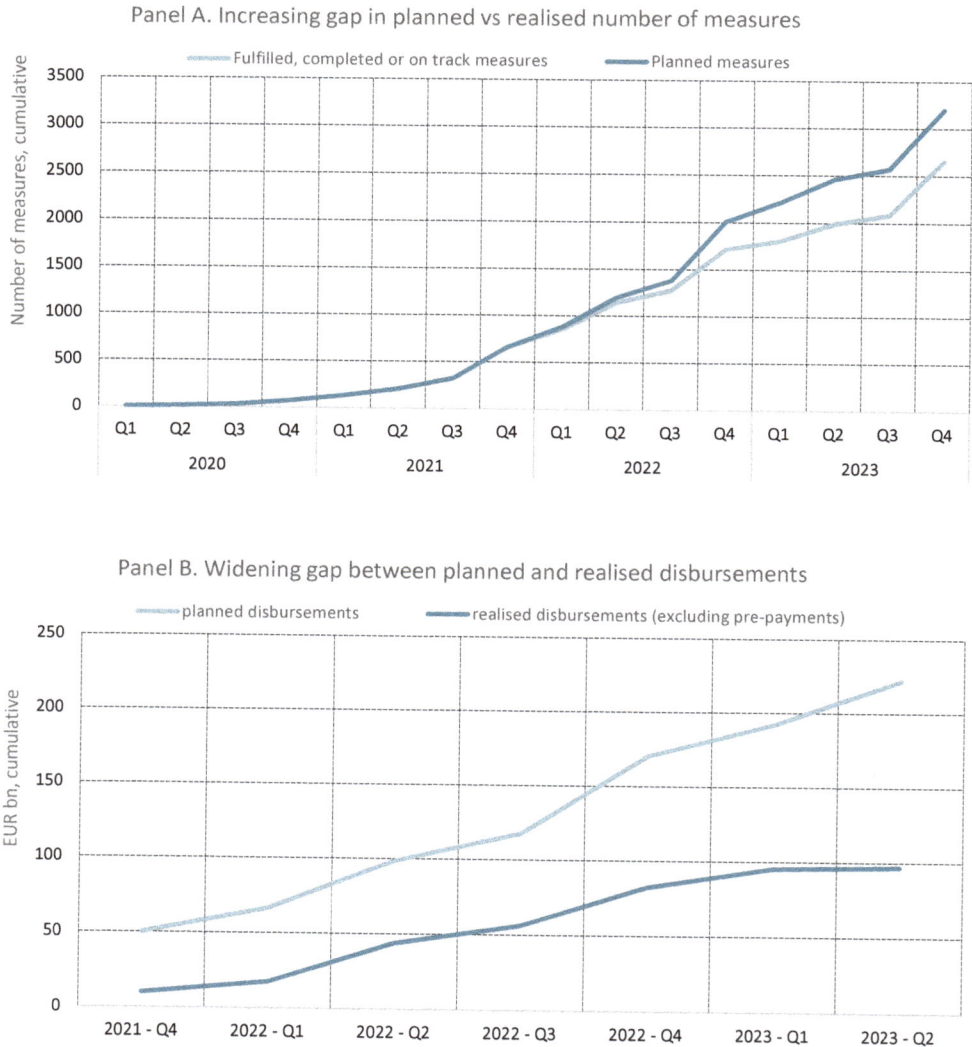

Fig. 1.8 A Gap between Plans and Realisations in RRF Implementation.
Source: Authors' calculations based on Member States' self-reported data on RRF implementation, RRF Operational agreements, and the Recovery and Resilience scoreboard.

Earlier reporting rounds made clear that the implementation of reforms has frequently been frontloaded in the plans, in preparation for structural changes. Also, the higher number of milestones and targets related to reforms in the past signals that investment-related projects might take more time to implement. In 2022, the number of not-completed investments and reforms were similar (corresponding to 21.5% and 21.7%, respectively). As Figure 1.9 shows, in 2023, there are a higher number of investments due than reforms, with the majority of them being on track (69.2%). Among delayed or not-completed measures in 2023, there are a higher number of investments than reforms (141 versus 111, respectively); however, these correspond to a smaller share (20.4% versus 22.4%, respectively). The higher number and share of anticipated delays among investments than reforms might signal the impact of price increases as well as remaining shortages and supply-chain bottlenecks.

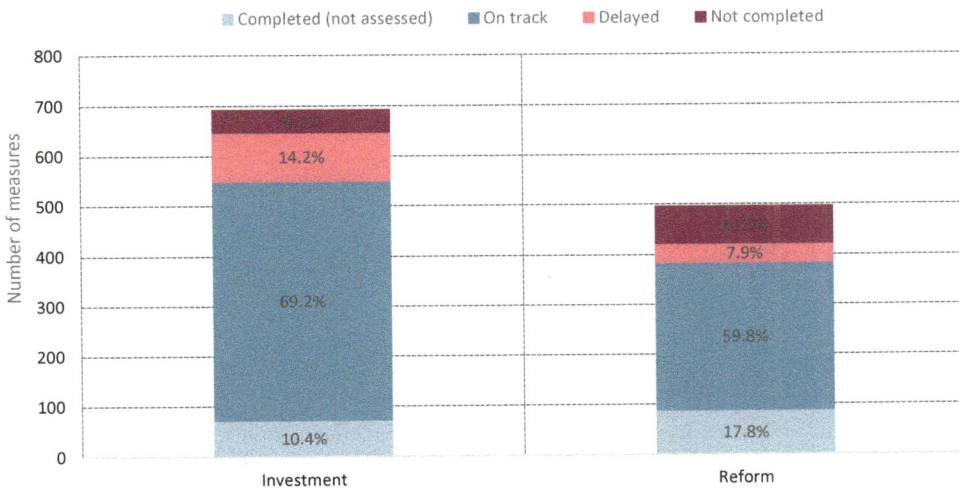

Fig. 1.9 Status of Investments and Reforms in 2023.
Source: Authors' calculations based on Member States' self-reported data on RRF implementation.

Looking at areas of implementation, which are closely related to the pillars of the RRF plans, some topics stand out either because their implementation seems to be on an improving trajectory or because there are more delays observable among them than among all measures on average. When looking at delayed measures, the areas of research or innovation are underrepresented. That is, measures related to these areas don't seem to suffer from any impediments of implementation (see Table 1.6a). This is indicative of the quarters ahead in 2023. When looking at not-completed measures, areas such as next generation or policy, and green transition, were also underrepresented, indicating that their implementation was also relatively faster in the past. However, the area of research and innovation was neither under- nor over-represented among not-completed measures, which signals that these areas' relative advantage in implementation was not yet observable in 2022.

Table 1.6a Areas with Relatively Faster RRF Implementation, 2020–2023

%	Research	innovation	next generation | policy	green transition
total	6.1	5.9	8.6	1.6
delayed	2.9	4.4	5.1	0.7
not completed	6.1	5.9	7.6	0.5

Note: The calculation is based on text search using the keywords indicated in the columns. In case of multiple keywords, the symbol '\|' indicates inclusive 'or'.
Source: Authors' calculations based on Member States' self-reported data on RRF implementation.

Among delayed and not-completed measures, the area of infrastructure is salient, with 7 p.p. higher share of delayed and 4 p.p. higher share of not-completed projects than infrastructure's overall share among measures (see Table 1.6b). When looking at the area including infrastructure or development or infrastructure and buildings, the results are similar. Infrastructure projects can suffer from delays when there are supply-chain disruptions or price increases, as these can affect the tendering process. Among delayed measures, we see the overrepresentation of some other larger areas (1. municipalities or authority, 2. solar or wind or hydrogen, 3. digital transformation, 4. digital or energy or twin or transition). These results point to potential capacity constraints in municipal authorities and in the specific areas of the energy and digital transition.

Table 1.6b Areas with Bottlenecks in RRF Implementation, 2020–2023

%	infrastructure	infrastructure | build	municipalities | authority	solar | wind | hydrogen	digital transformation	digital | energy | twin | transition
total	11.8	19.7	13.0	3.7	3.0	33.7
delayed	19.0	28.5	17.5	4.4	4.4	39.4
not completed	16.1	23.7	11.5	4.6	1.7	30.0

Note: The calculation is based on text search with the indicated keywords in columns.
Source: Authors' calculations based on Member States' self-reported data on RRF implementation.

In sum, the scaling-up of investments in specific areas, such as infrastructure, energy, and digital transition might lead to congestions, that is, slower implementation due to capacity constraints, in particular at a lower level of governance, for example, at municipality level. Supply-chain disruptions and price increases might add up to cause bottlenecks in the implementation of RRF measures, which can be illustrated by the visible gap building up between the planned and realised number of RRF measures as well as between the planned and actual disbursements that regularly follow the completion of RRF-measure packages.

Evidence from public procurement points into the same direction.[5] The share of RRF-co-funded procurement notices relating to public investment has so far been small, ranging between almost zero in Northern and Western Europe to around 10% in Southern Europe. Procurement for other EU-co-financed investments appears to follow the same pace as in 2022 (Figure 1.10). However, the number of RRF-related procurement notices is rising rapidly. This could lead to congestion when it comes to the award of contracts or the implementation of RRF-co-financed projects, which need to be implemented by 2026. This congestion could also affect less time-sensitive projects, such as those co-financed by EU cohesion funds of the 2021–2027 programming period, which only need to be implemented by 2030.

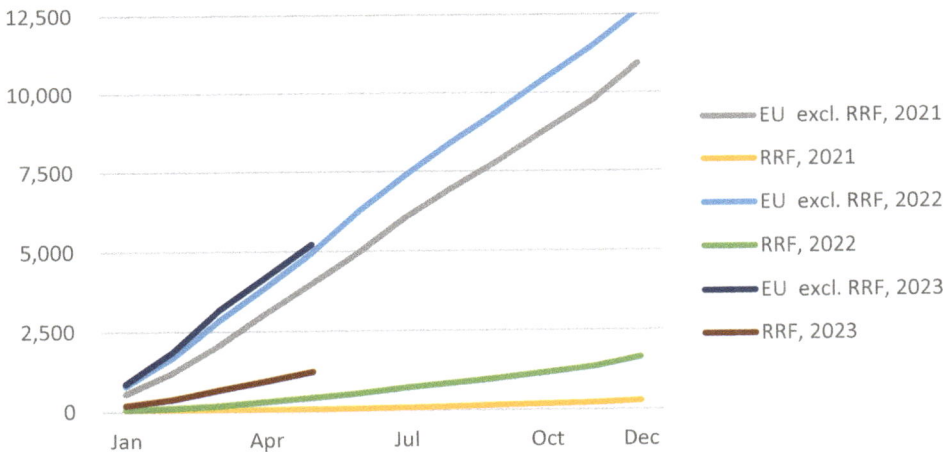

Fig. 1.10 Cumulative Issuance of Public-Investment-Related Procurement Notices Co-Financed by the EU, Southern and Eastern Europe, by Year.
Source: Authors' calculations.

Already, there are some signs that capacity limits in the public sector are slowing procurement processes already underway. The delay between the submission of

5   The following figures are estimates based on the information provided on public procurement in the TED database (https://ted.europa.eu/TED/main/HomePage.do), which exclude public procurement below certain value thresholds and may suffer from different reporting practices by different Member States. The estimates presented here are based only on contract notices and contract awards, including by utilities, of open tendering procedures, to make the dataset more homogenous. The large majority of procurement notices meets these criteria. Expert judgement has been used to allocate the types of works, goods and services that are procured to public investment, and to clean contract award values. The identification of RRF-co-financed notices is based on keyword extraction of descriptive text that most notices provide.

tenders and the signature of contracts appears somewhat larger for RRF-co-funded procurement than for nationally or EU-co-financed investment, at least for procurement related to construction (see Figure 1.11).[6] This might capture the delays related to infrastructure projects that can be picked up from Member States' monitoring of RRF projects (see above). However, the difference in the signature delays is small, and, given that the publication of procurement notices for RRF-co-funded projects only started to take off in 2021, the estimates of signature delays beyond 500 days become quite uncertain for RRF-related notices.

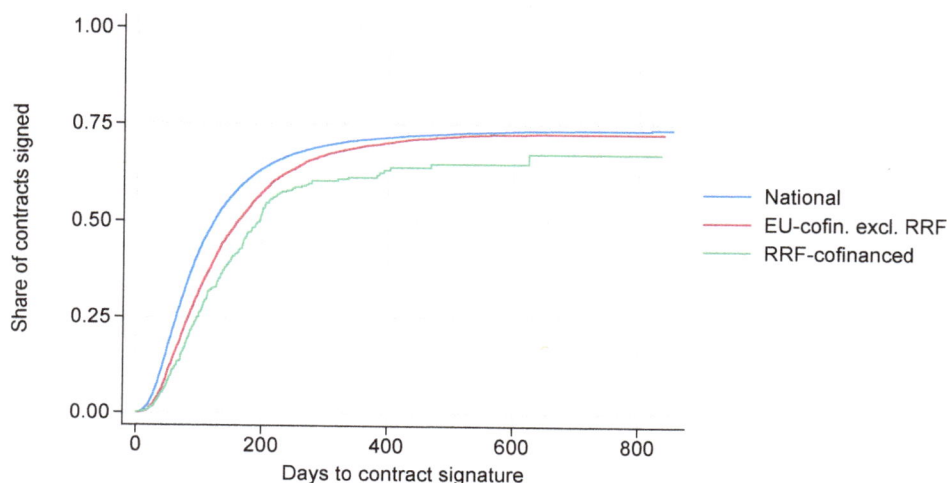

Fig. 1.11 Delay between Tender-Submission Deadline and Contract Signature.
Source: Authors' calculations.

In summary, evidence from the publication of procurement notices corroborates the findings from Member States' monitoring of the implementation of their Recovery and Resolution Plans: that bottlenecks have so far been small but may increase as the implementation of the planned investments gathers steam.

6   In the corresponding bivariate Cox regression, the hazard ratio is 15% lower for EU (excl. RRF)-co-funded investments than for nationally funded investments, and 35% lower for RRF-co-funded investments. Both estimates are statistically significant in that regression at the 1% level (50,000 contract awards, robust SEs). The share of contracts signed typically hits a ceiling at about 75% of contracts tendered in this dataset, including at longer horizons. This may reflect that some tendered contracts are never signed or gaps in the reporting of contract awards.

1.7 Concluding Remarks

The end of the pandemic and the outbreak of the Ukraine war added three new pairs of conflicting objectives to the EU's economic policy: to lower inflation while preserving financial stability, to preserve energy security while accelerating the transition to climate neutrality, and to consolidate fiscal budgets while softening the effect of the energy- and food-price shocks. On balance, monetary policy tightened rapidly, and public spending accelerated, especially for public infrastructure related to the green transition. The European Commission has introduced new tools like the Next Generation EU fund and the RePowerEU plan. It has also proposed adaptations to the fiscal framework that make it easier for Member States to undertake longer-term investment programmes without hitting the limits of the framework. In addition, in the guidelines for fiscal policy, it pushed for the expansion of public-investment plans. The Next Generation EU fund and the Recovery and Resilience Facility are already providing resources to the EU economy through 2026. However, it is still uncertain how the need to sustain high levels of public investment will interact with the new fiscal framework. Some pressures may well re-emerge after 2026, once the RRF expires.

Now, it is high time to implement the planned efforts. As delays start to pile up in specific areas, it is worthwhile to have a closer look at their nature and specificities. As expected, there have been some delays in implementing the Recovery Fund. This is due, in part, to abrupt price increases that have drastically altered the costs of infrastructure and construction projects. Other delays relate to the diffuse nature of the projects, which involve multiple levels of local government. Improving implementation capacity is key for the success of the existing plans. Preserving space for future investments is crucial for Europe to maintain a leading role in the needed digital, green, and energy transitions.

References

Fuest, C. and J. Pisani-Ferry (2019) 'A Primer on Developing European Public Goods' *EconPol Policy Report*. vol. 3, November

European Commission (2022) Recommendation for a COUNCIL RECOMMENDATION on the economic policy of the euro area COM (2022), 782 final

European Commission (2023) European Semester: National Reform Programmes and Stability/Convergence Programmes

European Commission. 'Recovery and Resilience Scoreboard', https://ec.europa.eu/economy_finance/recovery-and-resilience-scoreboard/index.html

European Commission (2023) Report from the Commission to the European Parliament and the Council on the implementation of the Recovery and Resilience Facility: Moving Forward. 25 September. 545 final/2

TED database, https://ted.europa.eu/TED/main/HomePage.do

2. Financing Public Investment in France

Mathieu Plane and Francesco Saraceno

The chapter first deals with the historical evolution of public investment and capital in France. While still high in comparison with other EU countries, it was significantly reduced since the early 1990s. A reversal of the trend, prior to COVID-19, was mostly due to local governments. After COVID-19, a rebound was followed by flat growth; investment in 2023 is barely at 2019 levels. The result of these trends is a significant drop in net public wealth (mostly of the central government) since 2008. Funding exhibits a growing diversity. Investment spending is increasingly characterised by co-financing involving multiple actors, reducing the central-government share. The chapter concludes with an assessment of the sustainability of France's public finances. The critical gap $(g-r)$ remains positive for France even in the current environment of high inflation and increasing interest rates. We conclude, with some caution, that there is no real cause, in the medium run, for concern regarding sustainability.

2.1 The Historical Evolution of Public Investment

From the end of the 1940s until today, public investment in France has passed through different phases. After a long period of sustained growth during the 1960s (5% of GDP on average; see Figure 2.1), public investment remained at a relatively high level during the 1970s and 1980s (4.4% of GDP on average). The first break took place during the 1990s, a period during which priority was given to reducing the public deficit to meet the Maastricht criteria and join the euro. This resulted in an adjustment to public investment that, on average, fell below 4% of GDP from the mid-1990s to the beginning of the 2010s, when a second shock occurred. Following the sovereign-debt crisis, the fiscal stance changed, and a substantial part of the fiscal adjustment was achieved by reducing capital expenditure. Indeed, the reduction of public investment during that period has contributed to almost a third of fiscal consolidation even though investment represented only 6% of public expenditure. The share of public investment-to-GDP from 2014 to 2022 fell to 3.5 % on average and, during the period 2015–2018, reached its lowest level since 1952. A recovery in public investment began in the two years before the COVID-19 crisis, with an increase of nearly 14% between the end of 2017 and the

https://doi.org/10.11647/OBP.0386.02

end of 2019. This shift was linked to the electoral cycle of municipal elections and the government's desire to preserve investment within the framework of the targeted budget contract with local communities.

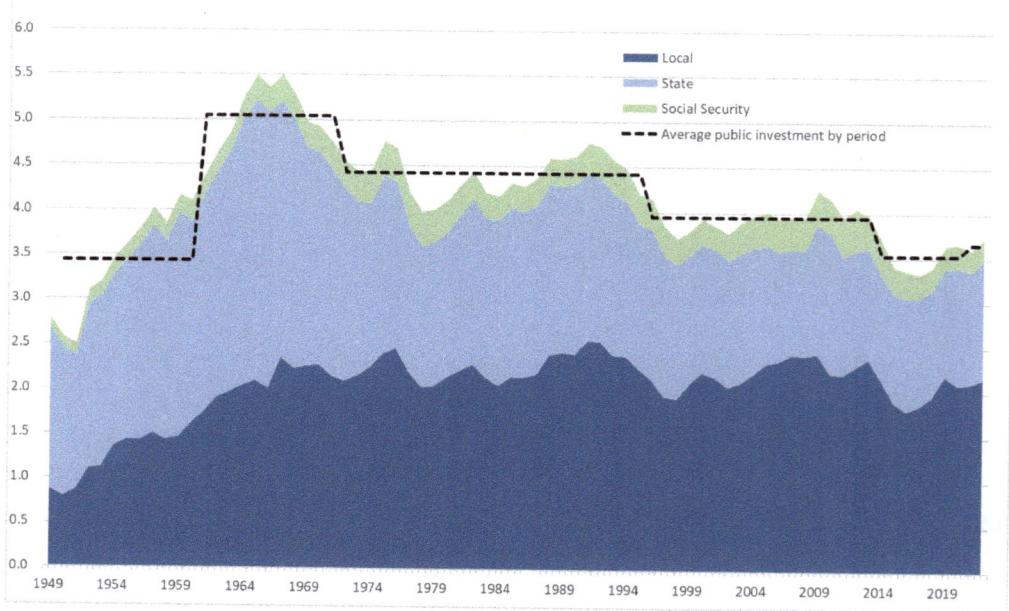

Fig. 2.1 Public Investment by Administrative Category, in % of GDP.
Source: Authors' elaboration based on data from INSEE.

2.2 The Public-Investment Dynamics since the COVID Crisis

Because of the political cycle, a partial reversal in public investment was to be expected after the municipal elections of 2017. Nevertheless, the drop observed in 2020 is out of proportion with that observed in previous cycles and is a result of the pandemic. Indeed, the COVID-19 crisis (and the first lockdown) led to a drop of 15% in public investment in the first half of 2020. By comparison, the three strongest half-yearly decreases observed for the previous seventy years were between 5% and 6%.

From the second semester of 2020, however, public investment nearly returned to the pre-COVID-19 level (-3 % at the end of the year 2020 with respect to the end of 2019), despite the second lockdown in November and December 2020 (Figure 2.2). In addition, the government voted in September 2020 for a hundred-billion-euro recovery plan ('Le Plan de Relance', see Plane and Saraceno 2021), partially financed (40bn euros) with funding from Next Generation EU. The 'Plan de Relance' includes a section on public infrastructure, with particular emphasis on the thermal renovation of public buildings, with increased planned investment from the beginning of 2021. Moreover, a new investment plan, 'Build the France of 2030', was announced in October 2021. This latter plan is intended to meet long-term challenges, particularly ecological ones, through massive investment to help the technological champions of tomorrow to emerge and to support the transitions of French sectors of excellence: energy, automotive, aeronautics and even space. These plans, presented by President Macron, identify public investment as central to the revival and strengthening of the economy as well as to the meeting of major future challenges, first and foremost that of ecological transition.

Despite these major announcements, public investment has remained surprisingly flat. In fact, it was, at the midpoint of 2023, almost at the same level as at the end of 2020. Public investment, therefore, had not returned to its pre-crisis level (-1%), yet GDP is 1.7% above its pre-COVID level (Figure 2.2).

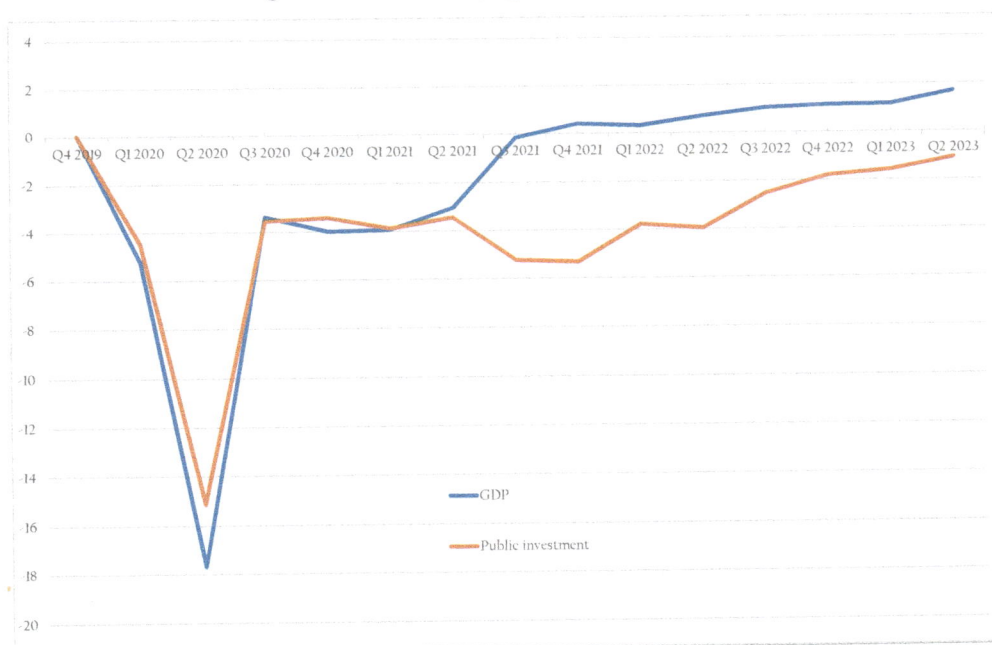

Fig. 2.2 Public Investment and GDP.
Note: 0 = 2019q4, in %, volume.
Source: Authors' elaboration based on data from INSEE.

It is also important to note that, while public investment remains mainly the responsibility of local authorities (carrying out 58% in 2022), the post-COVID dynamic is more on the side of the central government. Today, its investment is at a higher level than 2019, while local authorities and Social Security, have not returned to their pre-crisis investment levels (see Figure 2.1). Indeed, part of the investment programmes resulting from the Recovery Plan or 'France 2030' are implemented by the central government, and not by local authorities.

2.3 Net Investment Increases but the Pace of Public-Capital Accumulation is Still Low

The assessment of gross investment needs to be complemented by the analysis of the net flow of fixed assets (net investment) to assess the dynamics of the capital stock (abstracting from the effects of revaluation of the existing stock). Thus, if gross investment is larger (smaller) than the depreciation of capital (consumption of fixed capital, CFC, in national-accounts nomenclature), then net investment increases (decreases), and the stock of capital increases (decreases).

From the late 1970s to the first half of the 1990s, France's general government net investment was strong, averaging more than 1% of GDP per year (Figure 2.3). It even experienced a strong boom over the period 1987–1992, averaging above 1.4% of GDP per year. From 1993 to 1998, general government net investment declined sharply, reaching 0.5% of GDP in 1998, which amounted to a decrease of 1% of GDP over the space of six years. This, as was the case in other European countries, was mostly due to the effort to meet the Maastricht criteria in the run-up to the adoption of the euro: the cyclically adjusted deficit for France decreased from 4.6% of GDP in 1993 to 1.8% in 1998, and investment was the main adjustment variable. Net investment recovered in the next phase, then fluctuated between 0.7% and 0.9% of GDP over the 2000–2010 period, without ever returning to the level observed during the 1980s and the first half of the 1990s. Since 2011 and the Global Financial Crisis, net investment has been at its lowest level since the late 1970s, when wealth accounts were introduced.

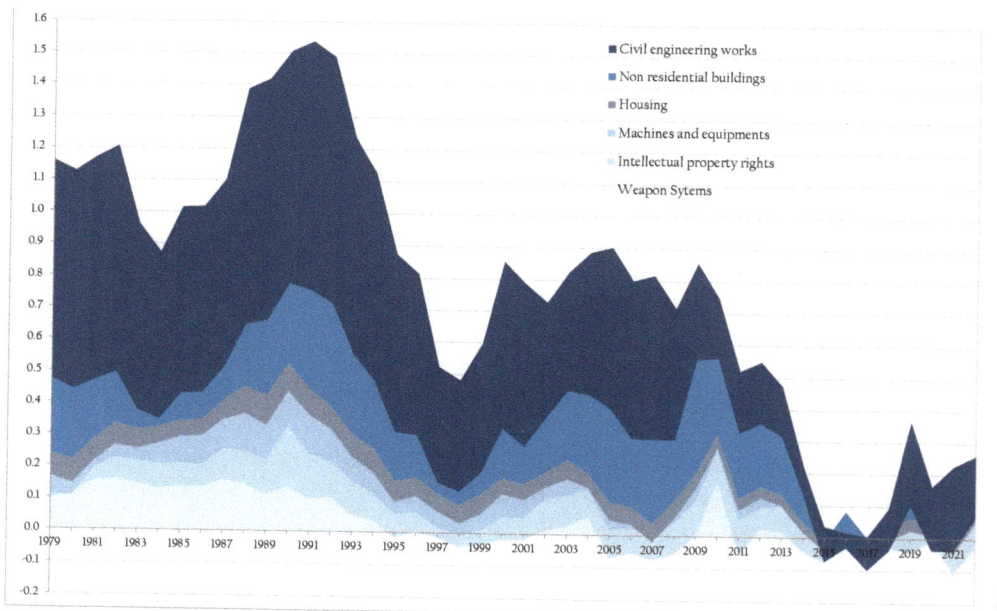

Fig. 2.3 Net General Government Investment by Component as a % of GDP.
Source: Authors' elaboration based on data from INSEE.

Thus, during the period 2014–2018, France spent about 0.7 percentage points (p.p.) of GDP (about €18bn per year in 2022 euros) less on net investment than it did during the period 2000–2010, and 1.4 p.p. (approximately €37bn per year in 2022 euros) less than during the period 1990–1992.

The picture that emerges from the analysis of stocks and flows is rather consistent and gives two main messages. The first is that, in France, public investment and the stock of capital have been largely affected by the macroeconomic cycle. In the two significant phases of fiscal consolidation—the run-up to adopting the euro in the 1990s and the aftermath of the sovereign debt crisis—investment was strongly reduced. Especially in the latter case, net investment turned negative to zero for all levels of government, thus reducing the stock of capital that, before the pandemic, was already at an all-time low. The second message that emerges, specifically from the analysis of stocks, is that, despite these trends in investment, the capital stock in France is still significant (and larger than in other countries). One might ask, then, if the effort of consolidation and the disproportionate burden that it has laid on public investment led, at least, to more sustainable public finances.

A comparison of the evolution over the last twenty years of non-financial assets' net flows in relation to primary net financial flow (financial assets — financial liabilities — interest expenses), which we consider here as a proxy of the net worth, clearly reveals the emergence of two sub-periods. The first, which runs from 1996 to 2008, can be seen as a period in which the additional public net financial debt (excluding interest expense) was more than offset by the net accumulation of non-financial assets, leading to a positive net value. This means that the general government stock of wealth increased in value over this period, even abstracting from price effects. The second period, which runs from 2009 to 2022, displays a new pattern in which the net debt increase is no longer offset by an increase in public non-financial capital, generating a sharp deterioration in the government's net worth. The economic and financial crisis has led to a sharp increase in public debt, and fiscal consolidation began to be implemented in 2011. On one hand, it partly reduced new financial commitments; on the other, it has been more than offset by a reduction in the net accumulation of non-financial assets. This is yet-further proof that the burden of fiscal consolidation was disproportionately laid on the shoulders of public investment. The sharp reduction in net worth, therefore, casts doubt on the effectiveness of fiscal consolidation in strengthening the public-finances outlook for France.

2.4 General Government Net Wealth: Still Positive but a Strong Decrease Since 2008

What is referred to as 'public capital' covers a wide variety of assets, such as land, residential buildings, ports, dams, and roads. It also includes intellectual property rights. It is necessary to break down the 'wealth of the State' into these different components to understand its dynamics, considering that price (most notably land price) and volume effects may play a significant role in explaining the evolution of the different components and of aggregate figures.

We use public data from the INSEE national accounts; our analysis covers the period 1978–2021. INSEE reports the consolidated level (general government) and its components, distinguishing between the central government, local governments, social-security administrations, and other government agencies.

In 2022, the consolidated public sector had a positive net wealth, despite the negative impact of the COVID-19 crisis (Table 2.1). Total assets held represented 167% of GDP, of which 103% was for non-financial assets. Financial liabilities totalled 134% of GDP. The net worth in 2022 was, therefore, 33% of GDP, around €12,700 per capita.

Table 2.1 Decomposition of General Government Net Wealth

	As a % of GDP			In euros per head
	1978	2007	2022	2022
Non-financial assets	60.8	90.4	102.9	39,920
Financial assets	27.6	52.6	64.0	24,820
Financial liabilities	33.7	84.9	134.2	52,040
Net worth	54.7	58.1	32.8	12,700

Source: INSEE and authors' calculations.

After reaching a record level in 2007 (58% of GDP), it has lost 25 points of GDP in the space of fifteen years. The reasons for this sharp drop are to be found on the net financial liabilities (debt) side, which increased substantially while non-financial assets increased slightly (see Figure 2.4).

This net worth is unevenly distributed among different levels of government. Indeed, it is very positive for local administrations (72% of GDP in 2022), very negative for the Central Government (-57% of GDP in 2022), and slightly positive for social-security administrations and other government agencies (8% and 10%, respectively). Broadly speaking, the central government—which runs recurrent public deficits — has accumulated public debt; low-debt local governments hold non-financial assets, be they land, buildings, or civil-engineering works. With the economic and financial crisis from 2008 onwards, the net worth of the central government deteriorated considerably as public deficits and debt increased. On the other hand, the net worth of local governments remained high and relatively stable over the same period due to a stable value of non-financial assets and their debt.

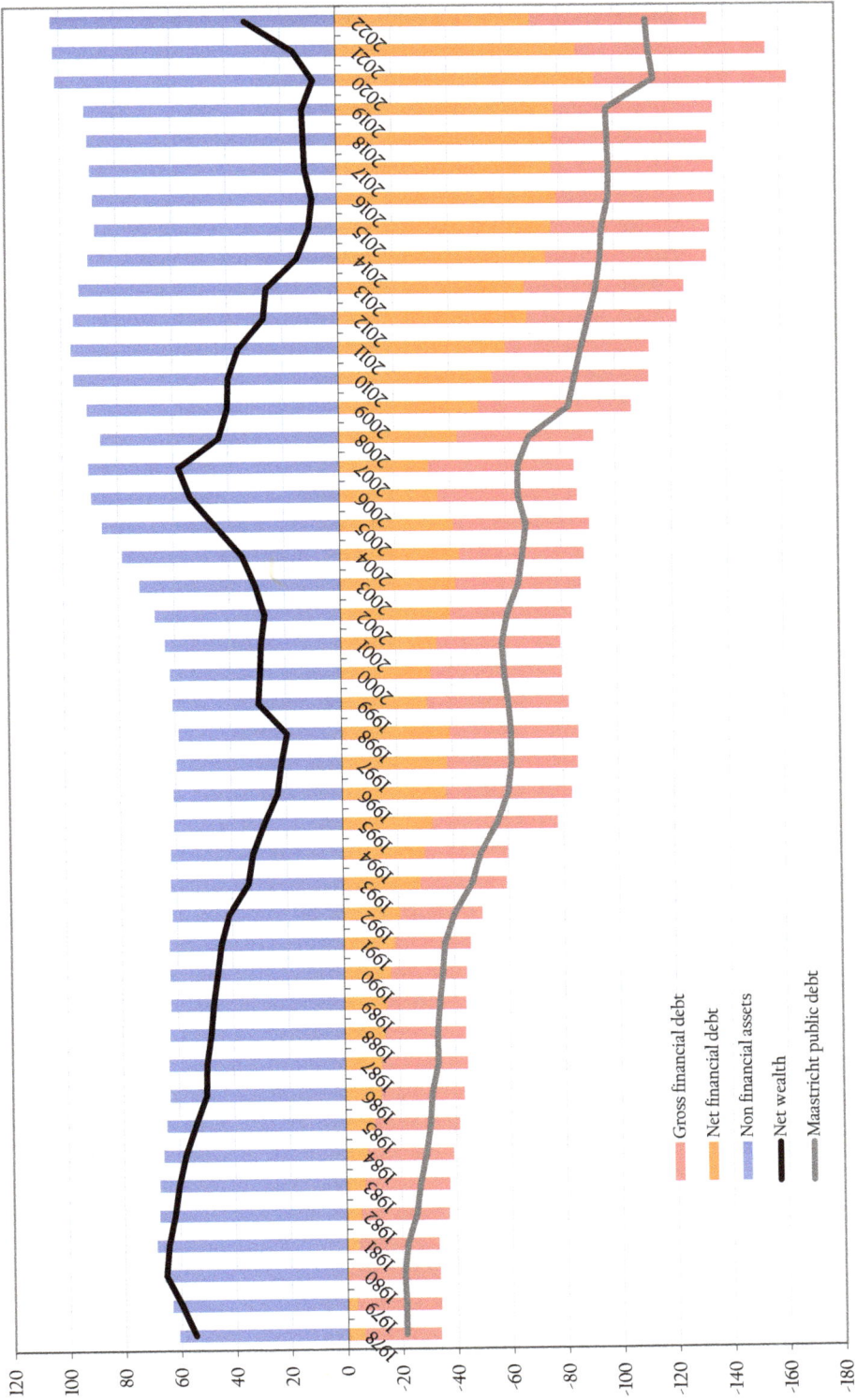

Fig. 2.4 Evolution of General Government Net Wealth as a % of GDP.
Source: Authors' creation based on data from INSEE.

Legend:
- Gross financial debt
- Net financial debt
- Non financial assets
- Net wealth
- Maastricht public debt

2.5 Savings and Investment Financing: The Large Gap Between the Central Government and Local Authorities

Historical developments show the extent to which the budgetary situation between the Central Government and local authorities has decoupled since the 1990s. Self-financing, which represents the ratio between savings and investment, although less than 100%, was largely positive for the Central Government and local authorities until the beginning of the 1990s. The use of debt to finance investment was moderate. But the fiscal situation of the Central Government deteriorated markedly from the 1990s: systematically negative savings replaced the previous, largely positive situation (1.2% of GDP on average over the 1980s). Conversely, local authorities saw their savings increase significantly during the 1980s. These were less than 1% of GDP until the beginning of the 1980s. They rose to 2% of GDP on average from the 1990s and reached the historic high of 2.2% of GDP in 2022. With a self-financing rate close to 100% from the mid-1990s to the present, local authorities have had little recourse to debt to finance their investment (Figure 2.5). The public debt of local authorities has thus varied very little since the beginning of the 1980s, oscillating only between 7% and 10% of GDP over more than forty years. Conversely, the Central Government, no longer generating savings from the 1990s, had to resort to increased indebtedness to finance its investment, despite scaling back on its investment projects. The effect was a reduction by one-third, in points of GDP, between the investment level for the last ten years and that of the end of the 1980s-beginning of the 1990s (see Figure 2.1). The debt ratio of the Central Government (including the various central administration bodies) has risen from 26% of GDP in 1990 to 92% in 2022.

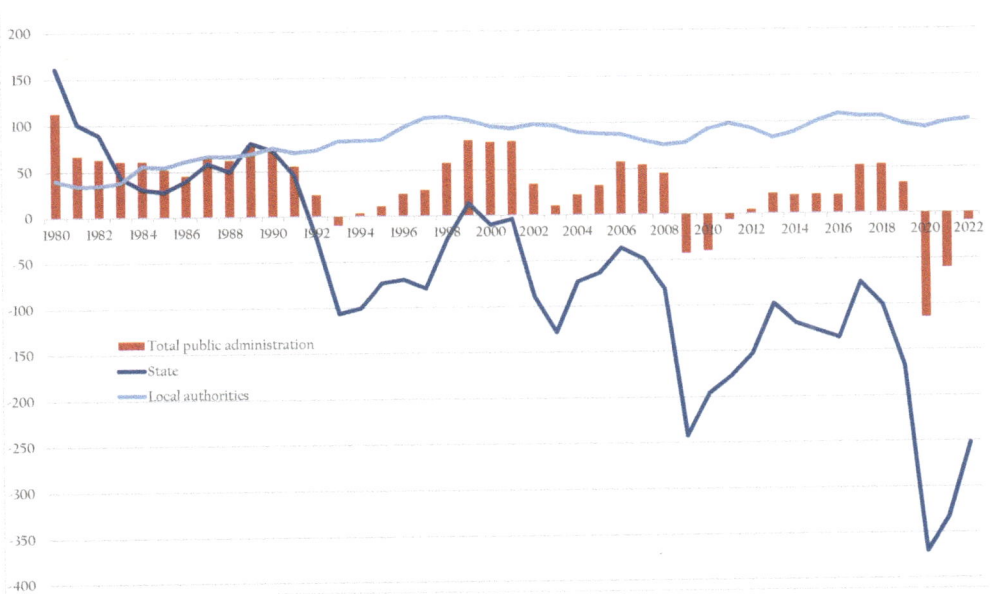

Fig. 2.5 Self-Financing Rate (Saving/Investment) by Administrative Category, in %.
Source: Authors' creation based on data from INSEE.

2.6 How is Public Investment Financed in France?

2.6.1 Who Does What?

In France, as in many European countries, public investment is primarily managed by local public administrations, accounting for 55.6% of the total in 2020. This figure is in line with the average of 54.8% across the European Union. The central government of France contributed 36.9% to public investment in 2020, while social-security administrations (SSA) contributed 7.5%.

Within France, defence is the central government's major focus for investment. It represents 71.1% of the expenditures from the general budget, according to the draft finance law for 2023. Other significant investment areas include the 'Justice' mission (5.9%) and the 'Security' mission (4.3%). State-operated entities, classified under central government in national accounts, predominantly invest in higher education. Local authorities, on the other hand, concentrate their investments on infrastructure, particularly in transportation and public facilities, including housing, water, and sanitation networks.

These investment priorities are, again, quite similar to other European countries. Defence and infrastructure (particularly transport and housing) constitute the majority of public investment, followed by health and education (see *Ministère de l'économie et des finances* 2023).

Due to their multi-year nature, investments are managed somewhat differently from other government expenditures. Categorizing these projects into commitment authorizations, multi-year appropriations, and annual payment appropriations is necessary to better anticipate future expenditure trends. This practice, customary for both the State and local authorities, was expanded to State-operated entities in 2012.

Since 2012, investment projects undertaken by the Central government, Social-Security Agencies, and other public actors are developed within a framework encompassing three tools:

1. An inventory of ongoing investment projects and a preliminary socio-economic assessment. The annual inventory supplies both the State and Parliament with an overview of ongoing public-investment projects. The inventory is carried out by ministries. The quantity and quality of information submitted is increasing but variable. While this remains the case, caution is warranted when interpreting figures from the ministry-completed forms.

2. The law mandates project leaders seeking State funding (or funding from related institutions) to conduct socio-economic assessments prior to application. The goal is to provide an objective analysis of costs and benefits for the community, thereby informing investment decisions.

3. For large-scale projects, the legislation also mandates an independent second expert opinion on the evaluation report. This procedure applies to projects exceeding 100 million euros.

These tools are mainly administered by the General Secretariat for Investment (Secrétariat général pour l'investissement, SGPI), operating under the Prime Minister's office to ensure coherence and oversight of the Government's investment policy.

2.6.2 Co-financing is Becoming the Norm

This management approach, though diversified, elevates the complexity of directing and steering investment strategies. Furthermore, the State, in tasking its operators with project management, has a declining influence on total public investment. While the central government's share in public investment has hovered between 35% and 40% since the late 1970s, the recent trend is for the growth of central government organisations (ODAC) and a reduction in the role of the Government itself.

Public-private partnership contracts are rarely utilized due to their commercial project requirement and restrictive administrative procedures. Most of financing happens through standard public-procurement procedures.

Funding structures, on the other hand, exhibit a growing diversity, concurrently reducing the Central government and its affiliated institutions' share in the total amount. Investment spending is increasingly characterised by co-financing involving multiple actors. Today, only a few major public projects are fully financed by the State, an operator, or a local authority. Each project has, on average, three co-financiers; consortia exceeding four members is common in real estate, higher education and research, and transport projects (*Ministère de l'économie et des finances* 2023). Notably, local and regional authorities, particularly regions, emerge as primary co-financiers. Furthermore, many public investment projects tap into European funding sources, such as the European Union or the European Investment Bank. Involvement of various stakeholders is necessitated by the substantial financial scale of these projects.

An important role is also played by the Caisse des Dépôts et des Consignations (CDC), the French National Public bank that manages the guaranteed savings by French households ('Livret A') and the pension funds of public actors, including central and local government and public corporations. The role of Public Investment Banks is analysed in Chapter 7 of this volume. Here, it is enough to say that the CDC finances public investment in, primarily, two missions. The first concerns the financing of social housing. Via the 'Livret A' savings account, the CDC collects funds, which it then lends to social-housing organisations. Its second mission is to support investment policies in territories: the organisation finances transportation-infrastructure projects and provides expertise on projects initiated by local communities. Since the launch of Next Generation EU, the CDC has also become involved in investment in green and digital transitions.[1]

2.7 Is French Public Debt Sustainable?

As the net worth of the French government has shrunk significantly in recent years, it is legitimate to ask whether public finances are still sustainable. The answer to this question is, with some caution and qualification, yes. Since the early 1990s, nominal interest rates have fallen significantly in almost all advanced economies, and more than inflation. The result is a decline in real rates, which has helped ease the debt burden. The apparent rate, the ratio of interest expenditure to public debt, has also declined despite a significant increase in the debt-to-GDP ratio. Figure 2.6 shows the case of France, but similar trends are seen elsewhere, in 'virtuous' countries as well as in those where public finances are most fragile, such as Italy.

---

1   The CDC has third mission which is to support businesses. It invests directly in companies to foster their development, but it also focuses on helping to secure financing for businesses or activities that would otherwise struggle, such as export financing for SMEs or financing for social and solidarity economy enterprises. To achieve this, it utilizes its subsidiary jointly established with the government: BPI France (*Banque Publique d'Investissement*).

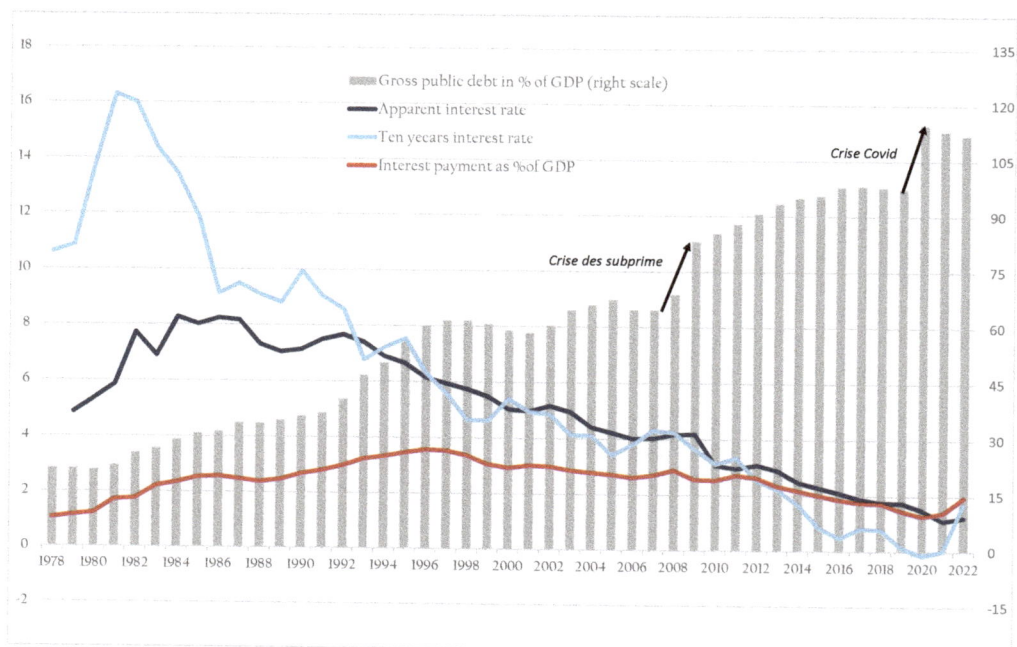

Fig. 2.6 Interest Rates and Public Debt, France.
Source: Authors' creation based on data from INSEE.

Recent literature has examined this long-term trend to try not only to understand the reasons for it but also to predict its future persistence. In a standard theoretical framework, the so-called 'natural' interest rate is that which leads to the balance between savings and investment at the level corresponding to the full utilisation of productive capacity; that is, it is the interest rate that neither stimulates nor depresses growth. This rate, which must be estimated, also dropped significantly over time. The analytical chapter of the most recent issue of the IMF *World Economic Outlook* (WEO) gives estimates for the natural rate that are close to zero for the largest world economies, and even slightly below zero for France and Japan (IMF 2023, p. 49).

Broadly speaking, a long-run downward trend in natural rates indicates a situation of chronic excess saving (which, in fact, describes a shortage of aggregate demand). What are the reasons for this chronic excess of savings? Since the late 1980s, and even more so since the early years of this century, global savings have increased dramatically. The reasons for this increase are multiple, from the recent increase in uncertainty and financial instability to the aging of the population, the increase in inequality, and the increase in private debt. In advanced economies, this increase in savings has been accompanied by a significant reduction in investment. Public investment, of course; but also, to an almost-equal extent, private investment. The decline of the latter is explained by the slowdown in productivity (France may be an exception in this, as, contrary to other countries, its decline of productivity is not matched by a strong decrease of private investment), the financial fragility of companies, and a general uncertainty that has compressed the 'animal spirits'. Platzer and Peruffo (2022) try to disentangle these factors for the United States and find that the slowdown in total factor productivity growth is the most important driver of the drop in the natural rate of interest, with demographics (a decline in fertility and a rise in life-expectancy) and inequality that are the second and third most important factors respectively.

To be sure, the decline in investment occurred only in advanced economies and, overall, it was offset by the boom in emerging market and low-income economies. However, the savings of the latter, in a search for 'safe assets', flowed into the financial markets of advanced economies, contributing to the widening gap with investment and the deflationary trend that central banks have been facing for at least a decade.

From 2021, we seem to be living in a new world. Supply-side difficulties (bottlenecks, rising production costs, geopolitical tensions, and the war in Ukraine) have led to scarcities in many sectors and slowly percolated to the whole economy. These challenges on the supply side of the economy have been compounded for some countries (such as the USA) by a strong increase in demand following the pandemic. In France, this demand boost has been relatively weak, with consumption still below its pre-pandemic levels and the savings rate still 3 p.p. higher than its 2019 level.

With inflation at levels not seen since the 1970s and growth that remains subdued overall, some have argued that secular stagnation is poised to become a thing of the past again, replaced by 'stagflation'. In fact, the risk of a 1970s-type stagflation is non-existent: Corsello et al. (2023) show how institutional differences (wage indexation and the independence of central banks) play a crucial role in explaining why the 2020s are not the 1970s. Nevertheless, and regardless of the risk of a repeat of the 1970s, the question remains: can we put secular stagnation behind us? Some elements might lead us to think so: it is certain that the organisation of production processes and the sectoral distribution of activity that will emerge at the end of this process will be quite different from those we are used to and that, for certain goods and sectors (think fossil fuels), prices are destined to remain permanently high. Furthermore, it is possible that the colossal investments necessary for the ecological and digital transition will support economic activity for decades to come. A recent report by *France Strategie* (Pisani-Ferry and Mahfouz 2023) details possible green-transition scenarios for France and lends some support to the view that inflationary pressures might build up between now and 2030.[2] It quantifies, in 2 points of GDP, the yearly additional investment needs for the French economy to stay in line with the 'Fit for 55' EU targets; it also notices that this additional investment, while boosting demand, might reduce potential GDP in the

---

2   Chapter 7 of the report details the sectoral-investment needs and quantifies them in 100 billion euros yearly of additional green investment, of which almost 90% is in transportation (€32bn) and housing (€54bn). If we net these numbers with the reduction in brown investment, the total is €66bn; transportation evens out, while, in housing, the lower brown investment is negligible.

short-to-medium run, that is, until 2030.[3] Furthermore, managing the transition (and ensuring a fair distribution of its costs) will likely involve higher energy prices—again, in the next decade or so—and higher public debt (in the order of 10 additional points from now to 2030, and of 25 points at the 2050 horizon). All this will lead to higher and possibly more volatile inflation in the next decade.

While the factors just mentioned may lead to think that secular stagnation is past us, almost all the reasons for the compression of consumption and investment that led Gordon (2016) and Summers (2016) to revive the concept of secular stagnation are still having an effect. It is even possible that these will play a larger-than-ever role in the future. Demographic factors and persisting high inequality will continue to push up savings. More flexible and precarious labour markets and an increasing debt burden (both public and private) will also likely have an influence on the savings rate. Last but not least, macroeconomic and geopolitical uncertainty will reduce the propensity to invest (especially in long-term projects) and feed precautionary savings. It is true, on the other hand, that geopolitical uncertainty could lead to a greater propensity to hold safe assets (thus pushing up demand for government bonds) and to make new public investment in previously neglected sectors, such as defence, thus contrasting the tendency towards secular stagnation.

While it is not possible to forecast which of these forces will prevail, it seems unlikely that the huge investments needed to set our economies on the path of ecological and digital transition will be sufficient to compensate for secular structural trends such as aging, rising inequality, uncertainty, and geopolitical instability. It is, therefore, reasonable to think that these forces will again dominate in the medium term and that policy makers will return in a few years to struggle with secular stagnation and deflationary pressures. This is a point also made by Blanchard (2023) and by the already-quoted WEO chapter (IMF 2023). The latter argues that, once the inflationary episode is over, we will return to an era of low interest rates; advanced countries will continue to suffer from reduced productivity growth and population aging, and emerging countries will see a similar situation as the dynamics of their economies catch up and converge with those of richer countries.

This has, of course, strong implications for debt sustainability—globally and for France. If interest rates are bound to remain sufficiently low, then fiscal space will be enhanced even with modest growth rates. In fact, by looking at the past, the growth-interest differential remained positive for most of the past decade (see Figure 2.7).

---

3   The ecological transition will require mostly capital substitution with the objective not of increasing productivity but of greening production.

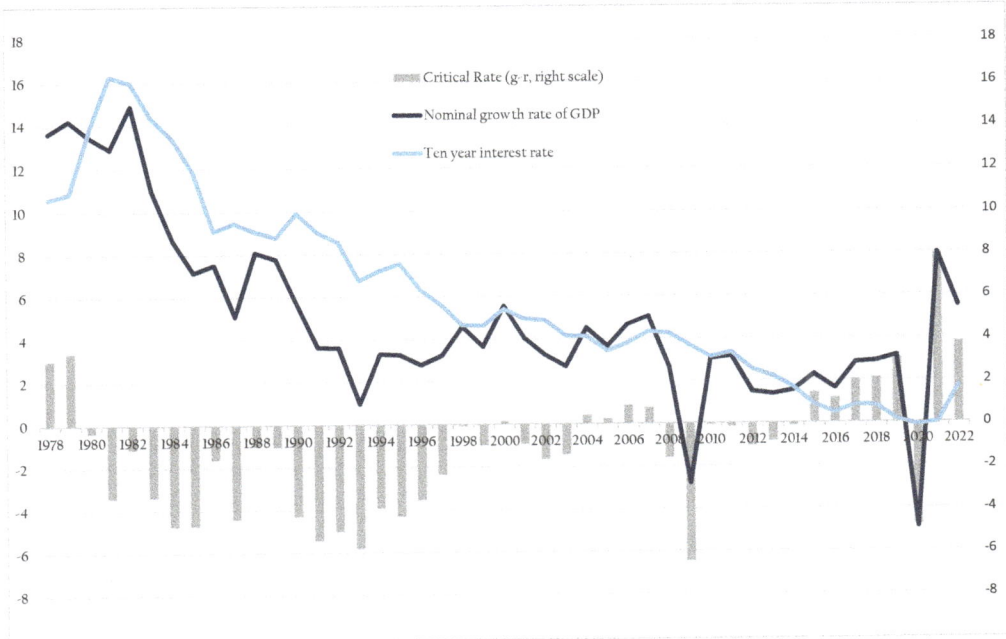

Fig. 2.7 The Critical Gap (*g-r*) for France.
Source: Authors' creation based on data from INSEE.

If this keeps being the case in the medium-term future, sustained investment may be compatible with a stabilization or even with a moderate reduction of public debt.

References

Blanchard, O. J. (2023) 'Secular Stagnation Is Not Over', *PIIE Realtime Economics Blog* January 24, https://www.piie.com/blogs/realtime-economics/secular-stagnation-not-over

Corsello, F., M. Gomellini, and D. Pellegrino (2023) 'Inflation and Energy Price Shocks: Lessons from the 1970s', *Banca d'Italia Occasional Paper*. 709 (July)

Draghi, M. (2012) 'Speech at the Global Investment Conference in London', ECB (26 July)

Gordon, R. J. (2016) *The Rise and Fall of American Growth: The U.S. Standard of Living since the Civil War*. The Princeton Economic History of the Western World. Princeton University Press

IMF (2023) 'The Natural Rate of Interest: Drivers and Implications for Policy', chapter 2 of *World Economic Outlook. A Rocky Recovery*. pp. 45–68. Washington DC : International Monetary Fund

Ministère de l'économie et des finances (2023) 'Évaluation Des Grands Projets d'investissements Publics', *Annèxe Au Projet de Loi de Finances Pour 2023*

Pisani-Ferry, J. and S. Mahfouz (2023) 'Les Incidences Économiques de l'action Pour Le Climat', *France Strategie, Rapport à La Première Ministre* (Mai)

Plane, M. and F. Saraceno (2021) 'From Fiscal Consolidation to the Plan de Relance', in F. Cerniglia et al. (eds), *The Great Reset—2021 European Public Investment Outlook*. Cambridge, UK: Open Book Publishers, https://doi.org/10.11647/OBP.0280

Platzer, J. and M. Peruffo (2022) 'Secular Drivers of the Natural Rate of Interest in the United States: A Quantitative Evaluation', *IMF Working Papers* 2022 (030)

Summers, L. H. (2016) 'The Age of Secular Stagnation. What It Is and What to Do About It', *Foreign Policy* (March/April), https://www.foreignaffairs.com/articles/united-states/2016-02-15/age-secular-stagnation

3. Germany Lacks Political Will to Finance Needed Public-Investment Boost

Katja Rietzler, Andrew Watt, and Ekaterina Juergens

After more than a decade of weak public investment, Germany has accumulated a substantial public-investment backlog. The requirements for additional public investment in the next decade are in the range of €600 to 800bn, implying a further commitment of 1.6 to 2.1% of GDP each year. The federal government had made provisions for much smaller programmes, evading the debt brake. After the federal constitutional court ruled that shifting € 60 bn to an off-budget fund is unconstitutional, even this is now under threat. The court ruling casts doubt over similar operations at the federal and state levels, and comes when fiscal policy was already tightening under the pressure of the reapplied debt brake and rising interest rates. As this publication goes to press Germany is engaged in a fierce debate how to resolve the budget crisis.

3.1 Situation and Recent Developments

After more than a decade of weak public investment, Germany has accumulated a substantial public-investment backlog, particularly at the local-government level. Investment needs, which range from roads and school buildings to the digitalisation of public administration, were already estimated in 2019 at €457bn over a ten-year horizon (Bardt et al. 2020). With the recently enhanced climate goals of the EU and the German government, additional investment needs in the health sector, as well as higher prices, the requirements for additional public investment and investment promotion in the next decade are more likely in the range of €600 to 800bn, which would imply a further annual commitment of 1.6 to 2.1% of GDP (Dullien et al. 2022; Rietzler and Watt 2022).[1] Whereas infrastructure investment should be raised substantially and smoothed—to avoid the problem of intermittency and procyclicality—over the

---

1   The estimate was based on 2022 GDP.

https://doi.org/10.11647/OBP.0386.03

long-term, investment to reduce greenhouse-gas emissions needs to be frontloaded, as the remaining carbon budget is shrinking rapidly. Investment to decarbonise the economy is mainly required in the private sector (in particular, production, transport, and heating), but the government plays a vital part in providing incentives for the private sector via investment grants in addition to carbon pricing and regulation. Furthermore, the government sector must decarbonise its own facilities, which amount to about 176.000 units at the local-government level alone (BMWi 2018). The current federal government is well aware of the requirements, having promised 'a decade of investment' in its coalition agreement (Rietzler and Watt 2022). Thus, one would expect a sustained and sizable increase in investment spending.

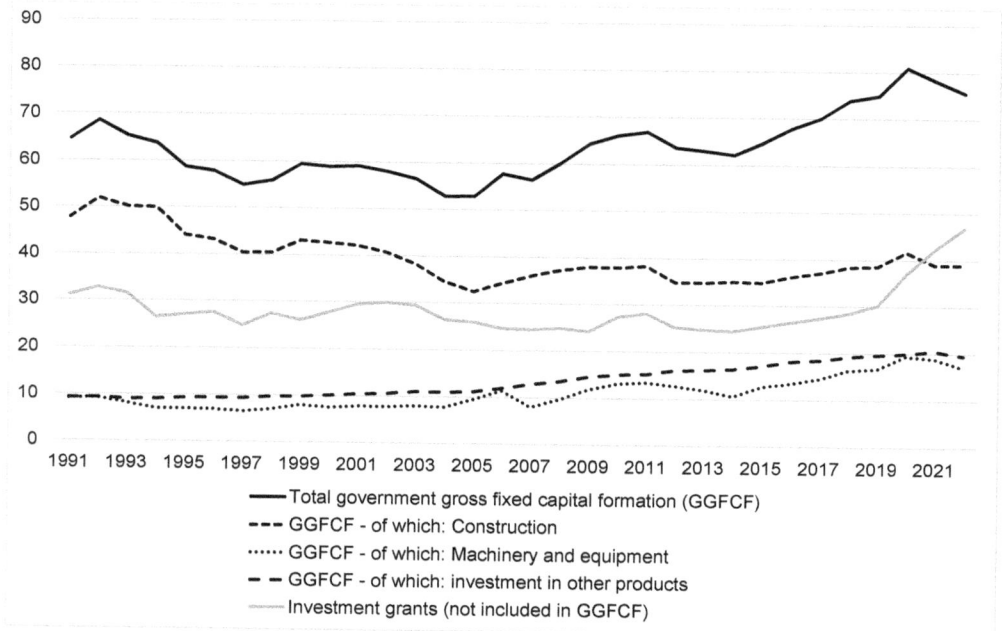

Fig. 3.1 Government Investment (GGFCF and its Components) and Investment Grants.
Note: in €bn, price adjusted, reference year 2015.
Source: Destatis, calculations of the IMK.

So far, the required massive additional public investment is nowhere to be seen in the data. Figure 3.1 shows that, after a strong increase in 2020 that was partly induced by the pandemic response, real government gross fixed-capital formation (GGFCF) declined again in the following two years. Investment in machinery and equipment, in construction, and in other products all dwindled. In early 2023, these trends showed little sign of reversing. In the first half of 2023, overall government investment declined by 2.7% compared to the second half of 2022, masking a strong decline of investment in machinery and equipment but somewhat stronger investment in construction compared to the previous half year; this was mainly at the municipal and state level, while federal-construction investment declined strongly even in nominal terms. Thus, part of the catch-up process since 2015 has been reversed.

Particularly in construction, double-digit price increases prevented nominal growth rates of a magnitude not seen since the German-reunification boom from translating into higher investment in real terms. In 2022, both nominal government construction investment and the respective deflator increased by 16%, leading to mere stagnation in real terms. In the first half of 2023, price increases for government-construction investment slowed somewhat. Municipalities, which accounted for 59% of the overall public-construction investment (almost three times the amount spent by the federal level), still report that their actual investment spending—85% of which is construction (cf. Figure 3.2)—regularly remains below what they had planned to spend. Municipalities face staff shortages in their administration and complain about capacity constraints in the construction industry (Raffer and Scheller 2023), both of which delay the roll-out of projects.

Unlike public investment itself, government investment grants to the private sector have increased massively since 2019 both in nominal and in real terms.[2] Here too, the expansion in real terms has recently been slowed by strong price increases.

3.2 What Does the German Population Expect? Results from an IMK Survey

Against the background of the accumulated-investment gaps, the adequacy of infrastructure has become a major barrier to economic activity in Germany—and Europe more generally—as firms report in surveys (European Investment Bank 2023, p. 69). Two other main barriers to private investment being voiced by managers are high energy costs and perceived uncertainty about the future (ibid.). These latter concerns could be at least partly alleviated, however, by improving the investment activity of the state. For instance, a more extensive public-goods provision in the renewable energy sector and the greater reliability of government investment spending could reduce uncertainty for private enterprises.

---

2   The deflator of private gross fixed-capital formation is used for price adjustment.

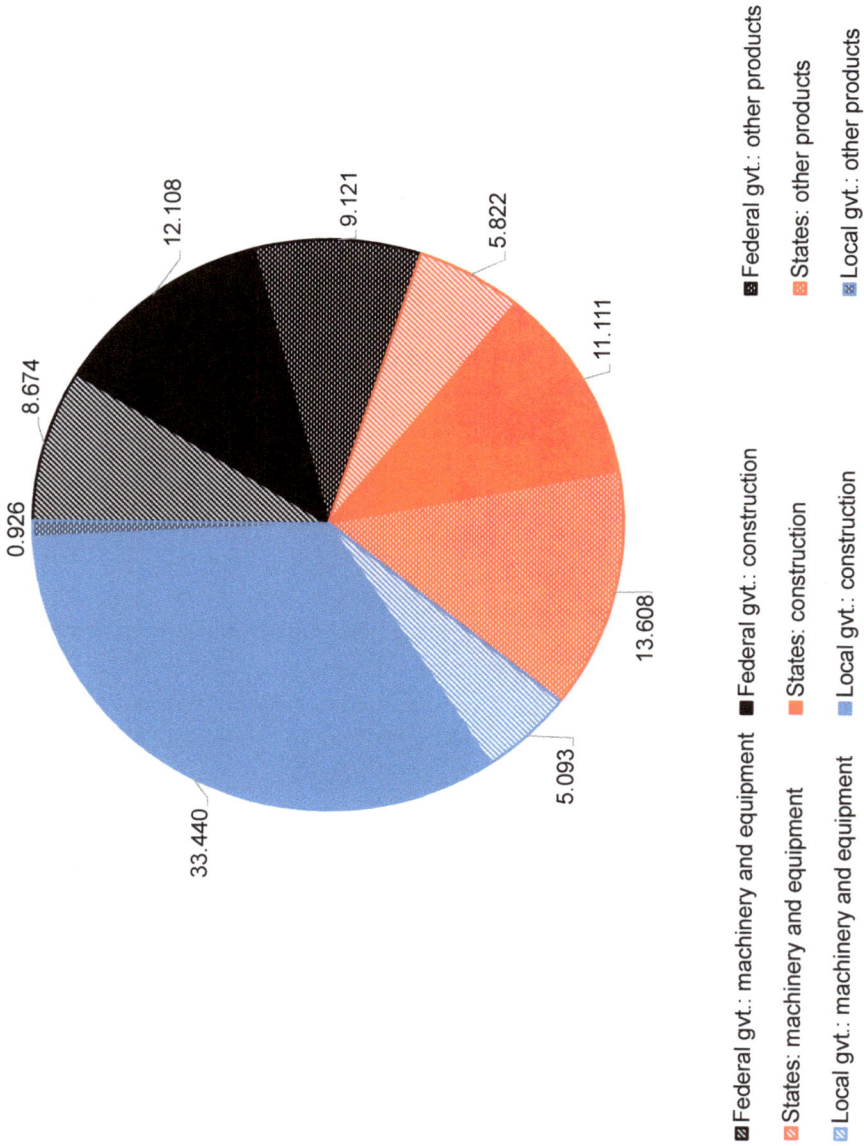

Fig. 3.2 Nominal Gross Fixed Capital Formation of Government Subsectors in 2022, on Federal, State, and Local Levels, in €bn.
Source: Destatis, excluding social security, which accounted for only €0.9bn or 0.8% of the GGFCF.

It is not only business leaders, however, who are concerned. A recent nationwide survey shows that German citizens and residents—whose votes ultimately determine the funding available for public-investment and spending priorities—are also discontented with the deterioration of public infrastructure and would prefer stronger public investment activity (Behringer et al. 2021; Henze et al. 2022). The survey examined public satisfaction with public infrastructure in various categories (see Figure 3.3) and attitudes towards government-investment activity in the run-up to the 2021 German federal election. The data was collected as a computer-assisted online survey, and the total dataset encompassed 8,483 individuals aged between 18 and 75, selected representatively according to main sociodemographic and geographic characteristics, such as gender, age, income, and federal state. The results of the survey reveal that, across all investment categories, the overall satisfaction with infrastructure is rather low and the desire for more government investment is strong in Germany.

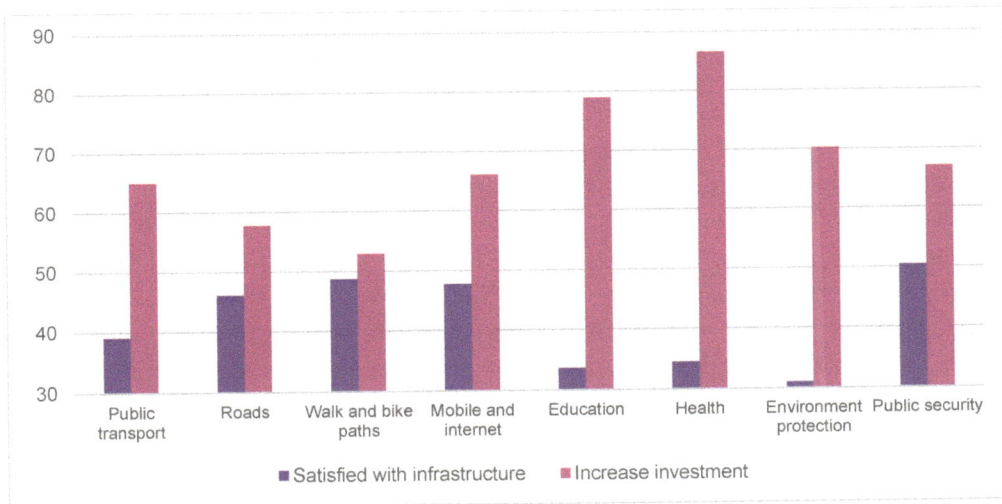

Fig. 3.3 Satisfaction with Public Infrastructure and Desire for More Investment, in % of Total Respondents.
Note: Respondents shown were 'somewhat satisfied' or 'very much satisfied' with public infrastructure, and their desire was that investment would 'increase somewhat' or 'increase substantially'.
Source: Henze et al. (2022).

As Figure 3.3 shows, satisfaction with the state of public infrastructure is low on average, being lowest for categories such as climate protection (31%) as well as education and health (34%). Accordingly, about 68% of surveyed individuals are generally in favour of an increase in government investment. The respondents see the greatest need for investment by far in the areas of health (87%) and education (79%), which is consistent with their dissatisfaction with the state of infrastructure. Since the survey was conducted during the COVID-19 crisis, these responses reflect the detrimental consequences of curbing investment in the health-care system that was vividly exposed by the pandemic. In addition, environmental protection is seen as an important area by more than two thirds of those surveyed.

Notably, the majority of respondents prefer an increase in public investment in almost all German federal states. In some of these, more than 70% see a need for additional investment (North Rhine-Westphalia, Schleswig-Holstein, Rhineland-Palatinate, and Berlin). Some significant differences in responses from urban and rural areas as well as from East and West Germany, however, are worth mentioning.

Firstly, residents of cities report a much higher satisfaction with public transport (48%) than those of rural areas (31%). Analogously, the urban population is much more content with internet and mobile networks (52% versus 44%). The quality of infrastructure in these categories is, of course, much higher in metropolitan areas than in the countryside. It is nevertheless striking that a relatively low satisfaction in rural areas does not translate into a proportionally higher demand for investment in public transport and digital infrastructure. This stands in stark contrast to, for example, health care, which shows an expected correlation between lower satisfaction and higher-investment desire in the countryside.

This interpretation does not imply that public-transport and digital-infrastructure issues are negligible in rural areas: there, a broad majority is in favour of more investment, too. However, while rural respondents seem to be more willing to accept cutbacks in public transportation, they report a higher interest in increased infrastructure investment benefitting private vehicles, such as roads and bridges (60% in the rural areas versus 56% in the cities. The difference is statistically significant). These patterns suggest self-selection between urban and rural areas and 'lock-in effects'. Residents of smaller towns must rely largely on cars for transportation. Since they don't use public transport, they do not express such an interest in investing in a better network, perpetuating the current situation, even though they are dissatisfied with it. The same phenomenon can be noticed in the case of bicycle infrastructure. Only 53% of all respondents expressed their preference for higher investment in this category, mirroring a still very low volume of traffic by bicycle in Germany. Accordingly, the need for the state to take an active role in providing alternatives becomes even more relevant: the green transition does not emerge by itself but builds on the systems already in place, and existing infrastructure shapes not only the current behaviour but also people's expectations of possible solutions and their plans.

Secondly, the biggest difference between East and West Germany is in the desire for more investment in environmental protection. While 73% of surveyed individuals voiced their preference for more investment in climate protection in West Germany, only 60% of respondents—still a majority—shared these demands in the East. The difference in responses of residents of East and West Germany does not reflect a lower objective need for environmental protection in the East. Rather, these are differences in the perceived urgency of climate issues in comparison to other economic and social concerns between the two groups.

Importantly, the respondents were asked how the additional public investment should be financed. This is necessary in order to elicit comprehensive preferences on public finance. Upon being confronted with the question of how to pay for the increase in public investment, about 6% of all survey participants who voiced a preference for this increase withdrew their request, and a further 7% of respondents could not answer the question. On the other hand, 17% specified that they would prefer the investment to be debt-financed; 62% (the majority) indicated that they would prefer other expenditures to be reduced; last but not least, 8% of the respondents were in favour of a tax increase to finance the additional public investment.

3.3 Financing Government Investment Spending

3.3.1 General Overview

Germany faces various challenges in overcoming its huge investment backlog and implementing the necessary investments for the economic transformation. Until the surprise constitutional court ruling on 15 November 2023, funding did not seem to be the critical issue. Staff shortages, both in relevant economic sectors and in public-sector administration, play a prominent role; and spending often remains substantially below plan (Raffer and Scheller 2023; Rietzler and Watt 2022). According to extrapolated survey data from the Research Institute of the Federal Employment Agency (IAB 2023), there were almost 1.7 million vacancies in the second quarter of 2023. This is an exceptionally high number by historical standards despite a decline compared to the fourth quarter of 2022. The ratio of registered unemployed persons to the estimated total vacancies was 1:1.5. In the second quarter of 2022, vacancies in construction were estimated to be above 162,000 and in public administration (including social insurance) nearly 30,000.

Despite two major crises, massive fiscal stimulus, and high deficits in some years; German public finances are in relatively good shape. The debt-to-GDP ratio of 66.1% at the end of 2022 is substantially below the euro-area average and has risen by much less than in the financial crisis. Employment is at a record level, and most forecasters, including the IMK (Dullien et al. 2023), expect declining deficits as the energy crisis is overcome and the spending on the 'electricity-price brake' and the 'gas-price brake' remains far below plan as gas prices have returned to pre-war levels (Figure 3.4).

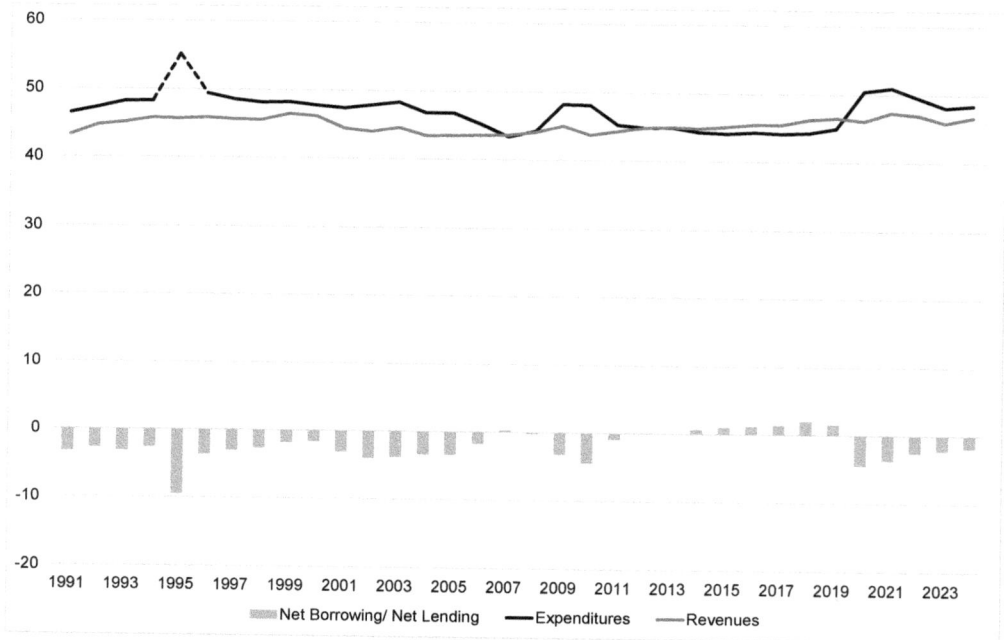

Fig. 3.4 General Government Revenues, Expenditures, and Net Borrowing/Net Lending, as % of GDP.
Source: Destatis, IMK forecast for 2023 and 2024.

Nevertheless, fiscal pressure was rising already before the court ruling. Recent income-tax cuts on top of extensive temporary measures to support household incomes in the energy crisis are causing permanent revenue losses. Unlike in the period before the pandemic, public finances no longer benefit from the tailwinds of declining interest rates that created additional fiscal space from year to year. On the contrary, interest spending has been rising since its nadir in 2021 and is now squeezing the fiscal room for manoeuvre. Its effect, in the case of the federal government, is exacerbated by booking discounts of new bond emissions immediately instead of spreading them over the term of the securities (Deutsche Bundesbank 2021). In this environment, the focus of fiscal policy is now clearly on consolidation. The German finance minister has announced his intention to restructure expenditures away from consumption and social spending towards more investment (BMF 2023a). While there is always scope for some efficiency gains, it is doubtful that double-digit billions of euros can be made available with this approach.

Against this general background, the financing options differ widely between government subsectors. These are now analysed in greater detail.

3.3.2 Fiscal Situation of the Federal Government

The debt-brake limits net new debt to 0.35% of GDP.[3] In addition, it allows for a cyclical component estimated according to the European Commission's production-function approach. Financial transactions, such as the purchase of shares in businesses or extended loans, are excluded. After a suspension for three years in the wake of the COVID-19 crisis, the debt brake was put back in force in 2023, one year earlier than the European fiscal rules. Due to a negative cyclical component of €15.3bn and financial transactions of €17.7bn, in addition to the permitted structural new debt of €12.6bn,[4] the federal government can take on new (net) debt amounting to €45.6bn in 2023, according to the budget plan. At €86.4bn, the planned deficit is almost twice as high. This is possible because €40.5bn of the €48.2bn in reserves accumulated before the pandemic are to be used (see Table 3.1).

Table 3.1 New Debt Permissions Under the Debt Brake and Planned Deficit in 2023

	Initial budget plan 2023
Permitted structural new debt	€12.61bn
Debt permitted due to negative cyclical component	€15.34bn
Balance of financial transactions	€17.67bn
Total permitted new debt	€45.62bn (1.1 % of GDP)
Planned fiscal deficit	€86.37bn
Deficit exceeding permitted new debt	€40.75bn
Use of reserves accumulated before the pandemic (Total: €48.2bn)	€40.50bn
Emission of coins	€0.25bn

Source: Haushaltsgesetz 2023, calculation in % of GDP based on IMK forecast (Dullien et al. 2023).

As a first reaction to the court ruling the federal government has decided to invoke the escape clause retroactively for 2023. An amendment to the federal budget is to be implemented mainly to legalise this year's spending out of the economic stabilisation fund, an off-budget fund to support households and businesses in the energy crisis. The amendment also affects the core budget, e.g. via an updated cyclical component.

---

3 GDP of the year before the draft budget is set up, that is, usually two years prior to budget execution.
4 0.35% of 2021 GDP.

The court ruling has made the draft budget for 2024 obsolete (and so it is not reported here). The strategy of the federal government had been to transfer credit permissions granted under the escape clause to off budget funds for future use. While the core budget was planned to be tightened somewhat, substantial room for manoeuvre was seemingly created in off-budget funds According to the constitution, the debt brake also applies to extra-budgetary funds as long as these are not legally independent bodies. Thus, in order to use so-called 'Sondervermögen' (special funds lacking a legal personality) to create fiscal space, the legislature also had to change the booking rules. This was done with a budget amendment for 2021 passed in early 2022, against which the conservative opposition (the Christian Democratic Union and the Christian Social Union) started legal action before the constitutional court. According to the old public-accounting rule, operations of the off-budget funds became relevant at the time of expenditure. This change of rules enabled the government to shift new debt to future periods. Table 3.2 provides an overview of credit permissions transferred to future years at the beginning of 2023.

Table 3.2 Unused Credit Permissions of Relevant Extra-Budgetary Funds ('Sondervermögen')

	Reserves (unused credit permissions) beginning of 2023	Planned withdrawals for 2023
Economic Stabilisation Fund ('WSF')	€169.8bn	€121.2bn (unrealistically high)
Climate and Transformation fund ('KTF')	€90.8bn	€14.1bn
Fund for the Army	€100bn	€8.4bn
Reconstruction Fund 2021	€14.0bn	€3.0bn
Digitisation	€6.4bn	€2.7 bn

Sources: Bundesrechnungshof (2023b), Deutscher Bundestag (2023b), estimates of the IMK.

The largest off-budget fund is the economic stabilisation fund (WSF), established during the pandemic and has been used to support gas suppliers and to implement the electricity- and gas-price brakes. Because gas prices have been much lower than forecast, actual disbursements have been substantially below plan. The emergency budget amendment 2023 seeks to bring past disbursements in line with the constitution. The fund will now expire in 2023, which means that other sources would have to be made available to fund the planned disbursements of roughly € 14 bn by April 2024.

The Climate and Transformation Fund (KTF) has so far been the government's key instrument to support climate-protection investment. Its regular revenue from carbon pricing is not nearly enough to finance the envisaged grants for climate investment and electricity subsidies for the German industry. The additional credit permissions were already insufficient as they were expected to be used up by 2026. Now the underfunding is becoming even more serious. In addition, the coalition agreement of 2021 had envisaged a 'climate allowance' ('Klimageld') that returns revenues from Germany's carbon tax to the population on a per-capita basis. This is one option for ensuring social justice in the transformation (Gechert et al. 2019) and, thus, bolstering acceptance, So far institutional-administrative weaknesses have prevented a direct 'climate payment' to the population, but if it is these revenues would not be available for investment or for transformation-related investment grants.

In principle the constitutional court ruling of November 2023 applies to all credit permissions made available to extra-budgetary funds under the suspended debt brake. It could thus also affect the Reconstruction Fund 2021, which envisages €2bn for the repair of federal infrastructure and up to €14bn to rebuild the regional infrastructure in Rhineland Palatinate, North Rhine Westphalia, and Bavaria—areas affected by torrential rain and flooding in summer 2021. Although the investment is not additional, it will modernise the regional infrastructure and can also include climate-adaptation measures. A cancellation is hard to imagine, but funding is now in doubt.

The other funds are of minor importance. Measures put in place to address massive needs, particularly the funding of digitisation, are quite insufficient. Progress on such projects, however, has been impeded not only because of funding issues but also due to the fragmentation of responsibilities between the levels of government and the lack of a coherent strategy (Bundesrechnungshof 2023a).

Unlike the other funds, the fund for the army setting aside €100bn for a modernisation of the German armed forces in response to the Russian aggression against Ukraine has been established outside the scope of the debt brake through a change of the German constitution, supported by a large majority in both the Bundestag[5] and the Bundesrat.[6] The envisaged spending is mostly classified as investment according to the national accounts, but it does not contribute to the modernisation of infrastructure or transformation.

If the court ruling is applied to all affected operations, the underfunding of the federal budget in the coming years may exceed €110 bn. As this publication went to press it is still not clear what the 2024 budget will look like, nor when it will be passed. The court ruling has triggered a fierce debate about whether and how to finance the originally envisaged spending. Some are calling for substantial social spending cuts, others for reductions in subsidies, particularly those harmful to the climate. The finance minister remains opposed to tax increases. Many, including previous supporters, are demanding a comprehensive reform of the debt brake or even its abolition, for which, however, there is not the required two-thirds majority. One option to provide the necessary funding for state support of the ecological transformation

---

5   The German federal parliament.
6   The representation of the federal states in the German legislature.

within the framework of the debt brake would be to endow the KTF with the same constitutional credit financing rights as the fund for the army. The overall volume could be comparable. However, this would also require a two thirds majority both in the Bundestag and the Bundesrat.

If the envisaged spending is scrapped or is now financed by other spending cuts or – less damaging – tax hikes, rather than borrowing, it is very likely to push the German economy into a recession once more in 2024. But the issue is not merely one of cyclical demand management. The planned investment in infrastructure and the support for businesses and households in accomplishing the needed decarbonization, while insufficient, is certainly necessary for Germany to modernise and address widely recognized weaknesses in its production model. Any serious cutbacks pose a threat to that endeavour.

The difficult fiscal-policy choices need, moreover, to take into account that substantial additional demands on the spending side will arise. The thirty-year redemption of debt incurred during the pandemic years 2020 to 2022 (€358.2bn) begins in 2028, while the debt incurred via the economic stabilisation fund (WSF) and up-to-€100bn debt incurred for the armed forces will also have to be paid off, beginning no later than 2031. Unless EU own resources are expanded, Germany will also have to service its share of the common debt assumed to finance the Recovery and Resilience Facility. (If the maximum underfunding of more than € 100 bn materialises – of course the redemption will be lower.)

3.3.3 Fiscal Situation of the Federal States

In Germany, the sixteen federal states play a limited role in public investment. They are directly responsible for research and development (universities) and education as well as some infrastructure and transport investment. They also play an important indirect role by supporting local authorities via regional fiscal-equalisation systems. Fiscal surpluses of the states taken altogether disguise large regional disparities, notably in terms of outstanding debt burdens per capita but also the challenges posed by structural change. Moreover, the financial situation at this level is rather opaque: numerous off-budget funds, differing debt-brake rules, and limited data complicate the assessment of the fiscal situation.[7] A number of states have resorted to similar practices as the federal government For instance, Saarland and Bremen—both poor states, with an important role for steel production—have invoked the emergency clause of the debt brake to create transformation funds. Saarland has set up an off-budget fund for the transformation while Bremen is using a 'crisis fund' within the core budget. Berlin

---

7   The scientific advisory board to the Stability Council has recently demanded more transparency concerning off-budget funds of both the federal and the state levels of government (Unabhängiger Beirat des Stabilitätsrats 2023). Cf. also Deutsche Bundesbank (2022).

decided to establish an off-budget fund for climate protection. All these models may now be at risk in the wake of the constitutional court ruling.

The states also face substantial fiscal pressures due to revenue losses from tax cuts and the end of the housing boom, which led to a large downward revision of revenues from the real estate transfer tax, the most important state tax. In addition, the states' VAT share is gradually reduced in favour of the federal government as a temporary crises-related increase and some federal programmes are phased out. By 2028, it is scheduled to decrease by 5.3 percentage points from 52.9% in 2020.[8] In addition, some states face noticeable budget burdens due to short redemption horizons for the debt incurred in the pandemic. The states cannot expect much additional support from the federal government. On the contrary, the federal ministry of finance argues that the federal government bears the lion's share of the crises-related expenditures and that it has reached a limit, where no further support of states and municipalities is possible (BMF 2023b). While it is true that the federal government has shifted substantial funds to the other government subsectors and incurred most of the crises-related additional debt, the states and municipalities are affected by decisions of the federal level—for example, offering shelter to refugees or setting standards. In this way, their capacity to conduct public investment at the regional level is limited.

3.3.4 Fiscal Situation of Local Government

Local governments play a vital role in public investment (Figure 3.2). However, their financial capacity to exercise this role is hindered even more severely, than on the state level. There are two key problems: permanently increasing assignments and responsibilities passed on from central government—for instance in the context of refugees, most recently from Ukraine—but with only limited additional funding; and substantial and persistent regional disparities (Raffer and Scheller 2023). High investment for years in wealthy Bavaria and low investment in regions going through structural change such as Saarland or the Ruhr Area (Ruhrgebiet) in North Rhine Westphalia are continuing to widen the gap. Both problems need to be tackled to overcome the investment backlog and at the same time invest enough in climate protection and adaptation. Local communities need additional revenues to finance long-term climate-related investment and sufficient transfers from the federal and state levels to finance expenditures related to the inflow of refugees (roughly one million from Ukraine alone). The growing population requires not only current spending, but also additional infrastructure investment, for example, in school buildings as refugees attending school in Germany from Ukraine alone exceed 200,000 (KMK 2023).

To overcome the problem of self-reinforcing regional disparities, more federal finance for social spending is required beyond the steps already taken and the

---

8   According to the most recent official tax forecast of October 2023.

distribution mechanism for the VAT share of the local communities, which currently favours economically strong communities, should be changed. However, such improvements for the municipalities would increase the fiscal pressure for the federal level.

Helping overindebted municipalities also remains on the agenda, as SPD, Greens and Liberals promised a solution in their coalition agreement but have yet to deliver. After several states (Hesse, Saarland and Rhineland Palatinate) started their own debt-relief programmes, North Rhine Westphalia, the most populous state, has announced its own programme (Landesregierung Nordrhein-Westfalen 2023). While such state debt-relief programmes receive much praise, it must be noted that the municipalities still bear a large share of the debt service burden under these programmes. This is particularly true in the case of North Rhine Westphalia, where the state hardly injects any funds of its own.

3.4 What has Been Achieved under the German RRF Plan?

As was noted in last year's chapter on Germany (Rietzler and Watt 2022), funding from the Recovery and Resilience Facility (RRF) is currently playing and will continue to play a minor role in financing public investment, in contrast to some other Member States. Originally, the German national plan to implement the RRF (DARP: Deutsche Aufbau- und Resilienzplan) foresaw €25.6bn in grants to be made available for projects from 2021–2026. Germany did not avail itself of the option to draw on RRF loans, because the interest rate on such loans was slightly higher than that which Germany, with its safe-haven status, enjoys on international bond markets. At the start of 2023, an additional €2.4bn were made available to Germany based on a recalculation of the RRF allocations to Member States, thus adding firepower of just under 10%. In addition, the REPowerEU programme, which was designed to help Member States to wean themselves off Russian energy as quickly as possible, made available to Germany an additional €2.1 for energy-related investment, specifically.

Despite these welcome top-ups, Rietzler and Watt's 2022 finding that EU programmes are of only secondary importance in Germany continues to hold true. This is the case because the substantial redistributional element in the original RRF targeted Member States severely affected by the COVID-19 crisis and those with GDP per capita below the EU average (Watt and Watzka 2020).

The end of 2023 marks the mid-point of the RRF programme. Assessing the progress made by the roll-out of RRF projects in Germany is not easy. At the time of writing (October 2023), Germany has only received the pre-financing which was paid out, unconditionally, in 2021. None of the envisaged five tranches, each of which requires detailed national reporting and approval by the EU Commission, has been disbursed, although a request for payment of just under €4bn was submitted in mid-September.[9] Correspondingly, the EU Commission RRF Scoreboard reports that Germany, to date, has not been officially assessed as having achieved any of the envisaged milestones and targets.

To a considerable extent, however, this situation reflects a processing delay that stems from the conceptualisation of the RRF facility. Only a 100% achievement score of milestone and targets triggers a full payment. Therefore, Member States shy away from submitting payment requests to receive their funding if all milestones and targets due for that tranche have not yet been achieved fully, so as to avoid receiving only partial payments, creating additional bureaucracy. An answer to a recent parliamentary question by the German Finance Ministry (8 June) indicated that the German government had, as of 30 April, itself designated 58 of the total 129 milestones and targets set out in the DARP as completed (Deutscher Bundestag 2023a: 36). Most milestones have been reached in the first two pillars of the DARP: decarbonisation (21) and digitalisation (11). Milestones in the other four pillars are in single figures: education (8), social inclusion (6), health (5), and public administration (7). In many cases, the inception-stage milestones achieved so far have been of a preparatory legal nature: passing/publishing legislation or administrative decisions enabling private-sector actors to claim various forms of support or bid for public contracts. In some cases, though, programmes have already been implemented with concrete and quantified outcomes; examples include support for electrical-vehicle purchases, tablets for teaching purposes, and the digitalisation and modernisation of hospitals. Changed circumstances led to the revision of 2 milestones, and the finance ministry is currently preparing to submit the first funding application, which will cover 36 milestones/targets.

Even if the RRF makes a relatively minor contribution to public investment in the German case, its expiration in 2026 will see this source of financing dry up. Unless EU resources are expanded, Member States including Germany will, moreover, be jointly responsible for servicing the loans taken out to finance the RRF. Discussions are ongoing about whether a successor facility, one likely to be differently structured and possibly permanent, will be put in place. To judge by the most recent EU Commission proposal (the Strategic Technologies for Europe Platform (STEP), June 2023), however, there does not seem to be much appetite for a centrally-funded facility of anything like the required order of magnitude.

---

9   Germany is not alone in this: a number of other Member States have, to date, not yet received funding by regular tranches.

3.5 Outlook

Germany's huge public-investment needs are widely recognized. Despite the pledge to initiate a decade of investment that the governing coalition made when it took office at the end of 2021, too little has been achieved. Understandably, recent focus has been on supporting households in the energy and inflationary crisis sparked by the Russian invasion of Ukraine (Watt 2022). As energy prices have declined from their peaks in 2022, the government is concentrating on its exit from the crisis mode. Already before the constitutional court ruling, the key objective was clearly the consolidation of public finances, not the raising of investment, however. The finance minister, from the liberal FDP, aimed to solve the trade-off between budget consolidation and additional investment via cuts in social and consumption spending (BMF 2023a). While this is politically popular insofar as it avoids the need for tax increases or higher borrowing, it proves difficult in practice to achieve spending cuts by orders of magnitude that would free up substantial additional resources. Most spending is on the basis of legal entitlements that are difficult to change substantially in the short run.

The government is still not prioritising public investment in the modernisation of Germany and its transformation to a low-carbon economy. It is not sufficiently understood that digital and ecological transformation are a once-in-a-generation challenge, like German reunification, which—among other instruments—was financed via a mixture of public debt and tax increases. Similarly, the modernisation and transformation of the economy should be financed using a mix of instruments. To the extent that future economic activity and, consequently, tax revenues are increased via public investment, debt finance in line with the golden rule is economically justified. Already politically difficult thanks to the debt brake, the constitutional court ruling has now seemingly ruled out deficit financing of a substantial proportion of the planned additional investment and accompanying support measures for business and households.

Given this, and the fact that climate protection and adaptation will not, in all cases, contribute to future growth and additional revenues it would make sense to finance some of the investment via additional tax revenues and also cut back ecologically damaging tax breaks. At the moment, however, there is a political majority for neither tax increases nor for a substantial reform of the German debt brake. Germany is also opposing reforms of the European fiscal rules which could increase the scope for public investment. It was already likely that public investment in Germany, even if there are increases in certain areas, would remain substantially below what is necessary. After the constitutional court ruling there is heightened uncertainty as to the path forward and a real risk of a substantial scaling back of the level of ambition.

References

Bardt, H., S. Dullien, M. Hüther, K. Rietzler (2020). 'For a Sound Fiscal Policy: Enabling Public Investment'. *IMK Report*, 152e, https://www.imk-boeckler.de/fpdf/HBS-007619/p_imk_report_152e_2020.pdf

Behringer, J., S. Dullien, C. Paetz (2021). 'Überwältigende Mehrheit der Deutschen will kräftige Investitionsausweitung'. *IMK Policy Brief*, 112, https://www.imk-boeckler.de/fpdf/HBS-008181/p_imk_pb_112_2021.pdf

Bundesministerium der Finanzen, BMF (2023a). 'Bundesfinanzminister Christian Lindner im Interview mit der Süddeutschen Zeitung'. 17 June, https://www.bundesfinanzministerium.de/Content/DE/Interviews/2023/2023-06-17-sueddeutsche-zeitung.html

—— (2023b). 'Schieflage der Bund-Länder-Finanzbeziehungen', in *BMF-Monatsbericht*. March: 8–13, https://www.bundesfinanzministerium.de/Monatsberichte/2023/03/monatsbericht-03-2023.html

Bundesministerium für Wirtschaft und Energie, BMWi (2018). 'Energieeffizienz in Kommunen. Energetisch modernisieren und Kosten sparen: Wir fördern das'. BMWi, Berlin, https://www.foerderdatenbank.de/FDB/Content/DE/Download/Publikation/Energie/energieeffizienz-in-kommunen-broschuere.pdf?__blob=publicationFile&v=2

Bundesrechnungshof (2023a). 'Bericht nach § 88 Absatz 2 BHO an den Haushaltsausschuss des Deutschen Bundestages Umsetzung des Onlinezugangsgesetzes Steuerung und Koordinierung'. 29 March, Bonn, https://www.bundesrechnungshof.de/SharedDocs/Downloads/DE/Berichte/2023/onlinezugangsgesetz-volltext.pdf?__blob=publicationFile&v=2

—— (2023b). 'Bericht nach § 88 Absatz 2 BHO an das Bundesministerium der Finanzen über die Sondervermögen des Bundes und die damit verbundenen Auswirkungen auf die Haushaltstransparenz sowie die Funktionsfähigkeit der Schuldenregel'. 25 August, Bonn, https://www.bundesrechnungshof.de/SharedDocs/Downloads/DE/Berichte/2023/sondervermoegen-volltext.pdf?__blob=publicationFile&v=6

Deutsche Bundesbank (2021). 'Federal Debt: Allocate Premia on Accruals Basis in Budgetary Interest Expenditure'. *Monthly Report*. June 2021: 47–51 https://www.bundesbank.de/en/publications/reports/monthly-reports/monthly-report-june-2021-868086

—— (2022). 'State Government Finances in 2021: Surplus and Additional Reserves from Emergency Borrowing'. *Monthly Report*. October: 13–28 https://www.bundesbank.de/en/publications/reports/monthly-reports/monthly-report-october-2022-898764

Deutscher Bundestag (2023a) 'Schriftliche Fragen mit den in der Woche vom 5. Juni 2023 eingegangenen Antworten der Bundesregierung', *Drucksache*, 20/7918, 9 June 2023 https://dserver.bundestag.de/btd/20/071/2007148.pdf

—— (2023b). Entwurf eines Gesetzes über die Feststellung des Bundeshaushaltsplans für das Haushaltsjahr 2024 (Haushaltsgesetz 2024–HG 2024), *Bundestagsdrucksache*, 20/7800, 18 August, https://dip.bundestag.de/vorgang/gesetz-%C3%BCber-die-feststellung-des-bundeshaushaltsplans-f%C3%BCr-das-haushaltsjahr-2024/302729

Dullien, S., A. Herzog-Stein, P. Hohlfeld, K. Rietzler, S. Stephan, T. Theobald, S. Tober, and S. Watzka (2023). 'Stark restriktive Geldpolitik verschärft Wirtschaftsflaute'. *Prognose der wirtschaftlichen Entwicklung 2023/2024. IMK Report*, 184. https://www.boeckler.de/fpdf/HBS-008701/p_imk_report_184_2023.pdf

——, K. Rietzler, and A. Truger (2022). 'Die Corona-Krise und die sozial-ökologische Transformation: Herausforderungen für die Finanzpolitik'. *WSI-Mitteilungen*, 75(4): 277–85 https://doi.org/10.5771/0342-300X-2022-4-277

European Investment Bank (2023). 'Resilience and Renewal in Europe'. *European Investment Bank Annual Report 2022/2023*, https://doi.org/10.2867/307689

Gechert, S., K. Rietzler, S. Schreiber, and U. Stein (2019). 'Wirtschaftliche Instrumente für eine klima- und sozialverträgliche CO2-Bepreisung: Gutachten im Auftrag des Bundesministeriums für Umwelt, Naturschutz und nukleare Sicherheit'. *IMK Study*, 65, https://www.boeckler.de/pdf/p_imk_study_65_2019.pdf

Henze, L. T., E. Jürgens, and C. Paetz (2022). 'Einstellungen zur öffentlichen Infrastruktur und zum Investitionsbedarf im Regionalvergleich'. *IMK Policy Brief*, 129, https://www.imk-boeckler.de/de/faust-detail.htm?sync_id=HBS-008383

Institut für Arbeitsmarkt- und Berufsforschung, IAB (2023). IAB-Stellenerhebung: Offene Stellen, https://iab.de/das-iab/befragungen/iab-stellenerhebung/aktuelle-ergebnisse/

Kultusministerkonferenz, KMK (2023). 'Abfrage der geflüchteten Kinder/Jugendlichen aus der Ukraine'. 38. und 39. Kalenderwoche (18 September – 1 October 2023), https://www.kmk.org/fileadmin/Dateien/pdf/Statistik/Ukraine/2023/AW_Ukraine_KW_39.pdf

Landesregierung NRW (2023). 'Landesregierung Nordrhein-Westfalen geht mit Programm für kommunale Altschulden in Vorleistung—zudem 6-Milliarden-Investitionsprogramm für kommunale Infrastruktur mit Fokus auf Klimaschutz und Klimaanpassung'. Press release. 19 June, https://www.land.nrw/pressemitteilung/landesregierung-nordrhein-westfalen-geht-mit-programm-fuer-kommunale-altschulden

Rietzler, K., A. Watt (2022). 'Public Investment in Germany: Squaring the Circle', in Cerniglia, F. and Saraceno, F. (eds). *Greening Europe—2022 European Public Investment Outlook*, Cambridge, UK: Open Book Publishers: 41–53, https://doi.org/10.11647/OBP.0328

Raffer, C., H. Scheller, (2023). *KfW Kommunalpanel 2023*. Kreditanstalt für Wiederaufbau, Frankfurt am Main, https://www.kfw.de/PDF/Download-Center/Konzernthemen/Research/PDF-Dokumente-KfW-Kommunalpanel/KfW-Kommunalpanel-2022.pdf

Unabhängiger Beirat des Stabilitätsrats (2023). 20. Stellungnahme zur Einhaltung der Obergrenze für das strukturelle gesamtstaatliche Finanzierungsdefizit nach § 51 Absatz 2 HGrG zur Sitzung des Stabilitätsrats am 2. Mai, https://www.stabilitaetsrat.de/SharedDocs/Downloads/DE/Beirat/2023/Stellungnahme/20230502_Stellungnahme_Beirat.pdf;jsessionid=FBA712DC9B95B9572EF0BE64FE9657AE.intranet632?__blob=publicationFile

Watt, A. (2022). 'Inflation and Counter-Inflationary Policy Measures: The Case of Germany', *IMK Study*, 183–10, https://www.imk-boeckler.de/de/faust-detail.htm?sync_id=HBS-008504

—— and S. Watzka (2020). 'The Macroeconomic Effects of the EU Recovery and Resilience Facility', IMK Policy Brief 98, https://www.imk-boeckler.de/de/faust-detail.htm?sync_id=9110

4. Italy's Public Investments. The NRRP and Beyond

Giovanni Barbieri, Floriana Cerniglia, Enzo Dia

This chapter provides the country report on Italy with an analysis of the role the Italian National Recovery and Resilience Plan in boosting public investment up to and beyond 2026. Italy's NRRP has 235 billion euros available for investments and reforms, making it one of the most remarkable modernization initiatives in the last seventy years. The impact of the NRRP is assessed and specific implementation challenges are highlighted, some of which have been caused by factors such as fragmented governance, a lack of effective monitoring, and compliance issues. Overcoming these difficulties is crucial for continuing to receive disbursements from the European Commission. The effectiveness of its governance is examined. An open question is how to ensure a positive capital-spending trajectory in Italy (especially after 2026) in compliance with the new rules set out in the Stability and Growth Pact.

4.1 Introduction

Italy's National Recovery and Resilience Plan (NRRP) is worth €235bn: €191.5bn come from the Recovery and Resilience Facility (RRF), €13.5bn from React-EU, and €30.6bn from direct Italian government funding through its Complimentary Fund.[1] Thus, over two hundred billion euros have been devoted to investments and reforms for Italy; it is one of the most impressive modernization plans of the past seventy years. If fully implemented, it could potentially generate one additional point of growth over the next decade. While this is a considerable amount, it is de facto equivalent to what was lost in the decade from

---

1   See Barbieri, G., Cerniglia, F., Gori, G. F., Lattarulo, P., (2022), 'NRRP—Italy's strategic Reform and Investment Programme', in F. Cerniglia and F. Saraceno (eds), *Greening Europe—2022 European Public Investment Outlook*. Cambridge, UK: Open Book Publishers: 55-70, https://www.openbookpublishers.com/books/10.11647/obp.0328; and Barbieri, G., F. Cerniglia, (2021), 'Relaunching Public Investment in Italy', in F. Cerniglia, F. Saraceno, A. Watt (eds), *The Great Reset—2021 European Public Investment Outlook*, Cambridge, UK: Open Book Publishers: 63-78, https://doi.org/10.11647/OBP.0280

https://doi.org/10.11647/OBP.0386.04

2009–2019 due to the economic and financial crisis of 2008–2009 and the austerity measures that followed to curb public spending that mainly impacted capital investments.[2]

Moreover, to truly tackle the existing North-South disparities in Italy, even greater resources are required than those currently available. While 40% of the NRRP funds are to be dedicated to the Mezzogiorno region and the reduction of the North-South gap is one of the Plan's transversal objectives, projections suggest that the resources from the NRRP will only decrease but not eliminate the gap. For example, the GDP per capita in the Mezzogiorno is currently 55% of that in central and northern Italy; in 2026 it should rise to 59%.

In addition, the NRRP is currently facing a series of implementation challenges. There is concern over the planning and spending capabilities of certain local governments, which are expected to receive a substantial portion of the allocated resources. There is also concern over the recent surge in raw material costs which act like a sword of Damocles, as the Plan was originally designed with lower infrastructure-expenditure commitments. In fact, the Italian government have negotiated with the European Commission to amend the Plan in order to facilitate the feasibility of the projects and coordination with the REPowerEU programme.

Public-investment flows over the coming year will be fuelled in Italy not only by the NRRP's resources but also by cohesion policies primarily focused on the Mezzogiorno region. The overarching goal of these is the reduction of territorial gaps. Here, again, much depends on the spending-planning capacity of local governments especially in the Mezzogiorno. Furthermore, there are growing concerns that the constraints imposed by the new European fiscal regulations, set to take effect (potentially) in 2024, may not ensure a consistent trajectory of public investment in Italy beyond 2026. Yet, a comprehensive programme, aimed at recuperating a decade of declining public investments and addressing the significant funding needs resources required posed by the digital and green transitions, call for a timeline and resources that go well beyond 2026.

The progress of Italy's NRRP and the constraints that could hinder the path towards sustained growth of public investments beyond 2026 are outlined in this chapter. An update on the current state of advancement is also provided. We evaluate whether the resources allocated by the Plan genuinely contribute to enhancing investment and assess whether Next Generation EU (NGEU) can be deemed successful, including as an experiment for a shared European-debt framework in funding critical public investments crucial for growth and EU convergence.

---

2   This progression has been extensively documented in the chapter on Italy of the previous *Outlook* instalments.

4.2 Italy's NRRP

The total resources available in Italy's NRRP from the Recovery and Resilience Facility are €191.5bn (which is 26.5% of the entire RRF), of which €68.9bn are grants and €122.6bn are loans. It is aligned with the strategic guidelines outlined within the NGEU and is divided into six missions: 1. Digitization, innovation, competitiveness, culture and tourism; 2. Green revolution and ecological transition; 3. Infrastructure for sustainable mobility; 4. Education and research; 5. Inclusion and cohesion; and 6. Health. The €191.5bn budget is allocated in the plan as follows: 21% for Mission 1; 31% for Mission 2; 13.3% for Mission 3; 16.1% for Mission 4; 10.4% for Mission 5; and 8.2% for Mission 6.

Italy's NRRP is designed as a performance-driven strategy rather than a mere expenditure programme. It is structured around reforms and investments, carefully timed through the achievement of milestones (a total of 213) and targets (a total of 314) by the set deadline: 2026. As a result, all measures within the NRRP are accompanied by a clear implementation schedule and a list of expected outcomes that must be fulfilled in order to receive the planned allocation of financial contributions or loans.

Each reform and investment are associated with a comprehensive description of the measure's objectives and with indicators that reflect the aims. The indicators serve as benchmarks for evaluating[3] progress and elaborate: a) milestones, that is, critical stages of implementation (both in terms of tangible progress and procedural steps), including the adoption of specific regulations, the full functionality of information systems, or the successful completion of projects; and b) targets, that is, measurable indicators that gauge the outcomes of public interventions (such as kilometres of constructed railways) or the impact of public policies (like reducing the incidence of informal employment). Table 4.1 shows, for each deadline, the number of milestones and targets corresponding to the total funds received, divided into grants and loans.

---

3   In accordance with Regulation UE 2020/852 ('framework to facilitate sustainable investment') and with the European Green Deal's objectives, the RRP's measures must comply with the principle of Do-No-Significant-Harm (DNSH) to provide a substantial contribution to protecting the ecosystem without significantly damaging the environment. See De Vincenti, C. (2022), 'Green Investments: Two Possible Interpretations of the "Do No Significant Harm" Principle', in Cerniglia, F., Saraceno, F. (eds), *Greening Europe—2022 European Public Investment Outlook*, Cambridge, UK: Open book Publishers, 2022:177–85, https://doi.org/10.11647/OBP.0328

Table 4.1 Grants and Loans Timeframe

Deadline	Milestones and Targets	Gross amount (€bn)			Disburse-ments (€bn)
		Grants	Loans	Total	
13/08/2021					24.9
31/12/2021	51	11.5	12.6	24.1	21
30/06/2022	45	11.5	12.6	24.1	21
31/12/2022	55	11.5	10.3	21.8	19
30/06/2023	27	2.3	16.1	18.4	16
31/12/2023	69	8.1	12.6	20.7	18
30/06/2024	31	2.3	10.3	12.6	11
31/12/2024	58	6.3	15	21.3	18.5
30/06/2025	20	2.3	10.3	12.6	11
31/12/2025	51	4.6	10.3	14.9	13
30/06/2026	120	8.5	12.3	20.8	18.1
	527	68.9	122.6	191.5	191.5

Source: italiadomani.gov

The disbursed instalments to date include:

- 13 August 2021: pre-financing instalment of €24.9bn (of which €8.957bn in grants and €15.937bn in loans), which represents 13% of the total amount allocated to Italy in grants and loans under the Recovery and Resilience Facility.

- 13 April 2022: first six-month instalment of €21bn (€10bn in grants and €11bn in loans), following the positive assessment of the NRRP targets that Italy had to reach by 31 December 2021.

- 8 November 2022: second semi-annual instalment of €21bn (€10bn in grants and €11bn in loans) following the positive assessment on the achievement of 45 targets and objectives. Some of the targets and objectives covered include reforms in public administration, public procurement, tax administration, and territorial health care. In addition, investments were made in key strategic sectors, including ultrawideband and 5G, research and innovation, tourism and culture, hydrogen development, urban redevelopment, the digitalisation of schools, and reducing the backlog of court cases.

- 28 July 2023: third six-month instalment of €18.5bn was approved by the Commission after accepting the Italian government's proposed revisions to the NRRP (see details in section 4.3 below). The European Commission did not approve the disbursement of the full instalment of €19bn (€10bn in grants and €9bn in loans); €500 million were deducted because the government had not reached a required objective on implementing measures to ensure more student accommodations (beds), which was one of the milestones that needed to be reached by 31 December 2022.[4]

- 22 September 2023: The request for payment of the fourth instalment was forwarded by the Government to the European Commission. The next milestones and targets will need to be reached by the Italian government to obtain the disbursement of the fourth instalment (renegotiated with the Commission) so as to obtain by end 2023 the total €35bn planned for the year.[5]

As mentioned above, in addition to investments, the NRRP commits Italy to a major reform programme aimed at improving regulatory and legal conditions in order to steadily increase the country's equity, efficiency, and competitiveness.[6] Figure 4.1 shows the number of investments and implemented reforms by Mission.

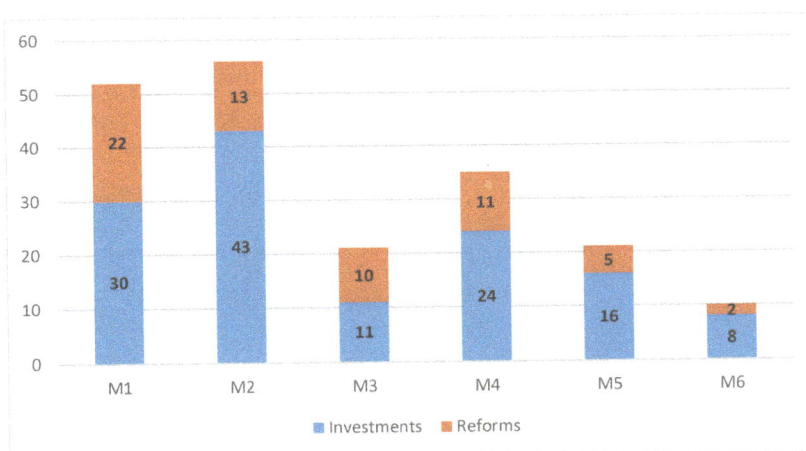

Fig. 4.1 Number of Investments and Reforms by Mission.
Source: Calculations of structure of NRRP Missions based on ReGiS data.

---

4   The initial target of assigning 7,500 beds by 31 December 2022—a target that the EU Commission assessed with exceptional precision—is now being transformed into a qualitative milestone (of reaching the larger objective of 60,000 beds by 2026). This adjustment is being proposed alongside ten previously submitted changes in order to receive the fourth instalment of the NRRP.

5   The EU Council adopted on 19 September 2023 the decision approving the amendments to Italy's RRP relating to certain goals and objectives to be achieved by 30 June 2023 for obtaining the fourth instalment of 16.5 bn euros.

6   The NRRP contains three main types of reforms: 1) horizontal or contextual reforms, that cross-cut across all the NRRP's Missions. These consist of structural innovations to the system, aimed at improving equity, efficiency, and competitiveness, thus contributing to the overall economic climate of the country (for example reforms within the public administration and the justice system); 2) enabling reforms, these reforms constitute a subset of contextual reforms and are directly aimed at ensuring the implementation of the NNRP and, in general, and removing administrative, regulatory, and procedural barriers that influence economic activities and the quality of services provided (for examples reforms related to public contracts, simplification of regulations and procedures, boosting competition, and the reduction of payment delays by public administrations; 3) sectoral reforms, included within each individual Missions that consist of legislative innovations for specific areas of intervention or economic activities aimed at introducing more efficient regulatory and procedural frameworks within their respective sectoral domains (for example, reforms related to the labour market and education).

Noteworthy is that €68.9bn in non-repayable grants have been allocated to Italy . This is not attributable to any specific negotiating activity between the government and the Commission but is simply the result of applying a calculation criterion that takes into account the size of the population, negative GDP growth, and the increase in unemployment in Italy compared to the European average. Non-repayable grants in principle have a neutral impact on the net borrowing balance, or could even improve it, since they reduce the deficit because they are considered as revenue. However, 'additional' loans are not considered as additional revenue from an economic point of view. Rather, they are considered financial transactions, the interest of which impacts public debt, worsening the net-borrowing balance. 'Replacement' loans, by contrast, do not have an impact on the general-government account, as they merely involve the replacement of already existing financing lines against expenditure already discounted in the public-finance forecasts. Grants and loans finance both 'new projects' (72%) and 'existing projects', that is, projects already financed prior to the NRRP. The choice of the distribution of grants and loans over time, coupled with the initial concentration of so-called 'existing projects' in the early years and the subsequent prevalence of new projects, distinctly impact the balances of the public budget. This effect is highlighted in a special dossier by the Chamber of Deputies.[7] In 2021 and 2022, the heightened emphasis on subsidizing pre-existing projects, which were already incorporated within the financial framework, created a fiscal leeway and a budgetary margin that favored the financial strategy of those specific years. The focus now is on new projects, accompanied by a gradual decrease in subsidies for loans. As a result, the overall impact of the NRRP on the government budget balance is turning negative, thereby constraining the government's flexibility and room for manoeuvre—see Figure 4.2 for a timeline of the disbursements of loans and grants.

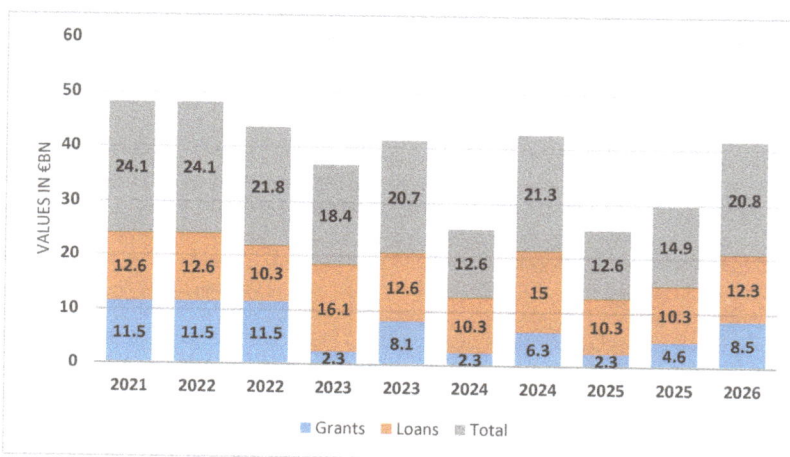

Fig. 4.2 Timeline of Loans and Grants.
Source: Calculations of structure of NRRP Missions based on ReGiS data.

---

7   Dossier by the Chamber of Deputies, *I profili finanziari del Piano Nazionale di Ripresa e Resilienza (PNRR)*, 7 November 2022.

The NRRP covers many areas of intervention and public-regulatory aspects. It is notably complex and covers a total of 187 'Investment Lines' (including the Complementary Fund), each designated for specific areas of intervention. The economic scale also varies significantly: 62% of the resources are earmarked for public investments, 12% for current expenditures and 19% for incentives. The remaining portion is for transfers to families and tax cuts. Measures resulting in tangible interventions dominate. This is a positive development, especially considering the substantial decline in public-infrastructure investments during the 2010s, given the drawn-out implementation timelines for public works in Italy.

This crucial aspect demands careful consideration. The NRRP employs a centralized governance structure, with the Presidency of the Council of Ministers assuming a central role. Regions played and continue to play a relatively minor part in the planning and execution of the NRRP; while social stakeholders and local governments contribute primarily in an advisory capacity. In August 2021, the responsibility for all NRRP measures was devolved to individual Ministries. This marked the start of the practical implementation phase: meticulous selection of interventions, criteria for allocation of resources to implementing entities, methods for carrying out investments. The NRRP, developed along sectoral-territorial lines, however, resembles 'organ pipes' that rarely intersect (Viesti 2023).[8]

In 122 of the 187 'Investment Lines', no indications are given regarding territorial devolvement. Consequently, projects come from the top down, with the obvious risk of not being able to capitalize on the available local expertise or tap into lessons learned in recent years. Currently, the transition from overarching NRRP guidelines to the specific identification of projects and beneficiaries takes place through various methods: (a) identified projects, that is, resources have already been allocated in the text of the NRRP or Complementary Fund for previously identified projects within a specific area. These are, to a great extent, investments entrusted to large stakeholders that are part of the broader public sector, as in the case of rail networks (almost all of which have been assigned to Rete Ferroviaria Italiana). The estimated amount of this type of investments is around 20% of the total budget; (b) direct procurement: some of the funds are directly overseen by local administrations responsible for managing the resources through procurement processes; for example, the digitalization of the Public Administration, modernizing judicial facilities, and developing broadband networks overseen by the Ministry of Innovation Technology and Digitalisation (MITD). Despite their significance, these allocations constitute a relatively minor portion of the overall funding, approximately 5%; (c) limited fund loans:

---

8   See also Viesti, G. (2021), 'Il PNRR e il Mezzogiorno. 80 miliardi, un totale in cerca di addendi', in *Quaderni di Rassegna Sindacale*, 2:53-62; Viesti, G. (2022), 'Un piano per rilanciare l'Italia?', in *Il Mulino*, 2:23-38; Viesti, G. (2022b), 'Il PNRR, gli asili nido e l'uguaglianza delle opportunità', in *Menabò di Etica ed Economia*, 3 July; Viesti, G., C. Chiapperini, E. Montenegro (2022), *Le città italiane e il PNRR*, WP Urban@it; Viesti, G. (2022), 'The Territorial Dimension of the Italian NRRP', in A. Caloffi, M. De Castris, G. Perucca (eds), *The Regional Challenges in the Post-Covid Era*, Milan, FrancoAngeli:201–18; Viesti, G. (2023), *Riuscirà il PNRR a rilanciare l'Italia?*, Rome, Donzelli Editore:53–62.

a share of the resources is allocated, upon request, to private individuals, businesses, or citizens. This applies to significant measures like the Transition 4.0 programme for business investments in digital modernization, as well as the 'Superbonus' and 'Ecobonus' for building renovations. It is estimated that these measures constitute around 15% of the available resources; (d) allocation plans: a share of the resources is distributed by the responsible Ministries to public entities based on regional-distribution plans. After the initial distribution, the regional administrations typically choose the projects or activities to be funded within their jurisdictions. These notably cover important interventions in healthcare or active labour policies. These measures are also estimated to account for approximately 15% of the Plan's resources; lastly, (e) calls for bids: a substantial share of the resources (around 45%) is and will be allocated through competitive calls issued by local administrations. These calls for bids require prospective public beneficiaries to prepare projects that involve ranking-based selections in accordance with the indications specified within the calls themselves. The main beneficiaries are mostly municipal administrations; others include water and waste-service providers and universities. Examples of some of the numerous projects in this category include schools and nurseries, urban-regeneration and quality-housing projects, a significant portion of water infrastructure, and measures that promote research, innovation, and partnerships between universities and businesses. The allocation and procurement mechanisms implemented thus far have differed greatly from case to case.

Moreover, each ministry reserves the right to choose projects deemed 'best' according to criteria they themselves define in the various calls for bids. Yet, in this way, investment implementation is decoupled from the endowment (and thus 'need'- based) indicators of the respective territories. Indeed, a shortcoming of the NRRP is that it lacks political guidelines regarding the principles that should govern the criteria for project selection and the territorial allocation of resources under each measure. Allocations between regions, cities, large and small municipalities, urban and inland areas result *ex post*: that is, they are the eventual outcome of the resource-allocation process and, specifically, of the call-for-bids mechanism. For instance, it is becoming evident that the process to address calls for kindergarten facilities has resulted in a territorial distribution of services that will only partially mitigate the significant disparities that exist nationwide in terms of providing young children and their families with the practical aspects to fully access their rights as citizens. In conclusion, this complex mechanism for allocating resources does not guarantee that the 40% resources target will be reached in the Mezzogiorno.

4.3 Challenges of the NRRP

The entire NRRP must be completed by 2026. This is an immense challenge considering the plan does not account for the steep rise in prices of raw materials, which have a significant impact on infrastructure costs that have become much more substantial compared to the initial, pre-Ukraine war, investment forecasts for each Mission and

Component of the NRRP. There is genuine concern that not all the infrastructure projects listed in the NRRP can secure funding and/or be successfully completed on time.

In light of the unforeseen challenges, some countries have requested the Commission to revise parts of their respective Plans.[9] The Italian government, on 7 June, submitted to Parliament a report on the status of the NRRP's enactment with an overview of the challenges that are emerging in the implementation of single interventions.[10] This is a significant step forward in terms of transparency and monitoring, fulfilling the government's required accountability to both Parliament and its citizens.[11] The report identifies challenges on a broad range of interventions. In fact, 118 out of 285 NRRP measures have been flagged as having critical aspects, but only 51 have significant issues. Collectively, these measures amount to €80bn, which is 42% of the NRRP's total budget (€191.5bn). The financial interventions that have notable challenges include 'Ecobonus' and 'Sismabonus' (approximately €14bn), high-speed railway lines to Northern Europe (€8.6bn), initiatives aimed at increasing resilience, territorial enhancement, and municipal energy efficiency (€6bn, for as many as 46,000 projects), an overall plan for nurseries and kindergartens (€4.6bn), and measures addressing flooding and hydrogeological risk management (€2.5bn). There are also NRRP flagship projects that are facing challenges; these include community healthcare involving the construction of social housing (€2bn) and community hospitals (€1bn). Of these, the most frequently reported issues regard regulatory hurdles (in 32% of the cases).[12]

Other problems include the low participation rate of companies in the bidding process and investments that are unattractive to market players. Delays in implementing the NRRP is another challenge. Municipalities are also having difficulty in carrying out projects effectively. Although they are the implementing authorities for nearly €42bn, they often lack the necessary planning capacity. What further aggravates the situation is that, since 2009, municipalities have been disempowered by the growing tendency to outsource essential public-policy tasks of a technical nature. Inflation is also a problem for municipalities since they have a high concentration of infrastructure contracts, like the kindergarten plan, that involve the purchase of goods and services which have seen significant price hikes this past year.

---

9   Estonia, France, Slovakia, Malta, Denmark, Spain, Slovenia, and Austria had their RRPs revised to include RePowerEU; while Germany, Luxembourg, Finland, and Ireland requested and obtained revisions of their RRPs for measures other than RePowerEU.

10 This detailed document presents an overview of the achieved objectives in the second half of 2022 regarding the disbursement of the third instalment (€18.5bn) of European funding. It also offers an initial assessment of the prospects for attaining the objectives set for the first half of 2023, which are associated with the fourth instalment of €16bn.

11 The report from the Court of Auditors (March 2023) had already highlighted a series of delays and challenges in the implementation of the actual spending phase envisaged by the NRRP.

12 See Rizzo, L., R. Secomandi, A. Zanardi, (2023), 'Criticità del PNRR tra rimodulazione e restituzione dei fondi', *Lavoce*, 16 June, https://lavoce.info/archives/101391/criticita-del-pnrr-tra-rimodulazione-e-restituzione-dei-fondi/

The NRRP's critical profiles include the ability to monitor challenges. This is a crucial issue both for an effective discussion between the Italian government and the Commission on the actual implementation process and for assessing the impact of current and future investments on economic growth. Timely follow-up is needed for a better assessment of macroeconomic and public-finance forecasts. Thus, the receipt of prompt and accurate information on the temporal distribution of resources regarding the actual economic nature of each initiative and the relative state of implementation is crucial. To date, that information is lacking. The primary official source for accessing the information is ReGIS.[13] However, the platform is limited in terms of completeness and updates (timeliness and frequency). For example, in some cases, lines of intervention have been executed but are not reported as such by the platform. Some of the stakeholders and municipalities have difficulty accessing ReGIS. Moreover, measures that are provided as incentives and facilitations for reporting require time-consuming audits by the Internal Revenue Service. Unfortunately, ReGIS, at least for now, does not provide consistent, timely information and cannot be relied upon to assess the NRRP's implementation progress (achieved and implementable expenditure).

Mapping the NRRP's weaknesses and, thus, the risk of delaying or failing to meet milestones and targets was obviously crucial in identifying possible revisions to the Plan. In fact, on 27 July 2023, Raffaele Fitto, Minister for European Affairs, South, Cohesion Policies and the NRRP, presented a revised proposal of the NRRP which included the creation of a dedicated chapter on REPowerEU. The following day, the European Commission approved the payout of the third NRRP instalment, which was linked to the achievement of the December 2022 targets. It approved the revised targets for the fourth instalment (due June 2023) and postponed some milestones to December 2023. The European Commission's disbursement decisions are based on confirmation of the achievement of the previous year's targets by end of year. This decision triggers the release of the corresponding payment, provided there is a positive assessment of the micro changes, and the EU Council approves the targets (which in the case of the June 2023 targets had not yet taken place). The proposed amendments to the NRRP, in relation to the fifth instalment, were sent to the European Commission on 7 August. These request the deferral of thirteen goals, the elimination of six goals (which can be covered with other sources of financing), and the integration of the milestone relating to the new measure of the single Special Economic Zone (reform). If all the proposed amendments are approved, as of 31 December 2023, the results to be achieved would reduce from 69 to 51, the number of targets from 46 to 30, and the number of milestones from 23 to 21.

The Italian government's revised NRRP proposal is worth some attention. It introduces a number of changes for 2023–2026. The new chapter on REPowerEU (as

---

13   This is an IT platform introduced in 2021 where central and other levels of government, local authorities, and other implementing entities are required to upload information relevant to the monitoring, reporting, and oversight of measures and projects funded by the NRRP.

per EU Regulation 2023/435[14] — a response to the energy crisis caused by the war in Ukraine) increases the financial provisions of NGEU. New resource allocations by the Commission, in the form of grants and loans to Member States, aim to facilitate a socially sustainable energy transition and to accelerate energy independence through the use of renewable-energy sources. Despite the fact that the proposal introduces changes to almost 1/3 (144 out of 349) of the goals originally set out in the NRRP, the affected amount is rather modest: €19.2bn, barely 10% of the total budget. Upon initial observation, it seems that the revision is mostly limited to dropping some of the original ambitious goals (that is, cutting the backlog in the justice system) and replacing them with less ambitious ones (that is, reducing tax evasion). If the Italian proposal is approved, it would mean an additional €2.7bn for Italy, equivalent to 13.8% of the additional €20bn provided through REPowerEU. These funds would be financed by issuing bonds for offsetting excess emissions through the Emission Trading System. Once again, Italy (this time with Poland) is the Member State that receives by far the most funds from the EU.

4.4 Italian Public Finance: Public Investment Beyond the NRRP

The trend forecasts of the General Government Income Statement (Conto economico consolidato delle Amministrazioni Pubbliche) shows a downward trend in total capital expenditure: 4.3% of GDP in 2026 compared to 5.1% in 2025.[15] The significant value for 2021–2022 is due to the resources allocated for the so-called 'Superbonus' for energy efficiency in buildings (3.3% in 2021 and 4.0% in 2022)—a scheme the government plans to suspend.

More specifically, in the DEF (the government's economic and finance document) forecast for 2022–2026, capital expenditure averages around 5% of GDP and public investment around 3.5%. Both figures are significantly higher than previous years due to the impact of additional NRRP-related measures. For the 2024–2025 period, the forecasted share of GDP (3.8% and 3.7%) is in line with the capital-expenditure peak of 2009, after which Italy experienced a dramatic slump in public investment that lasted twenty years.[16] NRRP resources — provided by the European Recovery

---

14   The Regulation was adopted in response to the energy crisis caused by Russia's war of invasion into Ukraine, it contains increases in the financial provisions of Next Generation EU with new resources that the Commission will allocate in the form of grants and loans to Member States in order to foster a socially sustainable energy transition and speed up energy independence with production from renewable sources.

15   Total capital expenditure consists of three components: i) public investment; ii) money transfers, for example to private companies, public institutions, citizens etc; and iii) shareholdings and provision of loans. Notably, ii) was 8.2% in 2021 and 7.7% in 2026.

16   See Barbieri, G., F. Cerniglia, G. F. Gori, P. Lattarulo, P., (2022), 'NRRP—Italy's strategic Reform and Investment Programme', in F. Cerniglia and F. Saraceno (eds), *Greening Europe—2022 European Public Investment Outlook*, Cambridge, UK: OpenBookPublishers: 55–70, https://doi.org/10.11647/OBP.0328; and Barbieri, G., F. Cerniglia (2021), 'Relaunching Public Investment in Italy', in F. Cerniglia, F. Saraceno, and A. Watt (eds), *The Great Reset—2021 European Public Investment Outlook*, Cambridge, UK: Open Book Publishers: 63–78, https://doi.org/10.11647/OBP.0280

and Resilience Facility (RRF) — accounted for 0.2% of Italy's GDP in 2022; they are expected to peak at 1.8% in 2025 (if all the funds received are actually spent), less than half of the investment forecasted for that year. In essence, the data show that Italy's positive trend in public investments, mostly driven by the NRRP, will end in 2026.

Hence, it is more important than ever that Italian budgetary policy support a positive public-investment trend beyond 2026. Unfortunately, the phase before us (already from this year) is one of great uncertainty. Fiscal policy must now reckon with lower internal economic growth prospects, and low growth in countries with which Italy has strong interdependencies. Italy's macroeconomic dynamics are also conditioned by the geopolitical turmoil triggered by the war in Ukraine, inflation, and restrictive monetary policies implemented by Central Banks, which have begun to drain liquidity from the economic system.

Key Italian macro- and public-finance data for the upcoming years, as provided in the DEF, are here reviewed.[17] The GDP growth trend in real terms is 0.9% for 2023, 1.4% for 2024, 1.3% for 2025 and 1.1% for 2026.[18] It should be noted that the highest growth (expected in 2024) should occur thanks to the large amounts of public investment over the period here considered. The new European fiscal rules — which will most likely put Italy on a path of deficit and debt reduction — will introduce enormous constraints, given the country's high public debt. Fom 2024, the so-called 'general escape clause', activated by the Commission in 2020 in response to the economic consequences of the COVID-19 pandemic, will cease to apply. As is well known, the European Commission had begun a discussion on reforming the Stability and Growth Pact's rules and the economic governance of the European Union before the effects of the COVID-19 pandemic became apparent. This discussion was last raised in November 2022 with the presentation of a series of guidelines.[19]

The Italian government, while supporting the main tenets of the European Commission's proposal, pointed out critical aspects on several occasions. Concerns were raised about the division of Member States into three categories, according to a debt sustainability analysis conducted by the European Commission and recommended greater involvement by the

---

17 Submitted by the Government to Parliament on 13 April 2023, to be followed by Update to the Economic and Finance Document (DEF) (by September 2023) and the Budget Law (December 2023) for 2024 and beyond. The DEF contains trends, forecasts, and real economic data.

18 NADEF updates (September 2023) are as follows: 0.8% in 2023, 1.2% in 2024 and 1.4% in 2025. As noted by the Parliamentary Budget Office, the projections presented in the DEF are subject to a notable degree of uncertainty regarding the execution of the NRRP. This uncertainty is further accentuated by the lack of tables in the DEF on annual expenditure forecasts. The DEF's forecasting methodology, encompassing both trend and programme-based projections, is premised on the assumption that expenditure will be fully implemented by 2026. See Testimony of the President of the Parliamentary Budget Committee during the hearing on the 2023 Economic and Finance Document, Rome 2023, https://www.upbilancio.it/audizione-nellambito-dellesame-del-def-2023/#:~:text=20%20April%20 2023%207C%20The%20President,e%20finance%20(DEF)%202023

19 https://eur-lex.europa.eu/legal-content/IT/TXT/PDF/?uri=CELEX:52022DC0583 by conducting a series of hearings and formulating final documents—see https://www.senato.it/service/PDF/ PDFServer/BGT/1372239.pdf and https://www.camera.it/leg19/824?tipo=A&anno=2023&mese=0 3&giorno=08&view=&commissione=05

Member States in the process. They also linked the review of economic governance to the ongoing discussions on the reform of state-aid rules and (re)designing industrial policies. A crucial aspect not yet addressed is how to show preference for public investment aimed at combatting climate change and promoting digital transition—two pillars of the NRRP—and supporting international commitments undertaken in defence spending.

In the 2023 DEF, the Italian government outlined its intention to gradually, but systematically, reduce its deficit and debt of GDP over three years (4.5% of GDP in 2023, 3.7% in 2024, and 3% in 2025). In 2026, however, the deficit target has been set at 2.5% of GDP. With reference to the debt-to-GDP ratio: it is expected to be 144.4% in 2022, 142.1% in 2023, 141.4% in 2024, 140.9% in 2025, and 140.4% in 2026.[20] Obviously, higher interest expenditure in relation to GDP than in previous years and higher average costs when issuing new debt will have a major impact on the expected decrease of (merely) four points.

The Parliamentary Budget Office has also developed some scenarios to consider the debt-to-GDP ratio, up to 2024, in the context of the new framework elaborated and proposed by the European Commission. These show that a decreasing debt trend is only possible with economic growth; furthermore, from 2033, the ratio could rise due to the progressive increase of Italy's aging population.

Moreover, the NADEF 2023, adopted in September 2023, confirms the Government's desire to fully implement the NRRP. The new growth forecasts, in fact, continue to incorporate the full implementation of the NRRP. The Government continues to move forward with its planned expenditure but spending flows have been slightly revised downwards for 2023, to a lesser extent for 2024, and revised upwards for 2025 and 2026. The Parliamentary Budget Office, in a letter validating the macroeconomic framework trend for 2023–24, has highlighted the risks of these continuous slippages in terms of supply bottlenecks, also in reference to the expertise necessary to manage and start the works.[21] It follows that overall investments—although supported by the NRRP—will be less dynamic in the short term than forecasted in the DEF (-11.7%).

To conclude, only by increasing public investment—even beyond 2026—can the debt-to-GDP ratio decrease at a faster pace, and, above all in times like these, allow the EU *in primis* to try to build a new framework capable of withstanding the new world powers. A massive public-investment programme funded by European fiscal capacity could enable the (re)construction of a European model that combines democracy, growth, cohesion, and welfare. It is likewise abundantly clear that major emergencies (like climate change) render public intervention hollow if limited to a single state or even groups of states, for example, if the EU alone were to act globally on green transition.

---

20   NADEF updates for deficit are: 5.3% in 2023, 4.3% in 2024, 3.6% in 2025. With reference to the debt-to-GDP ratio: 140.2% in 2023, 140.1% in 2024, 139.9% in 2025, and 139.6% in 2026.

21   See https://www.upbilancio.it/wp-content/uploads/2023/10/Audizione-NADEF-2023.pdf

References

Barbieri, G., F. Cerniglia, G. F. Gori, P. Lattarulo, (2022), 'NRRP—Italy's strategic Reform and Investment Program', in F. Cerniglia and F. Saraceno (eds), *Greening Europe—2022 European Public Investment Outlook*, Cambridge, UK: Open Book Publishers: 55–70, https://doi.org/10.11647/OBP.0328

Barbieri, G., F. Cerniglia, (2021), 'Relaunching Public Investment in Italy', in F. Cerniglia, F. Saraceno, and A. Watt (eds), *The Great Reset—2021 European Public Investment Outlook*, Cambridge, UK: Open Book Publishers: 63–78, https://doi.org/10.11647/OBP.0280

Bordignon, M. (2022), 'Europa: ecco le nuove regole fiscali', *Lavoce*, November, https://lavoce.info/archives/98748/europa-ecco-le-nuove-regole-fiscali/

—— and L. Ciotti (2023), 'La transizione verso le nuove regole fiscali europee', Osservatorio CPI, 24 March, https://osservatoriocpi.unicatt.it/ocpi-pubblicazioni-la-transizione-verso-le-nuove-regole-fiscali-europee

—— (2023), 'Nuove regole fiscali europee: è pur sempre una riforma', *Lavoce*, 16 May, https://lavoce.info/archives/101126/nuove-regole-fiscali-europee-e-pur-sempre-una-riforma/

—— and F. Neri (2023), 'Le regole fiscali europee per il 2024', Osservatorio CPI, 7 June, https://osservatoriocpi.unicatt.it/ocpi-pubblicazioni-le-regole-fiscali-europee-per-il-2024

Camera dei Deputati (2023), 'I profili finanziari del Piano Nazionale di Ripresa e Resilienza (PNRR)', *Documentazione di finanza pubblica*, 4, November, https://documenti.camera.it/leg19/dossier/pdf/DFP004.pdf?_1667911550919

—— (2023), 'V Commissione Permanente—Documento finale sulla comunicazione della commissione al parlamento europeo, al consiglio, alla banca centrale europea, al comitato economico e sociale europeo e al comitato delle regioni—comunicazione sugli orientamenti per una riforma del quadro di governance economica dell'UE, COM(2022) 583 definitivo', 8 March, https://documenti.camera.it/leg19/resoconti/commissioni/bollettini/pdf/2023/03/08/leg.19.bol0075.data20230308.com05.pdf

Caputo, G. O. and G. Viesti (2022), 'Il PNRR e le disuguaglianze italiane: potenzialità e criticità', *Il Mulino*, Autonomie locali e servizi sociali, 2, August: 199–220 https://doi.org/10.1447/105081

Commissione Europea (2022), 'Comunicazione sugli orientamenti per una riforma del quadro di governance economica dell'UE', COM(2022) 583 final, https://eur-lex.europa.eu/legal-content/IT/TXT/PDF/?uri=CELEX:52022DC0583

Corte dei Conti, (2023), 'Relazione sullo stato di attuazione del Piano Nazionale di Ripresa e Resilienza (PNRR)', March, https://www.corteconti.it/Download?id=bbd19bb6-f688-4cb4-ae21-ff1ac2b56466

De Vincenti, C. (2022), 'Green Investments: Two Possible Interpretations of the 'Do Not Significant Harm' Principle', in F. Cerniglia, F. Saraceno (eds), *Greening Europe—2022 European Public Investment Outlook*, Cambridge, UK: Open Book Publishers: 177–86, https://doi.org/10.11647/OBP.0328:177–85

Fabbrini, F. (2023), 'La revisione del PNRR: problemi sui tempi e sulla strategia', commento, Centro Studi sul Federalismo, 31 July, https://www.csfederalismo.it/it/pubblicazioni/commenti/la-revisione-del-pnrr-problemi-sui-tempi-e-sulla-strategia

Ministero dell'Economia e delle finanze (2023), Documento di Economia e Finanza 2023, https://www.mef.gov.it/focus/Il-Documento-di-Economia-e-finanza-2023-DEF/

—— (2023), Documento di Economia e Finanza 2023—
Nota di aggiornamento, https://www.mef.gov.it/focus/
La-Nota-di-aggiornamento-del-documento-di-economia-e-finanza-del-2023-NADEF/

Presidenza del Consiglio dei Ministri (2023), *'Terza relazione sullo stato di attuazione del PNRR'*.
31 May, https://documenti.camera.it/_dati/leg19/lavori/documentiparlamentari/
IndiceETesti/013/001/INTERO.pdf

Rizzo, L., R. Secomandi, A. Zanardi (2023), 'Criticità del PNRR tra rimodulazione
e restituzione dei fondi', *Lavoce*, 16 June, https://lavoce.info/archives/101391/
criticita-del-pnrr-tra-rimodulazione-e-restituzione-dei-fondi/

Senato della Repubblica (2023), 'Risoluzione della 5° Commissione Permanente sulla
comunicazione della commissione al parlamento europeo, al consiglio, alla banca
centrale europea, al comitato economico e sociale europeo e al comitato delle regioni—
comunicazione sugli orientamenti per una riforma del quadro di governance economica
dell'ue (com(2022) 583 definitivo)', doc XVIII, no. 1, https://www.senato.it/service/PDF/
PDFServer/BGT/1372239.pdf

Servizio Studi della Camera dei Deputati (2023), 'Terza relazione sullo stato di attuazione del
PNRR—I traguardi e gli obiettivi da conseguire entro il 30 giugno 2023', 14 July, https://
documenti.camera.it/leg19/dossier/pdf/DFP28f.pdf?_1683021396554

—— (2023), 'La terza relazione sullo stato di attuazione del PNRR—Focus sui profili di
riprogrammazione del piano', 20 June, https://documenti.camera.it/leg19/dossier/pdf/
DFP28_R.pdf?_1693483680910

—— (2023), 'Monitoraggio dell'attuazione del Piano Nazionale di Ripresa e Resilienza—Le
proposte del governo per la revisione del PNRR e il capitolo RePowerEU', 31 July, https://
documenti.camera.it/leg19/dossier/pdf/DFP28_Ra.pdf

Servizio Studi del Senato, (2023), 'Il bilancio dello Stato 2023–2025. Una analisi delle spese per
missioni e programmi', Servizio del bilancio del Senato, March, https://www.senato.it/
service/PDF/PDFServer/BGT/01372851.pdf

Svimez (2023), 'Dalla ripartenza coesa alle scelte per rafforzare equità e crescita: PNRR, Fondi
di Coesione, politiche industriali e diritti di cittadinanza', in *Anticipazioni del Rapporto
SVIMEZ 2023: L'economia e la società del Mezzogiorno*, July, Rome.

—— (2022), 'Le politiche di coesione: il contributo alla ripresa e alla resilienza', in *Rapporto
Svimez: l'economia e la società del Mezzogiorno*, Rome: 413–47

Ufficio Parlamentare di Bilancio (2023), 'Rapporto sulla politica di bilancio', June, https://
www.upbilancio.it/wp-content/uploads/2023/06/Rapporto_2023_pol_bil_per-sito.pdf

—— (2023), 'Audizione della Presidente dell'Ufficio parlamentare di bilancio nell'ambito delle
audizioni preliminari all'esame del Doc. LVII, n. 1 (Documento di economia e finanza per il
2023)', 20 April, https://www.upbilancio.it/wp-content/uploads/2023/04/Audizione-UPB-
DEF-2023.pdf

—— (2023), 'Audizione della Presidente dell'Ufficio parlamentare di bilancio nell'ambito
dell'attività conoscitiva preliminare all'esame della Nota di aggiornamento del Documento
di economia e finanza 2023', https://www.upbilancio.it/wp-content/uploads/2023/10/
Audizione-NADEF-2023.pdf

Viesti, G. (2021), 'Il PNRR e il Mezzogiorno. 80 miliardi, un totale in cerca di addendi', in
Quaderni di Rassegna Sindacale, 2: 53–62

—— (2022), 'Un piano per rilanciare l'Italia?', in *Il Mulino*, 2: 23–38

—— (2022b), 'Il PNRR, gli asili nido e l'uguaglianza delle opportunità', in *Menabò di Etica ed Economia*, 3 July, https://eticaeconomia.it/1307-2/

—— (2022c), 'The Territorial Dimension of the Italian NRRP', in A. Caloffi, M. De Castris, G. Perucca (eds), *The Regional Challenges in the Post-Covid Era*, Milan, FrancoAngeli: 201–18

—— (2023), *Riuscirà il PNRR a rilanciare l'Italia?*, Rome, Donzelli Editore: 53–62

——, C. Chiapperini, E. Montenegro (2022), *Le città italiane e il PNRR*, WP Urban@it, https://www.urbanit.it/wp-content/uploads/2022/06/20220701-citta-e-pnrr-viesti-chiapperini-montenegro-1-1.pdf

5. Public Investment, Deficit and Public Debt in Spain, 1995–2022

Francisco Pérez and Eva Benages

Over the past three decades, public investment in Spain has followed an extremely irregular trajectory, with periods of significant capital accumulation and others in which net investment has been negative. The sustainability of the pace of investment has been challenged by expenditure policies that are procyclical instead of stabilizing, in addition to fiscal regulations that have not been able to improve public-productive capital by following the golden rule. The revision of the EU's economic-governance framework should take into account this and other experiences to enhance the compatibility between fiscal rules and the expanded investment envisaged by the Recovery and Resilience Mechanism.

5.1 Introduction

Since the Maastricht Treaty came into force in 1993, Spain's public investment has gone through very different stages. The causes for these shifts are many. They include the changing overall conditions experienced by the Spanish economy, the scant attention given by spending policies to stabilization and sustainability objectives, the challenges of public-sector financing since the Great Recession, and the fiscal framework established by the Stability and Growth Pact (SGP) in 1997 and its subsequent revisions.

Member States have presented objections to the SGP. The first concerns its design, which gives prominence to the output gap, even though this variable is not observable and is subject to debate due to its dependence on the estimation criteria. The second objection concerns Member States' limited compliance with fiscal rules and the lack of consequences for non-compliance, leading to a decline in the Pact's credibility. The third relates to the framework's complexity, which raises questions about both its political acceptability and the European Commission's discretionary application of its rules (2022).

Warnings concerning the poor de facto safeguards for public investment in the EU fiscal-policy framework have increased since 2019 (European Fiscal Board 2019; Darvas and Anderson 2020), despite the loosening of deficit restrictions for that purpose. In October 2021, the European Commission relaunched the public debate

https://doi.org/10.11647/OBP.0386.05

on the review of the EU's economic-governance framework, and, in December 2022, it presented a communication about its reform (European Commission 2022) to the European Parliament, the European Central Bank (ECB), the European Economic and Social Committee, and the Committee of the Regions. This communication proposed a framework to address the financing of a green and digital transition towards a climate-neutral economy and to solve the issue of the high public debt-to-GDP ratios reached in the first decades of the twenty-first century. Both challenges require fiscal regulations that enable strategic investments and also protect the viability of fiscal policy.

This reformed approach requires closer attention to the trajectory of public investment than in the past because, while capital formation in the EU as a whole has not suffered significantly over the last three decades, some countries, such as Spain, have seen an important reduction in net investment since 2010. As a result, the public-capital growth rate has been cut in half.

These circumstances raise the question of whether the criteria for calculating the deficit that can be financed with debt should expressly contemplate a golden rule that protects net investment, given that the European Recovery and Resilience Strategy is committed to strengthening investments for the ecological transition; the digital transformation; smart, sustainable, and inclusive growth; social and territorial cohesion; social and institutional health and resilience; and policies for the next generation, children, and youth. It is a strategy that also contemplates investment needs for both tangible and intangible assets.

This chapter argues for an approach to deficit policy in line with the criteria of the golden rule by examining the trajectory of investment and of public-capital stock in Spain between 1995 and 2022. It also reviews the challenges of financing public investment in the context of high fiscal deficits since the onset of the Great Recession.

5.2 The Trajectory of Public Investment in Spain, 1995–2022

After becoming a member of the EU in 1986, Spain implemented a rigorous public investment strategy that was supported, in large part, by European structural funds. Much of this strategy coincided with the Spanish economic expansion between 1995 and 2008; it was fuelled by a powerful real-estate bubble. Figure 5.1 shows that, up until the onset of the financial crisis, public investment doubled in real terms, growing more than GDP. It also shows a sharp fall thereafter.

a) €m 2015

b) Real Evolution of GDP and
Public Investment, 1995=100

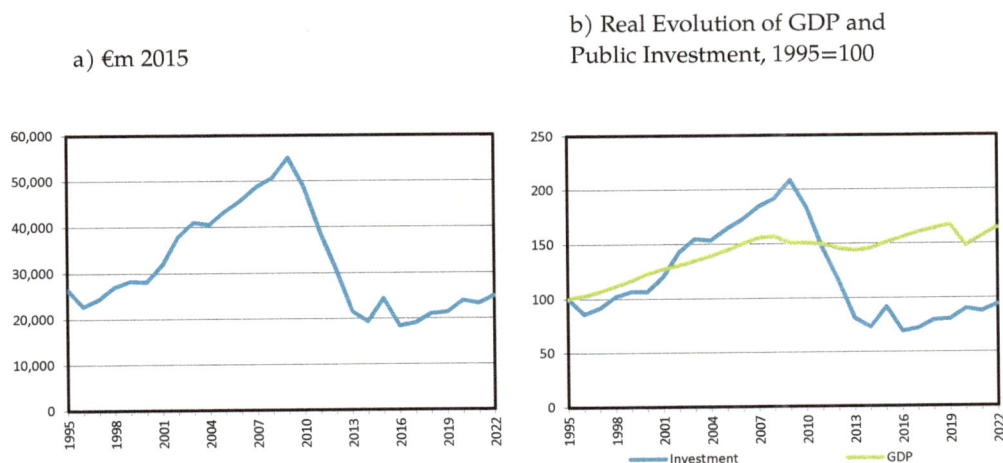

Fig. 5.1 Public Investment in Spain, 1995–2022.
Note: Public investment includes investments made by external agents in infrastructures for public
use (ADIF, AENA, State Ports, etc.).
Source: BBVA Foundation-Ivie (2023), INE (CNE), and authors' elaboration.

The pronounced procyclicality of the trajectory of gross-public capital formation shows that these expenditures have not been sustainable and have in no way contributed to stability. Instead, they have reinforced growth throughout the expansionary phase and accentuated the recession in the most difficult period of the crisis. Despite the recovery experienced in the last five years, gross public investment in Spain remains at lower real levels than in the initial years of the series, being 6% lower in 2022 that in 1995.

The investment effort of the initial long expansionary phase is mostly concentrated in productive infrastructures, mainly transport-related (particularly high-speed railroads). Gross public-capital formation in social infrastructures (educational, health, cultural, social services, administrative, etc.) is also highly important (Figure 5.2). Investment increased by two between 1995 and 2009 in both aggregates, but when the crisis struck, the decline in transport infrastructure was greater and more severe. The recent recovery has focused mainly on social infrastructure, which has returned to its 1995 levels, while productive or transport infrastructure is still 20% below its 1995 level.

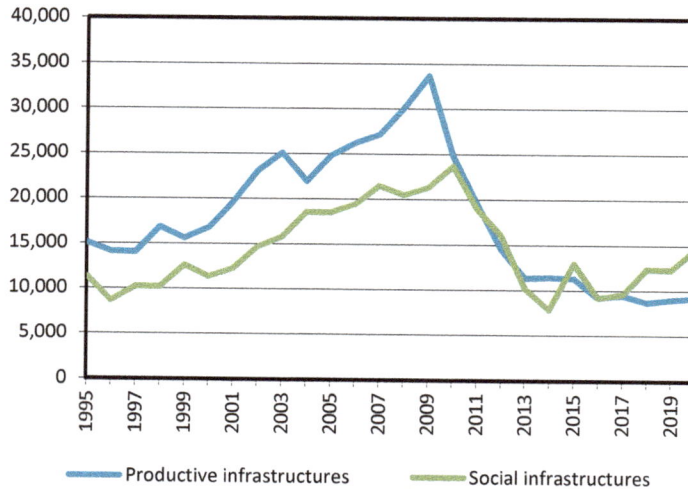

Fig. 5.2 Public Investment in Productive and Social Infrastructures in Spain, 1995–2020, in €m 2015.
Note: Public investment includes investments made by external agents in infrastructures for public
use (ADIF, AENA, State Ports, etc.).
Source: BBVA Foundation-Ivie (2023) and authors' elaboration.

5.3 From Investment to Capital Accumulation

The data on the trajectory of the public fixed capital stock allows us to determine how much of gross investment is absorbed to cover the depreciation of existing public capital and what part of net investment produces changes in capital stock.[1]

The rapid investment pace between 1995 and 2012 implies an increase in stock of 87%, largely concentrated in productive infrastructure (mainly transport[2]), which grew by 93%. Although public investment increased during the first two years of the Great Recession, from 2010 onwards it does not even cover the depreciation of the existing stock, which decreased by 5% since then (Figure 5.3).

The part of gross investment that is absorbed by capital accumulation amortizations is always significant (Figure 5.4). In the period of greatest investment effort, consumption of fixed capital represents around 50% of gross investment and the other half represents net investment, that is, that which constitutes stock growth. However, when gross investment fell sharply with the onset of the crisis, consumption of fixed

---

1   The analysis that follows is based on information from the database that has been developed by the BBVA Foundation and the Ivie for over twenty-five years, which corresponds to the information for Spain that is used in different international databases, such as EU KLEMS, funded by the European Commission's 6th and 7th Framework Program, as well as its successor, the EUKLEMS & INTANProd project, funded by the European Commission's Directorate General for Economic and Financial Affairs (DG_ECFIN) (EU KLEMS 2011, 2012). The database is available at BBVA Foundation-Ivie (2023). In addition, a report that accompanies the database is published annually. Furter details can be found in Pérez and Mas (Dirs.) (2020).

2   The latest data broken down by type of infrastructure (productive or social) corresponds to 2020.

capital represented more than 100%, making net investment negative from 2013 onwards and reducing the stock of public capital.

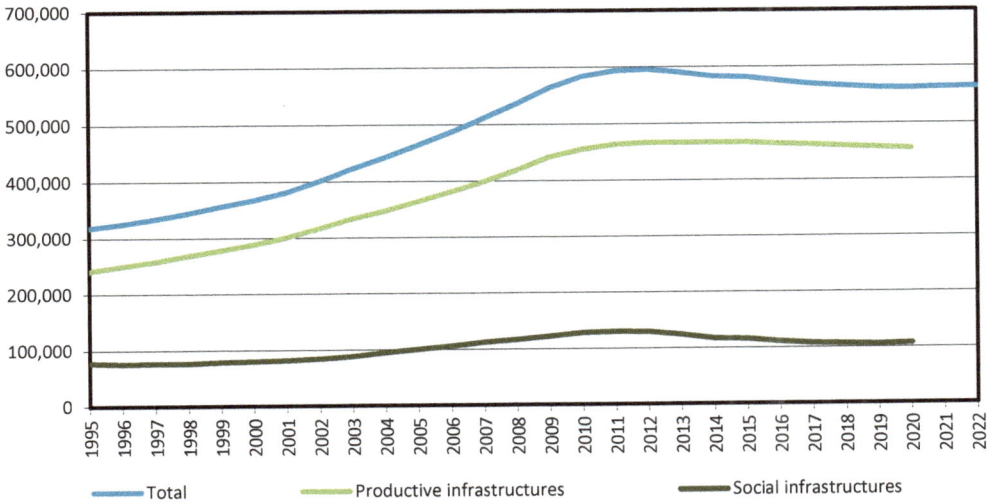

Fig. 5.3 Evolution of Public Capital Stock in Spain, 1995–2022, in €m 2015.
Note: Public capital includes privately owned infrastructures for public use (ADIF, AENA, State Ports, etc.).
Source: BBVA Foundation-Ivie (2023), INE (CNE), and authors' elaboration.

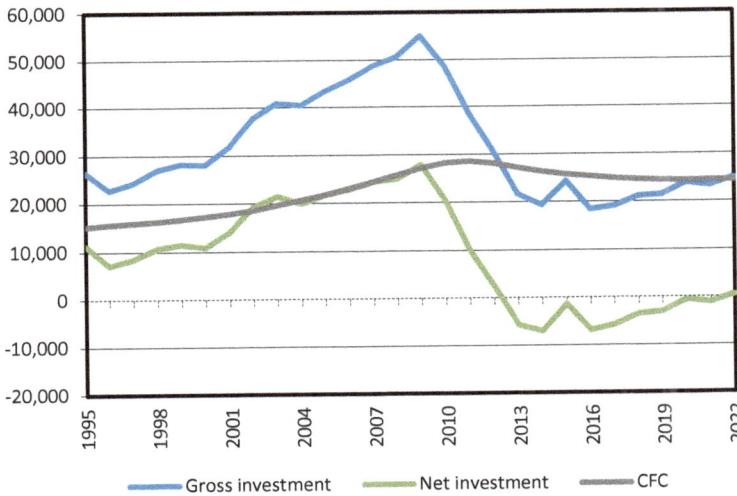

Fig. 5.4 Gross Public Investment, Net Investment, and Consumption of Fixed Capital in Spain, 1995–2022, in €m 2015.
Note: Public investment includes investments made by external agents in infrastructures for public use (ADIF, AENA, State Ports, etc.).
Source: BBVA Foundation-Ivie (2023) and authors' elaboration.

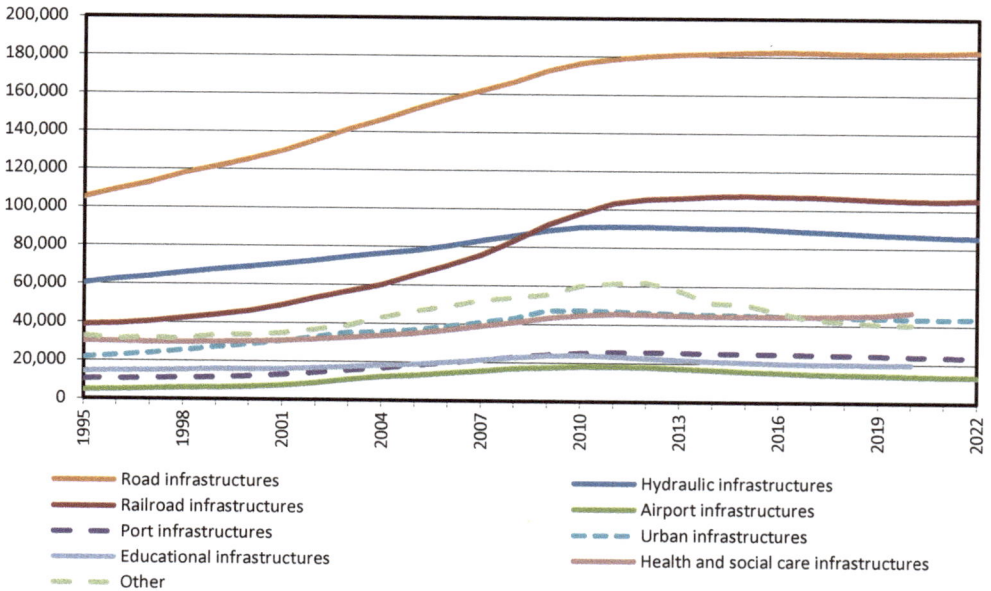

Fig. 5.5 Evolution of Public Capital Stock in Spain by Type of Asset, 1995–2022, in €m 2015.
Note: Public capital includes privately owned infrastructures for public use (ADIF, AENA, State Ports, etc.).
Source: BBVA Foundation-Ivie (2023) and authors' elaboration.

Figure 5.5 shows that all assets experienced a significant growth in the expansionary phase. When the crisis hit, accumulation stagnated, at least in all of them, and even fell significantly in some cases. Among the assets that failed to cover replacement, the ones that stand out are port and airport infrastructures, educational and social services infrastructures, with cumulative declines of over 9% from 2012 to present.

The gross capital formation of Spain's public sector has been so irregular that, during the past decade, it has not been possible to maintain the accumulated public capital. Since then, the consumption of fixed capital has absorbed all the gross investment and, because net investment has been negative, the capital stock has aged.[3] The question that arises here is: what factors led to the decline in public investment following the Great Recession?

5.4 Investment and Public Deficit Financing

The drop in gross public capital formation in Spain during the Great Recession and subsequent years was mainly attributable to the spending cuts that the central, regional, and local government were forced to implement in order to limit the strong

---

3   See a detailed analysis in Pérez and Mas (Dirs.) (2020).

fiscal imbalances that emerged after 2008. The administrations had to make significant adjustments in many of their expenditures. These changes had a greater impact on investment as a result of the Stability and Growth Pact and the non-accommodative monetary policy that implied sharp increases in the cost of financing and the risk premium.

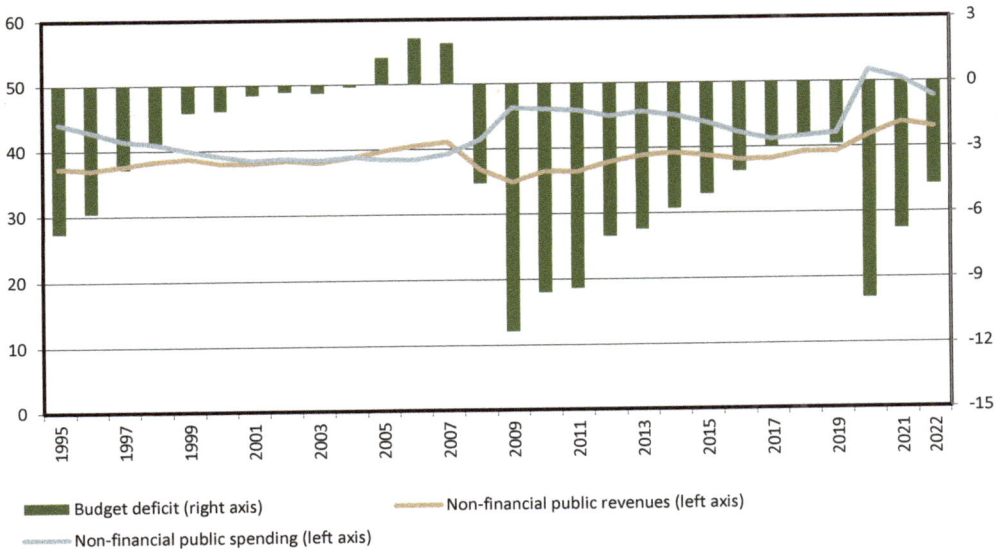

Fig. 5.6 Government Spending, Revenues, and Budget Deficit in Spain, 1995–2022 (% of GDP).
Note: Net public spending and net public revenues of aids to financial institutions have been considered.
Source: IGAE (2023a) and authors' elaboration.

Figure 5.6 shows that, during the expansionary phase that preceded the financial crisis, public revenues and expenditures followed converging paths that reduced the deficit and allowed for the achievement of budget surpluses between 2006 and 2008. However, the combination of a sharp fall in tax revenues in 2008 and 2009, which was much higher than in other European countries, along with the delayed recognition of the change in scenario on the expenditure side, led to immediate increases in the deficit, pushing it to unsustainable levels close to 10% of GDP in 2009. It remained above 6% until 2013.

A direct result of the evolution of the public deficit is the trajectory of the debt throughout the period analysed. In the initial period from 1995 to 2007, when the deficit was controlled and GDP grew rapidly, the debt-to-GDP ratio significantly decreased, reaching 35.7% in 2007. During the years of the Great Recession—of strong deficit and also falling GDP—the ratio soared to reach 105% in 2014. The recovery of growth from that year until 2019 and the efforts to contain the deficit interrupt the rising trajectory of the debt-to-GDP ratio. However, the COVID-19 crisis pushed the ratio up again, to a peak of 120.4% in 2020. The indicator remains at very high levels since then (113.2% in 2022) (Figure 5.7).

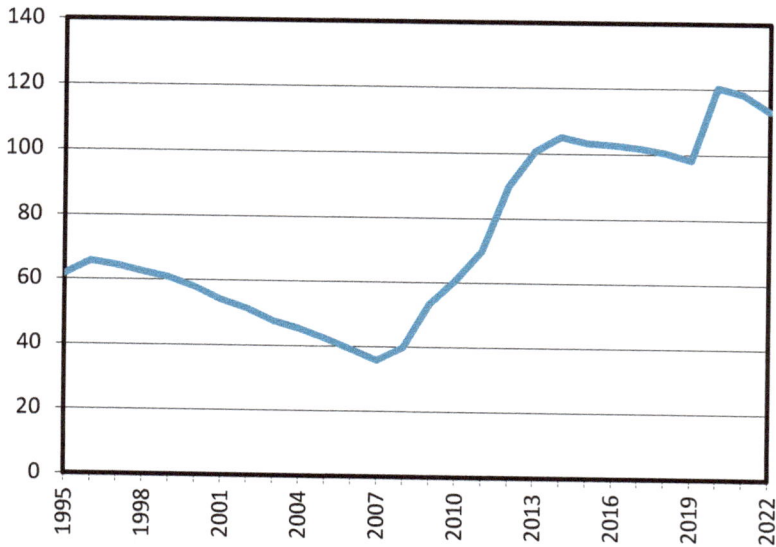

Fig. 5.7 Public Debt in Spain, 1995–2022 (% of GDP).
Source: Bank of Spain (2023).

Thus, despite measures to boost tax collection and reduce spending, efforts to reduce the deficit have not prevented a sharp increase in debt. Tax revenues began to improve as a result of various tax increases and thanks to the recovery of growth from 2014 onwards. Adjustments affected all levels of government but not all spending functions. Social protection was an important exception: there was an increase in spending on unemployment benefits and pensions, both of which are controlled by the central government. Other important social expenditures, such as education and health care, which are decentralized to regional governments in Spain, did experience a decrease.

As seen in Figure 5.8, total public spending stagnated between 2009 and 2017; public investment spending, meanwhile, which had been previously high, fell sharply from 2010 onwards. It remained at levels below those of 1995, despite a minor increase since 2016. With the arrival of the pandemic, public investment increased as a consequence of the different responses given by the EU to the new crisis. This has allowed Spain to rely on significant resources and funding from the Recovery and Resilience Mechanism (RRM) from 2020 onwards.

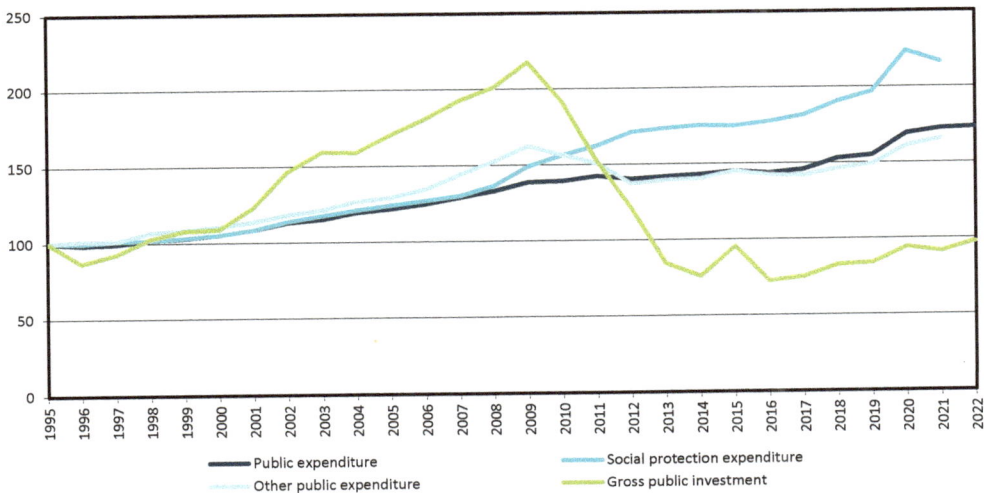

Fig. 5.8 Real Public Spending and Gross Investment in Spain, 1995–2022 (1995=100).
Note: Net public spending of aid to financial institutions has been considered. Public investment
includes investments made by external agents (ADIF, AENA, etc.).
Source: BBVA Foundation-Ivie (2023), IGAE (2023a, 2023b), INE (CNE), and authors' elaboration.

The decline in public investment during the Great Recession and its subsequent
stagnation was, de facto, a key tool for deficit control. The cost of this is that investment
was not protected when deficit surged with the start of the financial crisis. The public
sector faces the challenges of reducing many expenditures, particularly monetary
transfers associated with social protection, and adjustments are much more intensely
directed towards investment because they do not involve intense tensions with social
groups involving pensions, education or healthcare recipients.

Figure 5.9 illustrates how important these reductions in gross investment have been
in containing the deficit. It represents the ratio between the annual deficit and the
adjustment made in investment (the difference between each year's investment and
2008 gross investment). When investment adjustments began to be made in 2010, their
contribution to deficit control was modest, but this grew as investment remained low
and the deficit was gradually reduced. The investment adjustment is equal to 100% of
the deficit in 2018. In other words, the deficit would have increased by 100% if, all else
being equal, public investment had maintained its 2008 level in 2018. In more recent
years, the importance of the contributions of the investment adjustment to deficit
control is less significant, since the deficit increased once again with the arrival of the
pandemic.

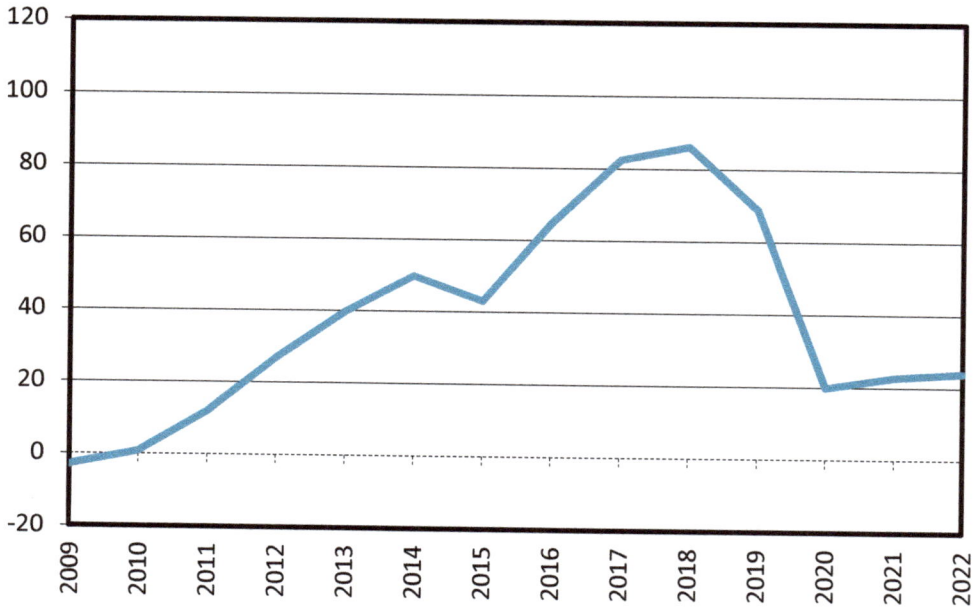

Fig. 5.9 Contributions of Investment Adjustments to the Reduction of Public Deficit in Spain, 2009–2022 (% of Deficit).
Note: Public investment includes investments made by external agents in infrastructures for public use (ADIF, AENA, State Ports, etc.).
Source: BBVA Foundation-Ivie (2023), IGAE (2023a), and authors' elaboration.

A joint analysis of the trajectory of Spanish public sector gross investment and its contribution to keeping the deficit under control shows that European fiscal laws, as they were implemented in Spain, have not served to protect investment. The justification for financing investment with deficits is that, if net investment is reduced in order to avoid imbalances that threaten the sustainability of public accounts, the consequences could be negative for growth and fiscal sustainability. By not undertaking productive investment projects, economic activity is reduced and tax collection is also affected. This is why the classic interpretation of the golden rule (Blanchard and Giavazzi 2004; Mintz and Smart 2006) contends that public deficits and indebtedness should be permitted if the goal is to finance net investment.

Figure 5.10 shows the trajectories of the government deficit, gross fixed capital formation, fixed capital consumption, and net investment, together with the horizontal line defining the 3% medium-term deficit rule. This rule attempts to prevent debt sustainability problems, while acknowledging that there are reasons that justify the financing of growth-enhancing expenditures, particularly potentially productive investment, with deficits. The figure shows two relevant features of the situation in the period in which Spain's public deficit has become a problem for compliance with the 3% rule, from 2009 onwards. The first feature is that the most important part of investment spending that is financed by the deficit is the consumption of fixed capital, that is, amortizations that allow the capital stock to be maintained, not increased. However, capital growth is what allows potential output to increase, and the stock does not grow because net investment is negative. Therefore, the growth of public capital is not what justifies the deficit. The second feature is that, despite the fact that the sharp adjustment of net investment makes a powerful contribution to controlling the public deficit, the notable gap between the two variables in the figure suggests that the most relevant part of the mismatch in the public accounts is the existence of recurring expenditure, both current and capital (such as consumption of fixed capital), which should be financed on a regular basis, but since they are not, they are financed with deficits.

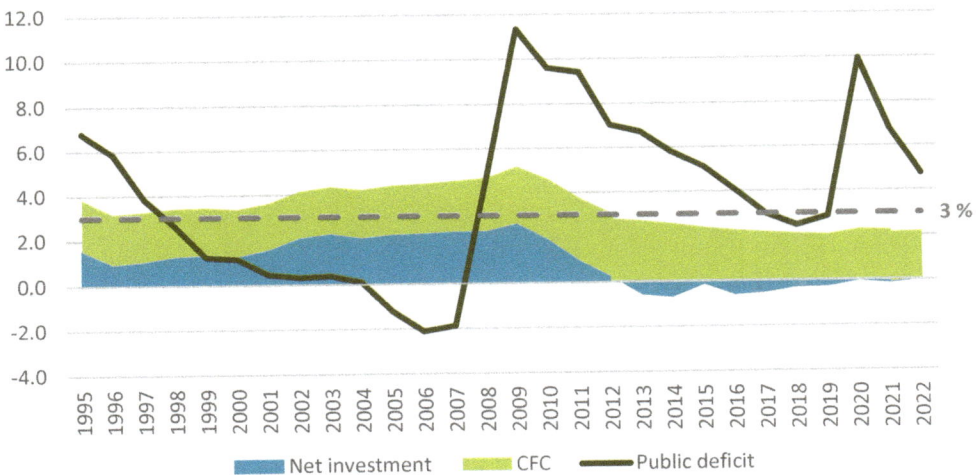

Fig. 5.10 Deficit Used to Finance Gross Investment and Fixed Capital Consumption: Net Investment, Fixed Capital Consumption, and Public Deficit. Spain, 1995–2022 (% of GDP). Note: Public investment includes investments made by external agents in infrastructures for public use (ADIF, AENA, State Ports, etc.). The net budget balance of financial institution aid has been considered. The deficit is represented in the graph with the opposite sign to allow comparisons. *Source*: BBVA Foundation-Ivie (2023), IGAE (2023a), and authors' elaboration.

5.5 Conclusions

This analysis shows that, in the case of Spain, European fiscal laws are consistent with a situation that presents several undesirable features that call for revision.

The first is that, despite the fact that the fiscal rules contemplate a flexible criterion to maintain investment and public capital stock, it does not exist in practice. This is shown by the negative values of net public investment of the most indebted countries, including Spain.

The second feature is that fiscal rules are not applied in accordance with the golden rule. They allow a large part of the authorized deficit to be used to finance the amortization of existing capital, but covering the consumption of fixed capital does not imply an increase in the capacity to produce goods and services in order to grow. Rather, it suggests the maintenance of the flow of services from public assets.

The third unfavorable aspect is that fiscal rules have not been operating as stabilizing mechanisms for demand and activity. However, they accentuate the cyclical profiles, especially (but not only) through procyclical adjustments to investment during expansionary and recessionary phases.

The European Commission's proposed review of the EU's fiscal governance should consider how to address these undesirable features observed in the implementation of fiscal regulations established during periods of high indebtedness in different countries, particularly in Spain. The review of the EU's economic governance framework should consider this and other experiences, in order to reinforce the compatibility between fiscal regulations and the investment targets set forth by the Recovery and Resilience Mechanism. If they are not protected, it will be increasingly challenging to improve the endowments of both tangible and intangible assets that contribute to the generation of European public goods with capacity to benefit future generations (Giavazzi et al. 2021).

References

Bank of Spain (2023). 'Statistical Bulletin'. Madrid,
https://www.bde.es/webbe/en/estadisticas/otras-clasificaciones/publicaciones/boletin-estadistico/boletin-estadistico.html

BBVA Foundation and Ivie (The Valencian Institute of Economic Research) (2023). 'El stock y los servicios del capital en España y su distribución territorial y sectorial'. València, March,
https://www.fbbva.es/bd/el-stock-y-los-servicios-del-capital-en-espana/

Blanchard, O. J. and F. Giavazzi (2004). 'Improving the SPG through a Proper Accounting of Public Investment'. *CEPR Discussion Papers*, no. 4220. Washington D. C.: Center for Economic and Policy Research,
https://cepr.org/publications/dp4220

Darvas, Z. and J. Anderson (2020). 'New Life for an Old Framework: Redesigning the European Union's Expenditure and Golden Fiscal Rules'. Brussels: European Parliament,
https://www.europarl.europa.eu/thinktank/en/document/IPOL_STU%282020%29645733

EU KLEMS (2009). *Growth and Productivity Accounts*: November 2009 Release, updated March 2011,
http://www.euklems.net/euk09ii.shtml

—— (2012). Growth and Productivity Accounts: Data in the ISIC Rev. 4 industry classification,
http://www.euklems.net/eukISIC4.shtml

European Commission (2022). 'Communication on Orientations for a Reform of the EU Economic Governance Framework. Brussels (COM(2022) 583 final',
https://eur-lex.europa.eu/legal-content/EN/TXT/?uri=CELEX:52022DC0583

European Fiscal Board (2019). 'Assessment of EU Fiscal Rules with Focus on the Six and Two-Pack Legislation'. Bussels: European Commission,
https://commission.europa.eu/system/
files/2019-09/2019-09-10-assessment-of-eu-fiscal-rules_en.pdf

Giavazzi, F., V. Guerrieri, G. Lorenzoni, and C. Weymuller (2021). 'Revising the European Fiscal Framework', https://www.governo.it/sites/governo.it/files/documenti/documenti/Notizie-allegati/Reform_SGP.pdf

IGAE (Intervención General de la Administración del Estado). Contabilidad Nacional. Operaciones no financieras. Serie anual. Madrid: Ministerio de Hacienda, https://www.igae.pap.hacienda.gob.es/sitios/igae/es-ES/Contabilidad/ContabilidadNacional/Publicaciones/Paginas/ianofinancierasTotal.aspx

—— Contabilidad Nacional. Clasificación funcional del gasto de las Administraciones Públicas. Madrid: Ministerio de Hacienda, https://www.igae.pap.hacienda.gob.es/sitios/igae/es-ES/Contabilidad/ContabilidadNacional/Publicaciones/Paginas/iacogofseries.aspx

INE (Instituto Nacional de Estadística). Contabilidad Nacional anual de España (CNE). Revisión Estadística 2019. Madrid, https://www.ine.es/dyngs/INEbase/es/operacion.htm?c=Estadistica_C&cid=1254736177057&menu=resultados&idp=1254735576581

Luiss Lab of European Economics (2023). EUKLEMS & INTANProd-Release 2023. Roma: Luiss University, https://euklems-intanprod-llee.luiss.it/

Mintz, J. M. and M. Smart (2006). 'Incentives for Public Investment Under Fiscal Rules'. Policy Research Working Papers, Washington D. C.: World Bank,
https://doi.org/10.1596/1813-9450-3860

Pérez, F. and M. Mas (Dirs.), E. Benages, J.C. Robledo, and I. Vicente (2020). 'El stock de capital en España y sus comunidades autónomas. Ajuste de la inversión pública y reducción del déficit'. *Working Papers*, no. 1/2020. Bilbao: BBVA Foundation, https://www.fbbva.es/wp-content/uploads/2020/01/DE_2020_DT_1_2020_Stock_de_capital_196-2017_Ivie_prot.pdf

PART II. CHALLENGES

6. Escaping Fragmentation and Secular Stagnation. The EU Policy Mix and Investment Financing

Pier Carlo Padoan[1]

The EU has be en impacted by multiple crises due to economic and geopolitical drivers. These crises have left scarring effects and may lead to fragmentation with serious permanent consequences. This takes place against the background of secular stagnation which makes the policy response more difficult. The main response strategy is the NGEU mechanism, based on public investment and structural reforms. It should deliver sustainable growth and structural change that allows to exit the multiple crises—pandemic, geopolitical, energy, inflationary—and puts the European Union on path of twin transformation (digital and green), reverting the drift towards secular stagnation. NGEU is an effective policy tool, provided it acts through policy packages of public investment and structural reforms and allows for time to complete the reform cycle. Its effectiveness must be seen in the context of a new policy mix fit to address the multiple-crises framework.

6.1 Introduction

The COVID crisis has prompted a joint response by EU Member States and by the European Commission. In the short-term, temporary measures such as the suspension of the Stability and Growth Pact and the temporary framework on state aid have minimized the immediate costs of the COVID shock. In the medium to long term, policymakers will have to address the challenges of the twin transition towards digital and green activities and to reinforce the EU-growth model. What will make this more

1   UniCredit is not to be held responsible for the contents of this paper. I thank Franco Bassanini, Marco Buti, Lilia Cavallari, Paolo Costa, Luis De Mello, Claudio De Vincenti, Daniel Gros, Paolo Guerrieri, Fiorella Kostoris, Marcello Messori, Alessandro Paladini, Debora Revoltella, Francesco Saraceno, and the participants of the Astrid seminar on european economic policy for useful comments. I also thank Roberto Fratter for excellent support in drafting the text.

https://doi.org/10.11647/OBP.0386.06

difficult are the consequences of the energy crisis and the inflation acceleration which impacts the dynamic of economic growth. Policymakers will also have to face the challenge of fragmentation generated by geopolitical tensions against the background of persistent secular stagnation.

To deal with the Covid crisis, the EU Commission has launched the Next Generation EU (NGEU) programme and activated its operational arm, the Recovery and Resilience Facility which is translated into National Plans of Recovery and Resilience (NPRR). The mission of the temporary instrument is to revamp EU growth in quantitative (how much growth) and qualitative (what kind of growth) terms. It does so by supporting public investment and structural reforms through substantial financing. €750bn in financing is provided by the EU budget and funded by the issuance of dedicated European bonds.

6.2 Phases of European Growth

In what follows, I consider the underlying logic of NGEU, linking the specific measures to the EU growth model to evaluate if and to what extent NGEU will be able to deliver growth and transform the EU economy towards its green and digital targets. I also look at the role of investment, both public and private, and the possible financing strategies, given the very large amounts of investment needed to complete the twin transition.

Post-war EU growth can be viewed as a sequence of subperiods characterised by growth-acceleration episodes (Hausmann, Pritchet, and Rodrik 2004). One way to identify subperiods is to mirror them with the evolution of the global economic and monetary system. From the Bretton Woods days to the present, the different subperiods exhibit characteristics that can be described as follows, with a specific focus on growth drivers.

1) Free Trade Area and Custom Union. This phase replicates the extension of the Bretton Woods (BW) system at the global level. The Bretton Woods regime was based on a domestic, demand-driven USA economy and an export-driven EU economy. The currency arrangement included a peg to the dollar backed by gold reserves. The main growth drivers in the EU were integration and trade openness. This structure generated a large positive supply shock for the EU, and the opening to international trade led to a significant reallocation of resources within countries. Resources were shifted from non-tradable to tradable sectors. There was no international capital mobility. Most EU countries ran a current-account surplus that reflected an excess of savings (savings > investments).

2) After the BW collapse in 1971, the dollar standard, and the two oil shocks, the EU struggled to converge. Sluggish growth highlights the fragmentation in the EU economy and the persistent risk of divergence between Northern and Southern members. Many EU countries adopted flexible exchange rates in reaction to dollar

flexibility. Northern members of the EU, however, established fixed exchange rates among themselves (giving birth to the 'D mark zone' in the first part of the 1970s) to enhance stability. Southern members' currencies devalued as oil prices raised inflation. Inflation differentials widened. Risks of divergence within the EU increased. Stagflation loomed.

3) In spite (or because) of the economic fragmentation in the global system, the EU's move from a custom union towards deeper forms of integration drove growth. Stability-growth tradeoffs in an inflationary environment are the key features of the macroeconomic system. Initially, flexible exchange rates were effective in absorbing shocks, but inflation in the EU accelerated at different speeds, which generated divergence in relative competitive positions. Excessive currency flexibility and volatility were seen as a challenge to the custom union. The European Monetary System (EMS) was established in 1979 as an attempt to provide stability and convergence in a stagflation environment. The move towards fixed exchange rates, with German monetary policy as an anchor, was seen as a way to enforce discipline and to restore integration. However, the EMS collapsed after a decade, when fixed exchange rates, full capital mobility, and national macroeconomic policies proved to be incompatible.

4) The Single European act. As monetary stability was reestablished, the EU single market and exogenous Total Factor Productivity (TFP) emerged as the drivers of growth. Evidence shows that economic and institutional complexity (such as the one associated with intra-industry trade and 'social capital') supports growth. Complexity as a feature of social and economic institutions that affects growth is more pronounced in northern EU members. However, not all TFP is exogenous. An endogenous component is driven by investment in innovation, research and development, and human capital. In spite of a self-sustained growth dynamics, an underlying tendency towards secular stagnation emerged, driven by demographics, inequality, and decreasing productivity. Growth below potential and, in some cases, declines in potential output characterised EU members and the Euro Zone, especially during the euro crisis (see 7, below). The sequence of EU enlargements in the 1980s also mark the start of acceleration episodes.

5) Growth gaps to potential output emerge in the Euro area. In a number of EU countries, structural impediments to growth (including the low quality of institutions) persisted in spite of efforts to complete the single market. This is particularly visible in the lack of a single market for services, which holds back productivity and innovation. Large output gaps also emerged in the USA. Globally, trade regionalism developed as a factor determining the nature of competition and conflict. Strategic trade policy became a policy option in support of national interests. Despite an increasing tendency towards regionalism, the global financial system remained dollar-based.

6) After the crisis of the European Monetary System, a 'corner-solution dilemma' emerged regarding the choice of exchange-rate arrangements (was it preferable to have fully flexible rates or a single currency?). The euro was introduced, but not all EU members joined the single currency. Initially, the introduction of the euro brought

convergence: the narrowing of spreads among members of the Euro was seen as a move towards a zero-risk or free-capital-mobility environment. A debt financed growth model also emerged, that is, one in which countries finance their growth through borrowing. This pattern generated imbalances that led to capital flows from excess-saving to excess-investment countries. Investment was directed, especially, towards low-productivity, non-tradable sectors. The lack of exchange-rate flexibility generated a deflationary pressure on deficit economies as surplus countries refused to reflate in order to allow for relative prices to adjust. The overall policy stance was restrictive, and the undervaluation of surplus countries' currencies was persistent. Integration did not progress.

7) Convergence turned into divergence, and risks of fragmentation increased significantly. In spite of large capital flows, or, rather, because of these, the eurozone proved to be unsustainable, an 'impossible trinity'. This 'euro crisis' and the bank sovereign doom loop prompted euro reform (most notably, the creation of a banking union). This policy response avoided the collapse of the monetary union. However, it shows the fragility of the collective agreement on which the euro was based. The reform was only partly successful, as a conflict between national and EU perspectives (risk mitigation versus risk sharing) persisted and the tendency towards divergence renewed.

8) Global imbalances and the global financial crisis. To accelerate recovery after COVID, the NGEU was launched. Its long-term structural orientation has been seen as the opportunity to reverse secular decline, replace external demand with internal demand, and change the composition of production and consumption in the twin transformation towards green and digital. However, these shifts require investment (both public and private), structural change, and an availability of non-tradable goods (services) to enhance TFP growth.

9) The current state of the EU (and global economy). The latest phase of the EU and global economy shows fragmentation both in financial markets and in trade relations. However, this fragmentation is not affecting Europe as much as other regions—an inversion of the case during the sovereign crisis. What is exceptional about this phase is the coincidence and interaction of multiple crises: geopolitical instability, the return of inflation, global fragmentation, and secular stagnation. This 'perfect storm' is reflected in an increase in global risk, monetary-policy dilemmas (inflation-financial fragility tradeoffs), and structural components of inflation.

Tensions will not subside soon, and global instability may rise. However, fragmentation will probably increase pressure on countries to join regional agreements or form agglomerations as a strategy to increase protection. A push for Member States' further integration may be proposed. Such a dynamic would likely be driven by geopolitical factors where Europe may play a leading role in shaping a reform of global governance, that is, a global-policy regime necessary to prevent further fragmentation. In this context, it is important to recall the conditions that enable cooperation and regime-building with multiple actors: a few key players must be identified, there must be repeated interactions between them so as to build mutual trust, adjustments must be available to accommodate differing preferences, and, finally, agreements are to be encouraged as a strategy to aggregate preferences among likeminded countries.

The impact of the geopolitical factor can be larger than the one activated by fragmentation. As we are in a framework of multiple crises, further crisis factors can play a role. An analysis of 'scarring' can shed some light on these effects. S. Nujin and Yu Shi (IMF 2022) show that different types of crises, including those related to geopolitical factors, can produce scarring effects (that is, permanent negative consequences) that differ at the aggregate and sectoral levels because of the different transmission channels at work in each. The largest impact of the recent crises is seen in service sectors. As supply-side channels of transmission have been interrupted or weakened, so too have capital and research-and-development investment, human capital, and other factors that impact TFP. The 'scarring', in this case, is the cumulative reinforcement of the negative medium-term impacts.

6.3 Secular Stagnation and the Growth Environment

The multiple-crisis mechanism evolves against a background of secular stagnation which is present both within the EU and globally as reflected in the declining real interest rate. The real interest rate is connected to the 'natural interest rate', r*, which is not observed and needs to be estimated. Estimates point to a decreasing natural interest rate for the Euro Zone over the past two decades. With all these caveats in mind, r* can provide useful evidence on the long-run policy environment and information to policymakers as they form their views on policy decisions. Last but not least, the decline of r* also reflects excess savings over investment, that is, growing savings and declining investment lead to lower r* and shrinking policy space. The negative trend is also related to TFP dynamics. More generally, declining r* and TFP reflect a weak effort in innovation, research and development, human and intangible capital accumulation, and demographic factors.

As already mentioned, in advanced economies, TFP is partially endogenous, that is, determined by investment in innovation and partly determined by policy which impacts on innovation activities. Evidence confirms the negative impact of TFP and demographic as well as the countervailing impact of fiscal policy on r*. The fall in TFP is generalized in advanced economies but significantly present in the EU.

Such a dynamic carries important policy implications. According to a view of the policy process in the long term (which is the one of interest here), a declining r* compresses the space for monetary policy since r* is the upper boundary of the policy rate. However, if r* increases, it compresses fiscal space to the extent that r* is related to the market rate. For a given growth rate, a negative difference with respect to the policy rate makes debt unsustainable. Policy can raise r* in the medium to long run through productivity-enhancing and demographic-improving measures. As a consequence, r* can increase and impact on fiscal-policy space. Put differently, the analysis of long-term growth factors provides indications of how to improve the policy mix and activate a virtuous circle as policy space is being created. Recently, pressures towards secular stagnation seem to have lost steam somewhat. Nevertheless, the underlying weakness of the economy, especially in the EU, does not support much optimism. In particular, there are no signs of significant turnaround in long-run productivity growth. In sum, to deal with the multiple-crisis environment, a new policy mix is needed, given that no single policy-instrument alone will support a new sustainable-growth acceleration.

Shocks interact and perpetuate themselves. They lower the long-term growth rates and may perpetuate secular stagnation. Fragmentation of global value chains generates supply shocks. Structural reallocation and appropriate industrial policies are needed. The impact of geopolitics feeds back on monetary policy via inflation and financial stress.

Monetary policy cannot be left alone. We also need fiscal and structural income policy as well as a global collective effort for regime rebuilding. This approach is consistent with the pattern of growth through accelerations and institutional change we have discussed above.

6.4 The NGEU Policy Response

EU policy design has made progress as a reaction to the crisis with the introduction of Next Generation EU (NGEU). In the current phase, NGEU is the single most relevant institutional innovation in Europe. It rests on the combined impact of public investment, structural reforms, and private investment. It can provide positive shocks similar to those related to the Single Market or the single currency. Let us look at this process in steps.

Step 1. The governments provide an immediate response to COVID-19 in terms of national budget resources to absorb the initial impact. The suspension of the Stability and Growth Pact provides the necessary fiscal space.

Step 2. Governments, in agreement with the Commission, define their structural-transformation strategy in terms of plans and sectors to be impacted by the resources made available by the Commission. The composition of the budgetary responses and the structural agenda reflect national preferences.

Step 3. The governments set the sequencing of measures related to investment and structural reforms. It is interesting to note that, on preparing their National Recovery and Resilience Plans, governments anticipated milestones relative to structural reforms with respect to those related to investment. The rationale for this is that the anticipation of reforms would make the implementation of investment faster and somehow smoother.

Step 4. A possible 'acceleration cycle' is activated as follows: 1) public investment is activated also with the support of structural reforms; 2) the public-investment component, in turn, activates accelerators and spillovers (see below); 3) private investment in the digital and green transformation is activated, and institutions facilitate the impact of reforms and allocation processes; 4) public-aggregate demand fills the output gap that may arise; 5) the impact of structural reforms, depending on the policy mix, may sustain acceleration.

We now look at some simulations of the possible impact of NGEU, relying on estimates produced by international organisations (Bankowski et al. 2022). The impact of NGEU is reflected in higher-potential output. The initial impact is largely due to investment, but, eventually, the contribution of TFP becomes the most relevant one by far.

In terms of the performance of NGEU, public investment would impact relatively more on acceleration (especially from the demand side of investment) while structural reforms would impact more on the sustainability of growth effects. This framework implies that the public-investment channel impacts directly on GDP growth while private investment and structural reforms impact on TFP and, hence, indirectly on GDP.

6.4.1 Public Investment

Demand effects of NGEU may be significant in the short run. They also facilitate structural-reforms implementation with benefits for supply that build up in the long-term. At the same time, as already mentioned, early implementation of structural reforms facilitates the impact of public investment.

The impact of NGEU on supply is not only such as to increase productive capacity, but it also creates the conditions to change the composition of supply towards a more digital and environment friendly configuration.

Within this framework, Member States allocate resources according to their specific priorities. Green investments are particularly prominent. Public investment impacts as a demand factor in the short-term but with multiplier effects that are particularly relevant for smaller countries.

Openness may be a decisive factor for the sustainability of accelerations. The deeper the economic integration among Member States, the larger are the spillover effects. Such effects are larger for smaller economies, given their relatively greater degree of openness. They also materialize in the early stage of the policy cycle.

Spillover effects are also present in the case of structural reforms. There are visible differences in the GDP response to public investment across Member States and financing instruments. GDP response depends on the content of public investment and on its financing characteristics. Evidence suggests that grants are used to finance shorter-term measures, while loans tend to be used to finance measures which impact more prominently on long-term growth. Finally, peripheral countries benefit more from public-investment boost. The impact on private investment depends primarily on the effectiveness of incentives.

6.4.2 Structural Reforms

The impact of structural reforms on GDP is more articulated and requires analysis of several aspects including the definition, functioning, and policy implications.

The quality of institutions helps (in part) to explain long-term growth performance in EU countries and elsewhere because these institutions impact on the effectiveness of investment and of allocation, as discussed above.

Growth accelerations are more likely when the spark-off is generated by a basket of policies. Combining reforms with expansionary macroeconomic policies, but also micro-policy measures, creates synergies to mitigate adjustment costs. This is the more important as reforms might entail transitory costs, such as temporary negative-demand effects or redistribution among segments of the population. A credible implementation of reforms allows future reform-driven income gains to be brought forward, as well as improving expectations of future benefits, thus mitigating short-term costs. The credibility of institutions that kick off reforms may contribute to enhance initial reforms-related gains. More generally, as shown by the literature, the acceleration, coordination, prioritization, and sequencing (or packaging) of reforms can generate benefits from complementarities and synergies.

However, the 'Structural Reform Cycle' (the sequence of steps that are needed to fully implement a reform measure) may be very long and difficult to complete. It follows that near-sighted politicians may find no interest in launching the process for structural reforms. The cycle begins the moment in which new legislation is introduced and approved by Parliament, to be followed by the adoption of administrative measures, their implementation, and possible revision. Consequently, it takes a long time for public opinion to appreciate the benefits of reforms (if it ever does at all).

The interaction between structural reforms and public investment is a key driver of acceleration in the implementation of NGEU. The 'impact stage' relates to the impact of reforms on the behaviour of firms, households, stakeholders, or entities exposed to the reforms, reflecting the change in incentives which the reform (should) produce. The very final stage implies firms' and households' (possible) perception of the reforms as having improved or degraded individual welfare. Possibly (but not necessarily) such perceptions may lead to an increase or decrease in approval and political support for the Government considered to be responsible for the change. In an integrated environment, national-reform programmes can generate significant spillover effects. This effect would add to the impact of public-investment and related spillovers we have discussed above. Note that the time horizon for the full benefit of reforms to materialize is quite long.

Last but not least, structural-reform programmes are very much country specific, reflecting national institutions and preferences. As such, there is no general policy recipe that can be applied to all countries without adaptation to national features.

6.4.3 Financing Needs and the Role of Private Investment

We now look at the financing mechanism for both public and private investment. Public investment in NGEU is financed through debt or grants. The cost of financing reflects the market reaction to the decision to launch the programme. Note that a virtuous circle may develop as follows: the announcement of NGEU, to the extent that it is credible, produces a positive impact on financial markets that, then, translates into a lower-interest rate and spreads.

The debt issuance that finances NGEU produces a decrease in financing costs which is self-fulfilling, as long as the operation is credible. This, in turn, implies that the design and implementation of NGEU projects are consistent with the mission of the overarching project. In terms of impact, an increase in government consumption has the most visible effect on private investment. Underpinning the NGEU, in this respect, is the temporary mechanism SURE—Support to mitigate Unemployment Risks in an Emergency. This scheme for financing, through the issuance of European bonds that are guaranteed by the EU budget, provides the required encouragement.

We now turn to consider private investment as green investment. Two symmetrical issues need to be addressed: to what extent is the private sector interested in investing in climate change, and to what extent are private investors interested in financing green activities?

Beginning with the first issue, EIB evidence shows that companies respond positively to investment in climate activities to the extent they have set climate targets, are energy intensive, have energy-cost concerns, and have adopted digital technologies. Other, less-prominent factors that affect companies' responses to green activities include their size and their adoption of advanced managerial practices.

Obstacles to green investment are also to be considered. Such obstacles include uncertainty about environmental regulation, lack of skilled staff, cost of investment, uncertainty about regulations referring to new technologies, uncertainty about climate change, lack of green finance. It is worth noting that, for all specific factors, the obstructing factor is stronger in the EU than in the USA. More generally, patent counts and research and development expenditure follow an upward trend and are highly correlated. The correlation is somewhat less pronounced in the USA. However, the share and count of energy-related startups in the USA and EU have been steadily declining in the decade 2008—2018. This is consistent with the declining dynamics of TFP.

The financing needs requested by the green transition are overwhelmingly larger than those provided by NGEU. Capital markets must provide private resources. And public policy must provide incentives to invest in green technology. The new climate strategy also requires new green technologies to fill the gap between the EU and the USA. More homogeneity could provide a boost to green investment. Currently, there is great heterogeneity across EU countries both in propensity to green innovation and in the use of green policies. The policy instruments impacting on performance are carbon taxes, research-and-development investment, and the mix between equity and debt (although debt finance seems to be ineffective in stimulating green innovation). Public policy can have a significant role in stimulating private investment by acting on the variables mentioned above. But this needs to be enacted at EU rather than national level: the banking channel which prevails in the EU is only modestly efficient in stimulating and sustaining innovation. At the same time, the Banking Union and Capital-Market Union are making little progress (Aghion et al. 2022).

Some progress is being made in green financing but a slow pace. In spite of increasing private-sector interest in ESG investment (Baker et al. 2022), in the case of public investment a virtuous circle of positive expectations about the success of NGEU could kick off and lead to an increase in private investment

6.5 Summary and Conclusions

The EU has been impacted by multiple crises due to economic and geopolitical drivers. These have had 'scarring' effects and may lead to fragmentation with serious and permanent consequences. Policy responses to prevent these consequences are made more difficult by the background of secular stagnation. We have looked at this issue by considering EU growth as a process based on a sequence of accelerations, sparked off by institutional changes and the ensuing structural breaks. Such acceleration episodes must be sustained with further policy measures. The main response strategy is the NGEU—a mechanism based on public investment and structural reforms. It should deliver sustainable growth and structural change that allows the European Union to exit the multiple crises (pandemic, geopolitical, energy-inflationary) and to move closer to a twin-transformation (digital and green) path, reverting the drift towards secular stagnation.

The response to the crises takes place within a framework of long-term growth characterised by different phases of convergence (and, at times, divergence) but being generated by one, very general, growth 'model'. In its bare bones, the long-run growth of the EU economy is based on two long-term drivers: (i) institutional change and (ii) total-factor productivity. Growth is amplified by the endogenous component of TFP, as firms invest in innovation and productivity-enhancing activities.

A framework of secular stagnation is identified by the decline of r*, the natural interest rate. The drivers of r* are linked to demographics and structural impediments; these are also reflected in a declining TFP. However, secular stagnation affects EU countries and sectors differently, with southern-EU Member States suffering more. This imbalance means that, other things equal, supporting investment is more difficult in Europe than in other economic regions, given the obstacles to investment that a low r* indicates. These effects are exacerbated by the impact of multiple crises. Nevertheless, a successful implementation of the reforms associated with NGEU should contribute to a reversal of the trend in r* and secular stagnation, thus providing policy space, both monetary and fiscal.

NGEU is based on public investment and structural reforms, but a third pillar should also be considered to provide incentives for private investment. Public investment impacts as a demand factor in the short term. It produces a boost to growth which is amplified through spillover effects, both in investment and in structural reforms. The deeper economic integration is among Member States, the more strongly these positive effects can occur.

Over the longer term, the major impact of policy measures is on the supply side. This impact has both an aggregate dimension, feeding potential and actual growth, and a sectoral dimension, which supports the twin transformation. Therefore, higher growth is obtained through structural change, facilitated by structural reforms.

The life cycle of structural reforms is generally quite long. The reform cycle describes the steps that need to be completed before the reform policy is translated from a political decision into an implemented policy with visible outcomes. Tradeoffs may arise between the duration of the reform cycle and the intensity of policy impact. Usually, reforms come in packages. Complementarities across reforms may generate positive-scale effects. However, growth-acceleration literature clarifies that packages and structural gaps are country specific (Hausmann, Pritchett, Rodrik 2004).

NGEU is an effective policy tool, provided it acts through policy packages of public investment and structural reforms and allows time to complete the reform cycle. Its effectiveness must be seen in the context of a new policy mix fit to address the multiple-crises framework. Such a policy mix should include the following items:

a) Monetary policies that stabilize inflation while avoiding financial stress;

b) Policy packages that are country specific and implicate the whole of the government;

c) A long-term perspective able to see benefits that are not immediate. This requires careful management of the transition phase to ensure it includes changes in the policy mix that are less expansionary in monetary and fiscal policy but are more supportive of the structural agenda;

d) Policy actions, both in investment and in structural reforms, that encourage the enhancement of benefits by spillover effects through EU countries. This will become more likely with the further opening of the EU economic space;

e) An openness to redesigning the EU fiscal framework. Irrespective of whether NGEU will be confirmed as a permanent instrument, it provides a convincing case of a policy built on a structural-conditionality system;

f) Incentives that can spark off private-sector investment and structural reforms but also minimize the misallocation of such investment;

g) Public-investment financing through the issuance of new European debt, provided such debt can deliver sustained growth. Private investment can be financed through financial markets as climate- and digital-related investment meet the interest of investors and households;

h) The increase in potential output generated by NGEU must, in the long term, be matched by an increase in demand from EU institutions;

i) The policy mix must include plans to reconstruct international-cooperation regimes to push back fragmentation. The conditions for cooperation with multiple actors are: few key players, repeated interaction to create mutual trust, the ability to adjust preferences. Finally, club-format agreements must be encouraged as a strategy to aggregate preferences among likeminded countries and, consequently, reverse stagnation pressures.

To conclude, Europe's exit from the multiple crises requires a new policy mix. Monetary policy will continue to provide price stability, while taking into account the impact on financial stability. NGEU should be the main driver of growth. Fiscal policy should be reinforced by establishing a central fiscal capacity. On a broader level, action is needed to reinforce the global-policy regime with a cooperative approach to fight fragmentation and escape stagnation. Europe should play a major role to support global cooperation.

References

Aghion, Philippe et al. (2022). 'Financial Markets and Green Innovation', ECB Working Paper, 2686, July, https://doi.org/10.2139/ssrn.4590501

Baker, Mark, Mark Egan, and Suproteem Sarkar (2022). 'How do Investors Value ESG?', NBER Working Paper, 30708, December, https://doi.org/10.2139/ssrn.4293621

Bańkowski, Krzysztof et al. (2022), 'The Economic Impact of NGEU: A Euro Area Perspective', *ECB Occasional Paper*, 291, April, https://doi.org/10.2139/ssrn.4095550

Hausmann, Ricardo, Lant Pritchett, and Dani Rodrik (2004), 'Growth Accelerations', *NBER Working Paper*, 10566, June, https://doi.org/10.3386/w10566

Jones, Charles (2021), 'The Past and Future of Economic Growth: a Semi-Endogenous Perspective', *NBER Working Paper*, 29126, August, https://doi.org/10.3386/w29126

Nujin, Suphaphiphat and Yu Shi (2022), 'Economic Scarring', *IMF Working Paper*, 22/248, December, https://doi.org/10.5089/9798400227257.001

7. From Crisis to Crisis, Can Europe Count on National Promotional Banks as Silver Bullets?

Laurent Zylberberg

The great financial crisis of 2008–2009 was a game changer for National Promotional Banks and financial Institutions (NPBIs) in Europe, with the COVID-19 pandemic and the Ukraine crisis reinforcing this shift. The 'Juncker Plan' shed a light on the investment gap and demonstrated that a dynamic European policy was possible. Thanks to the InvestEU programme, actors at the European level, such as the European Investment Bank (EIB), and the national level (via NPBIs and Financial Institutions) thrived in their specific role of fostering essential long-term investment throughout our continent. With this in mind, we need to have a different look at certain tools within practical accounting rules by integrating both positive and negative externalities.

7.1 Introduction

For many years, Europe has been experiencing a succession of crises that are sometimes limited to the continent or that reflect global developments. Many economists, including Schumpeter and Kondratiev, have explained that these crises can result from the conjunction of cycles and, thus, from evolutions of the economic model (Portier 2015). However, the instruments for responding to these crises are not indifferent to existing economic and societal models. At comparable economic levels, European countries will not provide the same response as those in Asia. Without erasing the differences in the processes of the legitimization of states and their instruments (Badie 1982), the dynamics generated by the construction of Europe had converging effects in the countries that compose it. One of these effects, the rise of National Promotional Banks and financial Institutions (NPBIs) as investment actors, has become increasingly prominent as the European Union implements investment policies aimed at reducing the gap with other parts of the world. These players, who occupy a specific place in the European economic model, have many differentiating elements but, overall,

https://doi.org/10.11647/OBP.0386.07

have enough strong common characteristics to gradually become one of the driving forces behind the implementation of European policies. This European specificity is a particularly important asset at a time when public actors and, in a comprehensive way, public action regain legitimacy. The COVID-19 crisis has drawn attention to the role of NPBIs as a 'shock absorber' for individuals and businesses, even as they also provide essential countercyclical elements. These actors in the European economy cannot act, however, if they are not differentiated from their respective Governments; they must maintain a public status and serve the general interest. Moreover, NPBIs shall also not be likened to private actors while acting in a competitive framework. Several key developments are still needed to give them the means to make full use of their capacities (Zylberberg 2020).

7.2 A Particularly Difficult Economic Environment for the European Union

7.2.1 Europe has been Facing Increasing Investment Needs for Many Years.

As the economist Pierre Jaillet has pointed out, long-term investors are essential 'to find a path of growth that is equivalent to or little less than that of the pre-crisis and to keep public debt on a sustainable trajectory' (2012: 169), but what type of investments are we speaking about? Whether we speak about productive investments, like the ones related to the renewal of the production tool—its modernization to achieve productivity gains and investments related to environmental adaptation (such as security and research and development or pure financial investments like primary and secondary debt, bond, and equity markets)—there is still the risk of missing out on many investments which can be described as social or the economic purpose of which is indirectly linked to the production apparatus. For example, social infrastructures that includes investments in health, education, and affordable housing are in a relative blind spot. Others not directly linked to investment in economic apparatus are altogether left out from the categorization seen above. This investment vision, therefore, can be misleading as demonstrated in the report by the former European Commission Chair, Romano Prodi and the former French Economy Secretary of State, Christian Sautter (Prodi 2018).

When simplified, the background noise indicates that private investment will naturally be directed towards profitable productive investment or financial investment, whereas public investment should be confined to social investment without the use of a viable economic model. This distinction misses the numerous interactions between the different types of investment. It neglects the study of externalities, whether positive or negative, and ultimately leads to a rigid and time-bound categorization of economic actors. The temporality factor, which distinguishes between short-term and long-term investment, however, is essential for understanding and guiding the behaviour of investors, whether they are public or private.

Against this background, the European Investment Bank (EIB) makes the same observation every year: how Europe is lacking investment compared to the USA. This differential is even more striking if we focus on productive investments, whereby the gap is nearly 4 points! (Figure 7.1).

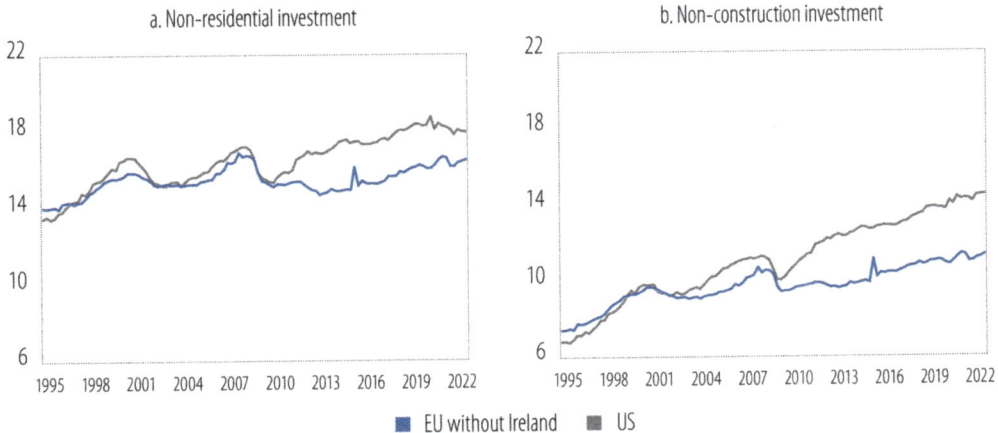

Fig. 7.1 Rest of Productive Investment in the European Union Compared to the United States since the Global Financial Crisis.
Note: Non-construction investment includes investment in machinery, equipment, and weapon systems, intellectual-property products, and cultivated biological assets.
Source: Eurostat and OECD national accounts statistics.

The financial crisis of 2008–2009 marks a clear separation of this trend. Investment in the USA reached its pre-crisis level in 2011, while, in Europe, it was necessary to wait ten more years for a return to the same level. In 2014, the European Union, faced with the acuteness of the problem, launched the 'European Fund for Strategic Investments' (EFSI). Unofficially known as the 'Juncker Plan', its objective was for the European Union to catch up with the same investment trend as it had experienced during the recovery that followed the previous crises of 1993–1997 (Le Moigne 2015).

In this regard, the Juncker Plan marks not only an economic but also an ideological turning point in the way the European Union looks at the role of public actors in investment. European actors are beginning to turn their backs on a system in which competition rules and the monitoring of public aid are the alpha and omega. By focusing on the ability of public investment to leverage, the Juncker Plan highlights the strength of public investors (including EIB and NPBIs).

7.2.2 These Needs are Part of Successive and Sometimes Simultaneous Crises

The 2008–2009 financial crisis resulted in a GDP with severe constraints on investment. But what stood out in this crisis was the difference in the recovery between the USA and the European Union, as shown in Figure 7.2.

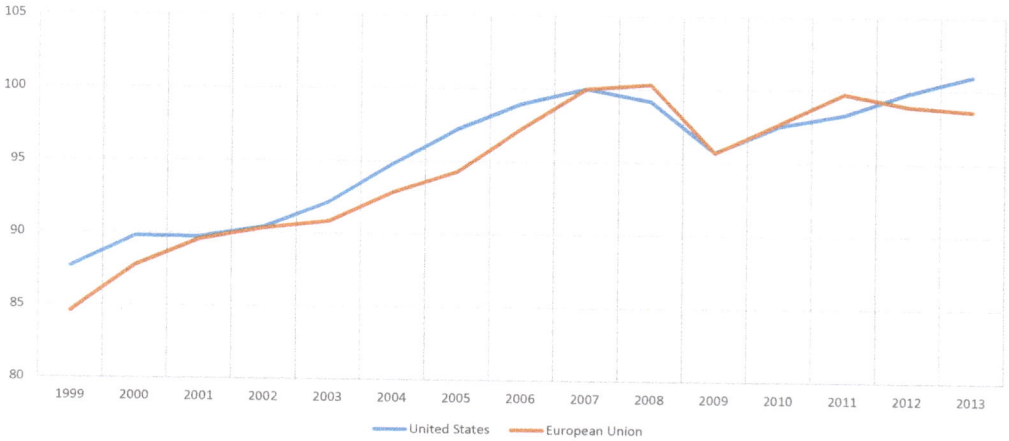

Fig. 7.2 Real GDP Per Capita: European Union versus United States (index 2007=100).
Source: World Bank.

This differential in GDP per capita has resulted in a corresponding weakening of investment.

How can one explain such a difference between Europe and the USA? The crisis of 2008–2009 was triggered in the USA by the real-estate boom of previous years. In Europe, if the real-estate boom was somehow mastered, the crisis was firstly a banking one and had long-lasting effects on the whole financial system (Jamet 2008; Figure 7.3).

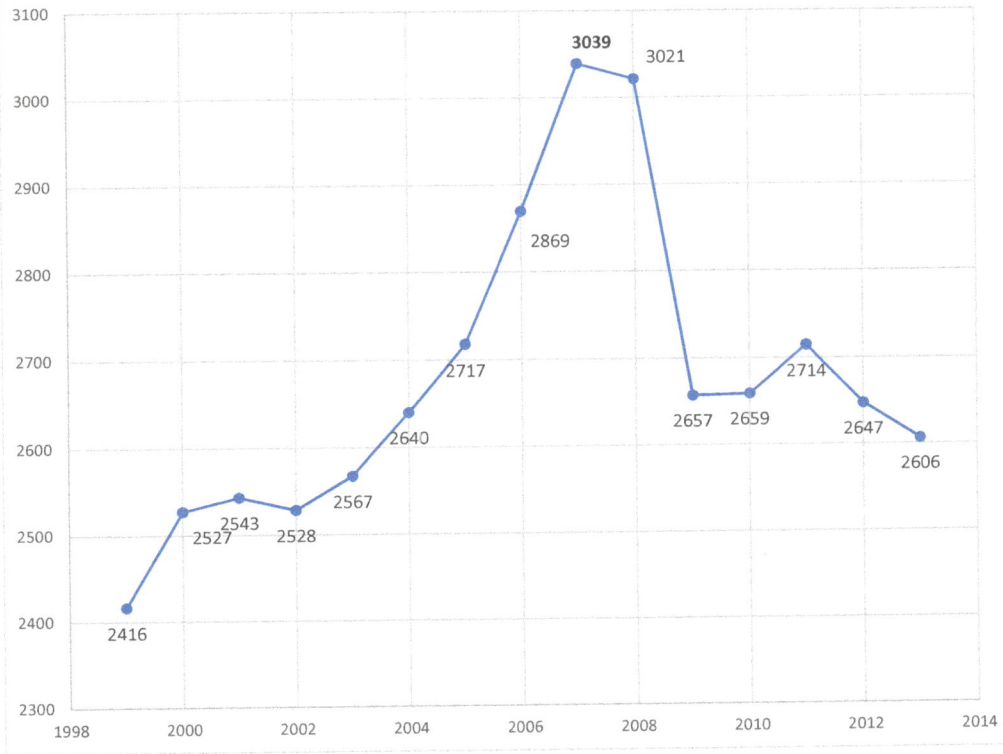

Fig. 7.3 Real Gross Fixed Capital Formation (EU 28, in 2013 prices, €bn).
Source: European Commission 2021.

This difference between geographical areas was alarming (Buti 2014), particularly in the way this lack of investment would induce long-term effects on the economy. Again, it is important to note that, while the USA was starting to raise its level of investment in 2011 (the lowest point having been reached in 2010), it was not the case in Europe. Lack of investment continued there until 2013, with a further significant decrease in 2011. This temporal disparity is largely due to differences in the financing of the economy between the two continents. We must remember that 'Banks are clearly the largest source of finance in the Eurozone (51%), unlike the United States, where bank credit would account for less than a fifth of the total financing of the economy' (CEPII 2015).

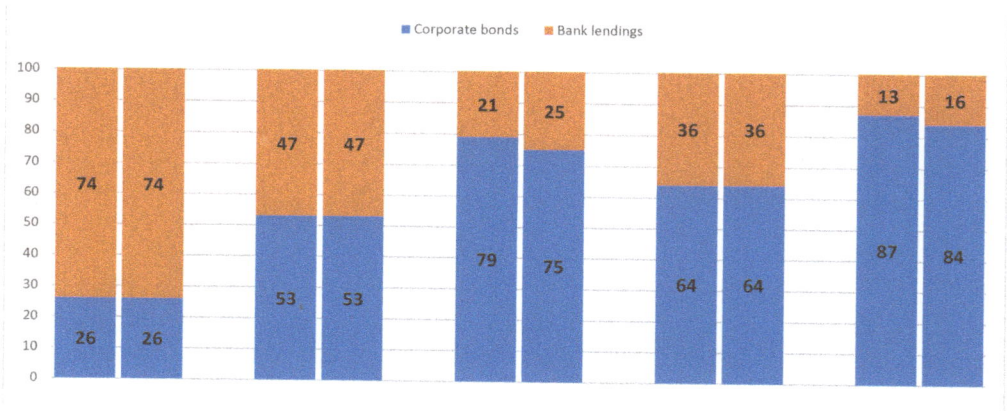

Fig. 7.4 Bank Lending versus Corporate Bonds (Corporate Bonds as a % of Corporate Borrowing
in the USA, EU27, UK, France, and Germany).
Source: Panagiotis, A., H. Eivind Friis, and W. Wright (2022).

As financing schemes clearly diverge between USA and Europe, measures taken after the 2008–2009 crisis produced differing impacts. One response was the strengthening of banking constraints to avoid falling back into the mistakes of the past. These new rules have increased the robustness of the European-banking model. To sum it up in one sentence: considering the causes of the 2008–2009 crisis, the remedies have had adverse effects on the recovery of the European economy.

While these new mechanisms were being put in place to boost growth in Europe, the COVID-19 health crisis occurred, which was unprecedented in all respects in recent global-economic history. Although we have experienced major economic crises or global epidemics in the past, we have not, in recent times, experienced both simultaneously. The impact on GDP was immediate, as shown in Figure 7.5.

Beyond the direct economic effects of the COVID crisis, what has had a lasting impact on economies is a return to the forefront of economic-sovereignty issues. While the globalisation of manufacturing chains was taken for granted, the COVID-19 crisis highlighted sovereignty issues that had been being largely ignored. Even worse, issues arose in unexpected areas (such as surgical masks or aspirin) that were never identified as key components prior to this pandemic.

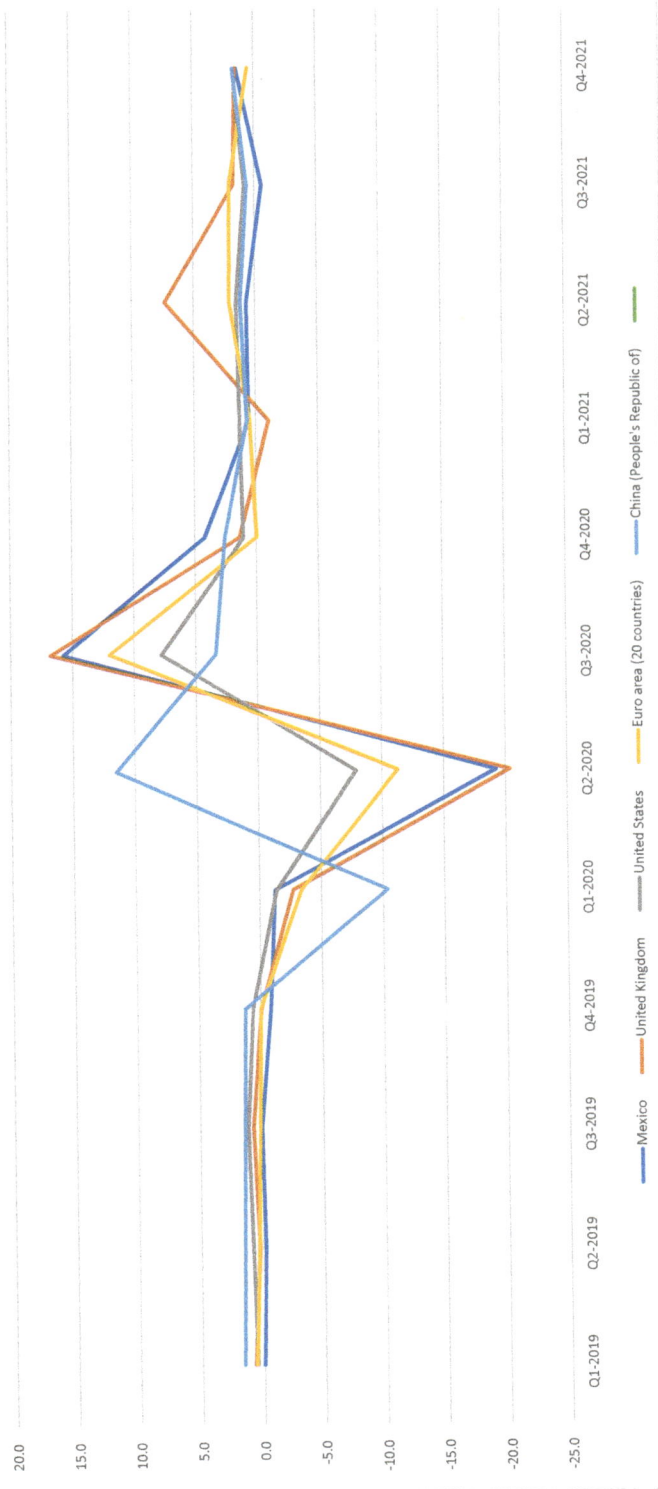

Fig. 7.5 Quarterly Real GDP Growth in % quarterly.
Source: OECD.

As the COVID-19 crisis came to an end, a new geopolitical crisis was breaking out in Europe that highlighted other, particularly energy-related, dependencies. One significant result of this compounding of crises is that NPBIs became the instruments of national sovereignty that were mobilised to act in various areas (ELTI 2023). Indeed, the invasion of Ukraine has had numerous, protean effects on European economies. We can mention a few of them: scarcity of energy sources, the economic impact of the sanctions put in place for companies working with Russia and Belarus, the hosting of refugees, etc. To cope with this economic shock, NPBIs were mobilised both in their traditional functions and, often, beyond their usual remits. They supported national economies through loans, some of which were subsidized; provided suitable financing for undertakings directly affected by the conflict, either via their commercial outlets or their own supplies; and launched emergency-housing programmes in neighbouring countries. They also undertook other actions to support Ukraine in budgets and in various donations.

In addition to these essential measures aimed at those most directly affected by the conflict, NPBIs provided help to other economies as they adapted to the new situation. Their interventions in the energy sector are a good example of their ability to respond quickly to immense needs. Europe's largest NPBIs, not to mention the EIB (or the 'European Climate Bank' as it likes to be called), were already heavily involved in the energy sector; they were at the heart of financing the energy transition, notably by funding renewable energies. The war in Ukraine posed new challenges that required focus on immediate needs. While maintaining their commitments to participate in the energy transition, NPBIs were asked to participate in the financing of very short-term solutions to address the end of the energy supply from Russia. Thus, the German NPBI (KFW) became the financier of the three new ports for Liquified Natural Gas (LNG) terminals in Germany, whilst the Italian National Promotional Bank (CDP) and its subsidiaries participated in the financing of a new terminal. In a country like France, where nuclear power plays a major role, Caisse des Dépôts (CDC) were tasked to examine the possibilities of financing the renewal of the nuclear-power plants.

Beyond energy, the entire scope of national and European sovereign financing was impacted by the Ukrainian crisis. Because NPBIs have both very large resources and the capacity to rapidly redirect these funds, they have been called upon to meet these new demands.

Environmental transition requires significant funding over a long period of time. On one hand, there is a need to change our production methods to achieve greenhouse-gas-emission neutrality by 2050 and, on the other hand, to adapt our economies to climate change. Although it is difficult to determine the precise requirements, with variations being quite large depending on the methods of calculation (Meltzer 2016; Li 2023), the order of magnitude amounts to tens of billions of dollars per year per European country. Two elements are clearly established. The first issue is linked to the temporality of the return on investment. Green investments need to mobilise actors coming from different parts of the economic spectrum. The co-ordination between them is quite difficult as, in terms of temporality, the expected return on investment differs from one actor to another. Secondly, the public sector alone does not have the means to meet the needs, but the private sector will not mobilise for profitability that seems either too low or too uncertain. A combination of the two is necessary, therefore, to achieve the required funding.

Indeed, beyond the amounts, the problem in the search for funding is the time differential between immediately identifiable needs and returns, which are sometimes hypothetical but always deferred. Moreover, Pisani-Ferry et al. (2023) have recently pointed out that a large part of these investments will not increase growth potential since most will be used to finance fossil-fuel reductions without increasing production capacity. Another challenge to the environmental transition is that efforts must be made in three directions: the substitution of capital for fossil fuels, the reorientation of technical progress, and, finally, in sobriety. The first of these will command the lion's share of investment efforts with, according to the authors mentioned above, 85% of the total amount. Sobriety in using energy for daily life will contribute for a mere 15% to 20% of the energy use. Households and companies have to adapt their behaviour in order to reduce the global use of energy.

7.2.3 The European Economic Environment is also Characterised by Other Penalizing Factors

A multitude of factors led to an increase in the financing requirements for the European economies. This situation is more shocking since two penalizing factors play a disabling role. The first of these factors is the return of inflation in Europe (Figure 7.6). After many years without increasing prices, we have now entered a new cycle, which may be limited in time, but, in any case, will have medium-term effects on the European economies (De La Rosière 2023). This is especially true for households wherein current expenditure is increasingly constrained (Cusset 2023).

This change in inflation has had a direct effect on interest rates. Of course, this allows long-term investments to regain attractiveness by differentiating themselves from short-term investments, and in time, will recover their value. Conversely, inflation- and interest-rate rises will have a delaying effect on borrowers who may fear that their debts will rapidly increase. It is also this logic that encourages precautionary savings (BPCE 2023).

In general, one of the main drivers of inflation is energy-price growth. There is a strong correlation between the price of energy, in its form of final consumption, and inflation (Pisani-Ferry et al. 2023). It is certainly possible to envisage a differential increase in the price of energy, since fossil-fuel sources would be used less as renewable-energy sources become more readily available. There will be complex mechanisms to manage if market mechanisms are left alone to decide the price of energy. Indeed, the fall in demand for carbon-based energy could lead to a fall in prices, or a smaller rise, while the uptick in demand for renewable energy coupled with a high entry-cost mechanism would make the latter, at times, less competitive. This logic invites public financial institutions to play a major role in directing financing towards investments with stronger positive externalities.

Even before this inflation rise, Europe had been experiencing a significant increase in its public debt relative to GDP since 2007. Admittedly, this increase is not specific to Europe and dates back a long time; however, debt represented 100% of world GDP in 1970 (De La Rosière 2022), while the International Finance Institute estimates that, in 2023, the global debt reached more than 305 trillion dollars, or more than 360% of the global GDP. It should be noted that this is the total debt, of which the public debt represents 40%. The most problematic aspect of this increase in debt, and particularly in public debt (and not just budgetary debt), is that it has not been directed towards investment (McKinsey 2021).

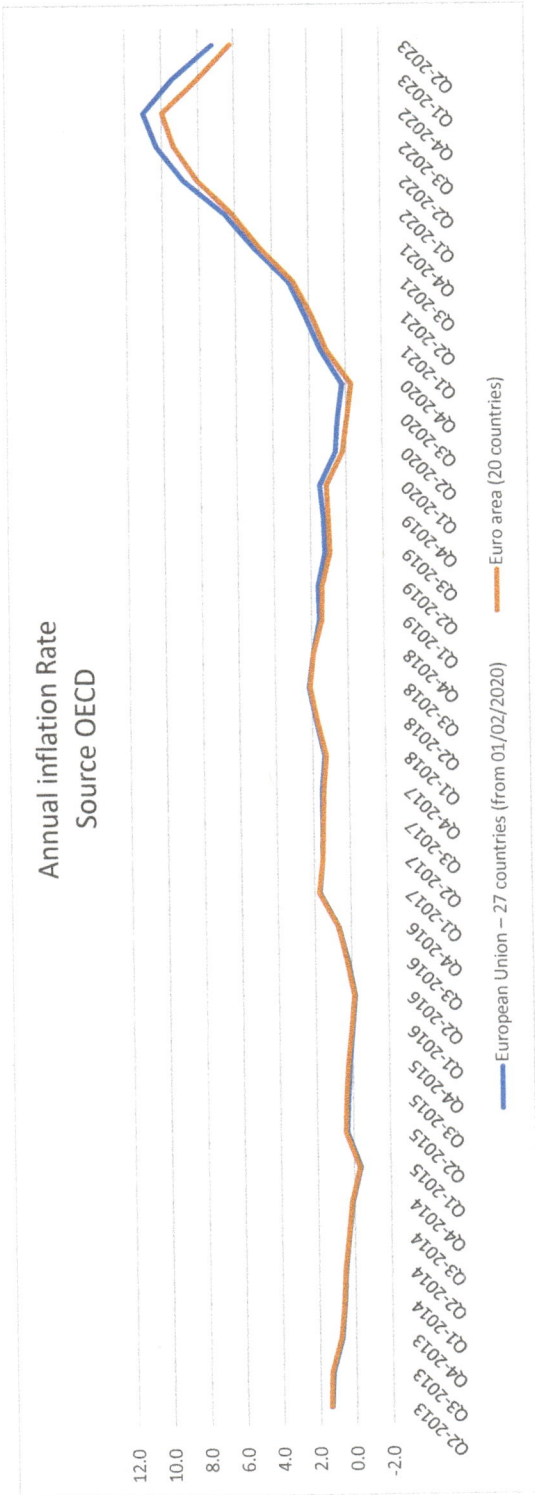

Fig. 7.6 Annual Inflation Rate.
Source: OECD.

In this context, we are witnessing a decrease in the capacity of governments to use the budgetary tool to intervene in the economy and, especially, to act as a catalyst for investment. According to the French National Statistics Office (INSEE 2022), of the five European Union countries with the highest debt in 2007, three (Italy, Greece, and Portugal) are still in the same group in 2021, and the two countries joining them, France and Spain, represent two of the biggest economies in Europe.

Since 2007, entities which have benefitted from low to very low interest rates are governments, for their budgetary needs, and private financial actors, for their short-term profitability. Debt rose sharply as low interest rates weakened the banking and financial system, encouraging the survival of non-viable enterprises and leading savings towards liquidity by discouraging the financing of long-term investments, that is, the classic Keynesian 'liquidity trap'. This unavoidable reduction in budgetary margins means that it is necessary to seek other sources of financing. Some authors (Cingolani 2017) argue for concerted action by the European Central Bank, the European Investment Bank, and the European Commission in order to support strengthened European programmes. These institutions would be financed by a grant component from the European budget and a loan component financed by monetary creation from the European Central Bank. This approach, developed before the rise in inflation and interest rates, seems difficult to implement for several reasons. Firstly, the intervention of the ECB implies the leaving-aside of countries of the European Union that are not members of the Euro. Secondly, it seems difficult to reconcile this action with another priority of the European Central Bank: to fight inflation. The temptation would be too great to reduce the creation of money by reducing participation in these programmes. Finally, such a plan misses out the growing role of National Banks and Public Financial Institutions as an essential link in European policies on the ground. Not being constrained by the budgetary rules of the States, NPBIs are able to attract savings and other private resources and to channel these, in alignment with European programmes, into long-term investments.

7.3 Assets to Meet These Major Challenges

7.3.1 A Dense Network of Strong, Robust NPBIs Anchored as Close as Possible to the Ground

Over the years, most European countries have developed national banks and public financial institutions (NPBIs). These institutions are very diverse in terms of size, resources, and goals. This is, of course, due to the varied nature of European countries and their own history. This variation attests to the very strong correlation between NPBIs and their own country; indeed, the structuring elements of the NPBIs are directly related to structuring elements of their country of origin. To take just a few examples, KFW in Germany was created in 1948 to finance the reconstruction of the country with funding from the Marshall Plan. The French Caisse des Dépôts was created in 1816, in a country broke and broken after the Napoleonic Wars, to mobilise savings and to finance infrastructure works on the eve of the second industrial revolution.

More recently, the fall of the Berlin Wall highlighted the immense financing needs of Central and Eastern Europe. To this end, three instruments were to be mobilised: the enlargement of the European Union to the East, the creation of the EBRD to finance the transition to the open-market economy via international financing and, finally, the establishment or reestablishment of national promotional banks—in some countries, this meant the creation of new institutions; in others, it meant giving back consistency to those that were on standby. BGK in Poland is a good example of the latter. Created in 1924 to finance local authorities, defence industries, and industrial development, this bank was put on hold between 1948 and 1989, at which point it resumed its activities to become one of the main Polish financial players. In other Central and Eastern European countries, new banking institutions were set up, such as MFB in Hungary, which dates to 1993, or SID in Slovenia and HBOR in Croatia, both of which were established in 1992.

The most recent of these financial institutions have often concentrated on three priority sectors: the financing of small-and-medium enterprises (SMEs), which have difficulty accessing funds from the commercial-banking sector; the raising of capital for start-ups, particularly for venture capital; and export financing. They also often contribute to the financing of three other sectors (infrastructure, local authorities, and housing) to a lesser, but equally significant, degree.

While discussions on the precise definition of NPBIs are ongoing (Marodon 2021), these institutions are defining themselves by their actions. As we know 'the proof of pudding is in the eating' (Engels 1975: 19). The combined members of the European Association of Long-Term Investors (ELTI), a consortium of NPBIs (more on this below), have made investment commitments amounting to more than €2,600bn. Decades ago, the French European founder Jean Monnet insisted that 'Europe will be forged in crisis' (Monnet 1978: 417). Those words could apply to NPBIs today as crises are revealing just how efficient they are as counter-cyclical actors.

In June 2020, a few months after the outbreak of the European COVID-19 crisis, an initial assessment of ELTI initiatives found that more were focused on grassroot measures adapted to local specificities (2020). These institutions were able to double the total amount of their funding between 2019 and 2020. What is remarkable is that this doubling includes not only loans but also direct capital investment. The protean character of NPBIs allows them to rapidly increase their volume of interventions and to modify the very nature of them. The 'Banque des Territoires', which brings together various entities of the Caisse des Dépôts in France, invested more than €2bn in 2022, representing more than three times the amount invested in 2018. The total portfolio is over €7bn for this institution. But the COVID-19 crisis also highlighted a capability to quickly mobilise huge amounts of funds for recovery schemes. In 2020, Caisse des

Dépôts launched an emergency recovery plan for a total of €26bn over a five-year period. The NPBIs remained active during the crisis that followed the invasion of Ukraine by Russia. As we know, this crisis has had a cascading effect on the entire economy: neighbouring countries have had to manage the direct influx of people, the direct impact of higher energy prices, and many other more-indirect effects.

In a market economy, public investors avoid crowding out other economic players, seeking, rather, to attract them by means of a leverage effect. Some players have set out rules to guide their investment in equity. The Caisse des Dépôts, for example, establishes their status as a minority shareholder by calculating the leverage effect on the global amount mobilised.

In fact, the concept of leverage poses formidable problems with definition and scope (Chelsky 2013; OCDE 2016). Many terms, such as 'catalytic effect', 'additionality', and 'mobilisation' are referred to indifferently even though they may refer to different realities. Do private savings become public money when invested by a public actor? Should a public institution's own resources be recorded as private when they have been capitalised by pure market mechanisms? Jeff Chelsky highlights the distinction between direct and indirect effects. Competition authorities largely consider the latter when assessing the effects of dominant market players, but an even more complex measure could be employed to assess the leverage effects. The World Bank measures all the catalytic effects in the environment of the operation. To take a trivial example, the capacity to attract private financing will be higher when supported by institutional actors with recognisably strong legitimacy and track records, such as the EIB or the largest NPBIs. Faced with these difficulties, the aphorism (attributed to Albert Einstein) 'Everything that can be counted does not necessarily count; everything that counts cannot necessarily be counted' may serve as a guide. An effective strategy to catalyse private funding will always have qualitative and quantitative dimensions, and we can add a third factor related to the additionality sought by public investment. In 2021, the Association Française de Gestion and Mazars (AFG 2021) pointed out that nearly half of respondents define contributions (ex-ante) and achievements (ex-post) as necessary elements for the analysis of change, but almost 60% agree that it takes five to ten years to have a relevant analysis. In other words, the allocation of funding based on additionality criteria require five to ten years to be analysed with some credibility!

7.3.2 A Dynamic Started with the Juncker Plan and the Role of the EIB

The Juncker plan marked a clear break in the vision of European financing. For many years, European funding had concentrated on subsidies and ensured that it did not interfere significantly with market rules. The investment deficit we have described above has appeared strong enough for European leaders to embark on a new path by mobilising the balance sheet of the European Investment Bank, while providing a guarantee from the European Union and relying largely on NPBIs for deployment in the territories. It should be noted that even before the outbreak of the COVID crisis, it was decided in 2018 to deepen the Juncker Plan by increasing the total amount of projects financed from €315bn to €500bn.

The initial aim of the Juncker Plan was to mobilise a relatively limited amount of financing (€15bn European Union guarantees and €6bn EIB contributions) to then exert a double-leverage effect. First, a multiplier of 3 with EIB Group financing, with a more usual 'risk-and-return' profile, and then a new multiplier of 5 with public and private financing. The expected leverage was, therefore, 15 compared to the initial stake.

This programme has succeeded in achieving its quantitative objectives by exceeding the €500bn total amount of projects, obtaining an interesting distribution at both the geographical and the sectoral levels (see Figure 7.7). The Juncker Plan's success is directly linked to the engagement of local NPBIs. Their mobilisation was key for launching the programme and identifying local needs. The very existence of a local NPBI was an enabler for enforcing the Juncker Plan in the best possible way.

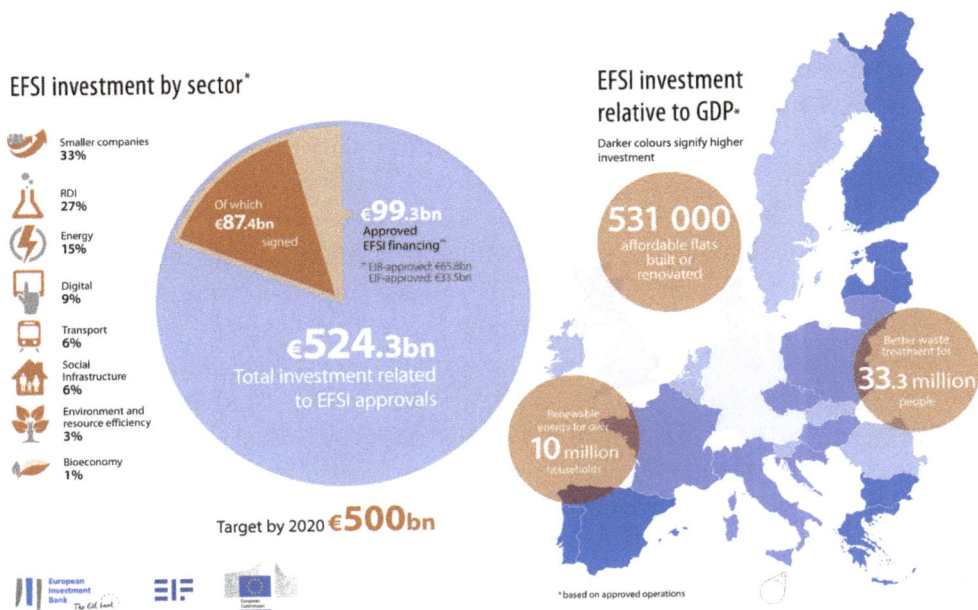

Fig. 7.7 EIB Group Figures (as of 31/12/2021).
Source: EIB (amounts in € are based on the exchange rate of the event (approval/signature)).

This success highlighted four key elements for the European economy:

- The need for investment was massive and the European market was, and still is, in a position to absorb considerable amounts of money without having a crowding-out effect on the private sector.

- The presence of an NPBI in a country is a formidable asset in directing investments towards projects strategic for Member States.

- Some sectors have benefitted greatly from these investments, particularly Small and Medium Enterprises (SMEs) and Mid-Caps, research and development, and the energy sector.

- Europe was able to set up this mechanism in a timely manner, going against the principles heralded in previous years—like State aid or competition rules—that led to the construction of a market in which immediate economic interventions were slowed.

Beyond the figures, the Juncker Plan has also brought significant changes to public financial actors. The EIB Group has been led to think beyond traditional lending and to transform its approach. Through the Juncker Plan, the EIB has recognized the logic of using long-term investments as well as of taking more risks than before (Griffith-Jones 2020).

In addition to this change of approach, which has been beneficial to the European economy, the EIB and other NPBIs have strongly developed their cooperation in this new framework. Their complementarity quickly emerged as a guarantee of the success of the Juncker Plan. EIB had the financial tools provided by the European Union but did not have the capillary network close to the ground that characterises most NPBIs. Conversely, even the most powerful NPBIs only had a limited European approach and, above all, did not have this access to European financial instruments. This complementarity did not erase the competition that might exist on certain projects or divergent modes of operation, however. In the end, the essential question was who would carry the final risk in a project involving all of these actors.

Overall, the Juncker Plan has been successful, but some elements could have been better developed.

Firstly, some sectors have generally been missed out by EFSI. Social infrastructure or transport have only marginally benefitted from the Juncker Plan. Social infrastructures are long-term investments by nature with limited returns whose positive externalities are undeniable; thus, they could have legitimately been fully part of the Juncker Plan dynamic. In the end, they represent only 6% of the financing (Prodi 2018). The situation for transport is different because these investments, with variable returns, often require direct or indirect subsidies. As EFSI did not offer this type of financing, another tool was adapted. The Connecting Europe Facility, which was built on the work of NPBIs since 2020 rendered those institutions responsible for identifying the projects to benefit from a European grant as well as investment from the local NPBI. Here, the leverage effect will be important and will make it possible to find funding in line with the projects.

The Juncker Plan also has a relatively greater impact on the EIB Group's risk model than on its products. The European Investment Bank is primarily a lending bank, unlike several European NPBIs, such as the Caisse des Dépôts in France and the Cassa Depositi e Prestiti in Italy. The European economy needs equity financing which is significantly harder to mobilise than loans. EFSI had the ambition to respond to this lack on certain projects—such as the financing of the Marguerite 2 infrastructure fund—but this part of the dynamic remains marginal. We cannot say that EFSI produced a structural shift of the EIB balance sheet in favour of equity, but it is true to say that EIB Group took more risks under EFSI via dedicated projects.

Finally, small projects (those under €50m) remain difficult to finance. They incur fixed costs of the same order of magnitude as larger projects, but their risks are more difficult to assess. To monitor such projects is costly in staff and other terms. Therefore, there is a natural tendency to finance larger projects. Furthermore, smaller projects are more difficult to identify. Developing thematic platforms would surely help to tackle this issue. By bundling different projects together, it becomes easier to reach the minimum critical amount and to propose a financing model. The risk profile of such a bundle is not easy to assess, however. Yet, this is where the detailed, local knowledge held by the NPBIs is a very important asset. To implement these field-based platforms, it would have been necessary for the EIB to establish a large-scale delegation capable of working with NPBIs, but this was difficult since EFSI was directly on the balance sheet of EIB. Otherwise, NPBIs should have been granted direct access to EFSI, but this case was not foreseen. To summarise: while small-scale projects have received a little more support than in the past, the Juncker Plan has not succeeded in making them a major focus of its deployment.

7.3.3 Enabling NPBIs to Make Full Use of their Potential

After the Juncker Plan in 2021, the European Union put in place new tools to allow a more direct involvement of NPBIs while keeping EIB as the main implementing partner. Having national and European actors working together covers both political and financial issues. One of the regular complaints about EFSI was that it was a little bit far from the ground. Because of the multiple intermediaries, the final beneficiary was often not aware that the loan benefitting them had resulted from the Juncker Plan. It was especially true for SMEs and Mid-Caps with the mechanism of guarantee for lenders. Including NPBIs directly in the loop was a major and positive change as they have a capillary network on the ground and a long history of cooperation for the implementation of European policies in territories (Zylberberg 2018).

After the Juncker Plan, the European Union launched the InvestEU programme in 2021 with the ambition of simplifying the multitude of existing programmes while facilitating access to actors other than EIB Group. Originally conceived in a context of growth, it also had to be adapted to the very significant recession resulting from the global economic shutdown due to the COVID-19 crisis. InvestEU differs from previous programmes in three major ways (European Commission 2021).

The first is that it brings together 14 previously dispersed specific programmes, each with different rules, under one single mechanism. This simplification facilitates the diversity of actors involved in their implementation and makes the overall investment policy of the European Union more visible.

The second change is about priority-setting. Under EFSI, there was a single envelope of funds for all projects, and the primary objective was to recover investment without setting sectorial priorities. Under InvestEU, four windows have been established, and each has a dedicated financial envelope. The four sectors are (1) sustainable infrastructure; (2) research, innovation, and digitalisation; (3) SMEs and medium-sized enterprises; and (4) social investment and skills.

Finally, InvestEU is a programme in which institutions other than the EIB may participate once they have satisfied the evaluation process—known as 'pillar assessments'. Entities eligible to become implementing partners include international organisations or their agencies; public institutions, including organisations of Member States; and, finally, private law organisations provided that they are entrusted with public-service tasks and that they provide adequate financial guarantees. This openness to NPBIs, as well as to institutions such as the EBRD or the Bank of the Council of Europe, is a major development insofar as it enlarges the potential partner pool for the European Commission. InvestEU recognises that European investment policies require complementarity between the European level and national levels: it is essential to have implementation partners who are closer to the ground and to the projects themselves.

Against this background, there is an increasing cooperation among NPBIs with an exchange of best practices and through joint positions without forgetting the establishment of the Marguerite 3 Investment Fund. Marguerite is a leading European infrastructure investor having managed three funds since 2010. It was created at the initiative of the European Investment Bank and five National Promotional Banks from Italy, France, Germany, Poland, and Spain, it has evolved into a fund manager with private investors and the support of EFSI and InvestEU.

The rise of the European Association of Long-Term Investors (ELTI) reflects this collective dynamic. This association brings together over thirty members of various sizes and balance sheets. It is important to underline that those new annual commitments of ELTI members increased by nearly 30% between 2018 and 2021, reflecting a particularly dynamic period of activity. Most of the amounts committed are in the form of loans, but some NPBIs do not refrain from intervening in the form of equity, which exerts a much greater leverage effect. Large groups are also emerging at national level. The Caisse des Dépôts, which includes entities such as BPI France and La Poste Group with Banque Postale, represents an aggregate balance sheet of more than €1,300bn. Regional cooperation can be seen in the '3 Seas Initiative', also known as the 'Baltic, Adriatic, Black Sea Initiative' (BABS). Further evidence of a move towards financial partnership is political scheme that has transformed into an investment fund with nine first-level sponsors. The main funder is BGK in Poland, but other NPBI partners in the scheme are Altum (Latvia), SID (Slovenia), BDB (Bulgaria), HBOR (Croatia), and VIPA (Lithuania). These public financial institutions work alongside the Estonian Ministry of Finance, banks, and guarantee agencies (such as EximBank in Romania and Hungary).

7.4 One Step Beyond...

With its large and widespread network of NPBIs, Europe already has the necessary tools to act. However, over many years, public finance has had to face headwinds from two directions: some proponents of the market economies regard the institutions as intruders in the economic game, and some actors in the public sphere consider NPBIs as potentially illegitimate actors that would be at the service of the public interest without necessarily being dependent on governments (Attali 2022). Today, things seem to have evolved. NPBIs are recognised as essential, but do they have the means to act as efficiently as they could?

From time to time, NPBIs must apply supervisory rules primarily intended for other, mainly commercial banks. They also have to abide by accounting norms wherein long-term funding is regarded as irrelevant; however, a long-term approach that includes positive externalities in investment calculations is a necessity to overcome short-term challenges.

A financial actor is, above all, a structure that will attract liquidity in order to transform it before it is returned, that is, before it has seen a loss or profit. This financial-intermediation mechanism varies according to the types of actors, yet the supervisory rules minimize these differences for legitimate reasons. This transformation impacts both the level of risk and maturity. Thus, liquid or short-term liabilities will become long-term assets. This change is made possible by appropriate management strategies and by the existence of sufficient capital to cope with the eventual materialisation of the residual risks. During crises, any prudential requirements, which define the risk-management framework and the level of capital needed to address identified risk, have gradually been reinforced with the aim of strengthening the resilience of actors and the system. As we have already seen, these requirements may have reduced the ability to take risks. Even worse, we contemplate the emergence of what is called 'the overcompliance' in different domains. Applying prudential rules to different actors is not a simple task. The trivial thing is to distinguish the actors based on their playing field (banks, insurance companies, etc.) but this essentialist approach does not take into consideration some specificities. From a practical standpoint, this tends to ignore long-term investors like NPBIs. Their specificity as countercyclical agents is ignored as prudential rules lead to pro-cyclical behaviour. Nevertheless, it is also true that supervisory rules are aimed at making financial actors robust and resilient to prevent the recurrence of crises from the past. They are not tools of economic policy, although they can heavily influence it.

Prudential rules are structural elements of the strength of intermediaries and are therefore essential to enable patient investment. The risk-management system must therefore be based on an assessment of long-term risks and returns adapted to the specific characteristics of the players. Since some actors, like NPBIs, have objectives other than short-term financial profitability, these tools lead to a distortion between the indicators used and the purposes of the institutions. Faithful to their core business, regulators give absolute priority to financial ratios alone without considering the positive externalities sought by NPBIs.

Climate risk is a good example of this distortion, and it is worth noting that attempts are made to integrate it into risk assessment. Other elements could also be considered, such as the protection offered by a diversified, long-term investment portfolio. The same is true for the reference horizons of indicators which are often short term.

If a prudential framework is considered essential to the stability of the financing system and, thus, to the continuous functioning of the economy, some measures could promote a better orientation of savings towards long-term investment while maintaining a secure framework. In other words, there is a penalisation of equity investment which makes the key function of NPBIs—transforming liquidity into long term investment—more difficult at the very time it is the most needed.

The long term remains the poor cousin of accounting standards despite recurring alerts on this subject (Demaria 2016). It is worth pointing out that both accounting standards and prudential rules have, for the most part, pro-cyclical effects. Accounting standards lead to gregarious behaviour and leave little room for long-term strategies. Asset valuation is based on the concept of 'fair value', which is, in fact, increasingly akin to market value. Quarterly reports have short-term consequences for investor behaviour. International Financing Reporting Standard (IFRS) 9, introduced in 2018, further reinforced this trend. The increasing volatility of valuations are making it more difficult for financial players to devise long-term strategies. To avoid the perception of valuations as artificial or even misleading, asset-valuation mechanisms must be carried out continuously based on the concept of 'fair value'. As the market is a beauty contest at a given moment (Keynes 1936: 156), it can hardly apply to any long-term perspective. Rather, it fosters an appreciation which, without doubt, is close to the consensus at a given moment, but does not consider the future. This 'fair value' valuation, therefore, appears not only to be unsuitable for the management of long-term investments, but also acts as an effective deterrent of them.

In this context, it is becoming more important than ever to think about building a long-term accounting framework to avoid using a ten-decimetre ruler to measure the length of a highway!

The quality of information is crucial for making informed investment choices, but it is not enough. In a modelling-resistant environment where externalities are numerous, the need to be prioritized. It is up to the public authority, which alone has the necessary legitimacy, to shed this indispensable light. Putting priorities into perspective is part of an effort aimed at investors and, especially, savers. Sometimes, what makes products unattractive is a lack of financial education; however, more often, it is the lack of legible priorities that drives behaviour in these groups. The hierarchy of externalities, whether positive or negative, is key for establishing incentives. They are often put forward progressively without being placed in a global perspective. Clarifying political choices by establishing a hierarchy of externalities can only be done by politicians at the global level, thus proving that the European model makes sense. By establishing a venue for arbitration that bring together experts, politicians, and civil-society representatives at European level, an analysis grid could be proposed to characterise long-term investments. This grid could then be included as a governance instrument for European financial instruments. It could also serve as a basis for characterising long-term investments at national or European level.

The NPBIs have shown in recent times, marked by all these challenges, that they are in a position not only to play their full role as countercyclical actors but also to shape, in part, a new restructuring of our economies. In today's progression of the world economy, Europe has demonstrated its strong assets with these public institutions as well as highlighting their strong legitimacy. The challenge today is to fully mobilise their means to succeed in this transformation without their resources being taken up by governments concerned with either filling their budget deficit or financing short-term policies. To paraphrase a famous author, 'Banks and Public Financial Institutions of all countries, unite!'

References

AFG, Mazars (2021). 'Finance à impact: les pratiques et défis des sociétés de gestion', https://www.afg.asso.fr/wp-content/uploads/2021/11/afg-enqu-impact-211122web.pdf

Attali, B. (dir.), Zylberberg, L. (coord.) (2022). 'Investing for the Long Term, a Short-Term Emergency (Some Food for Thought)', *Report for Caisse des Dépôts*, https://www.eltia.eu/images/20201210_texte_VF_EN_FINAL.pdf

Badie, B. and P. Birnbaum (1982). 'Sociologie de l'Etat', 2nd edn, Grasset et Fasquelle, coll. Pluriel

BPCE (2023). 'Hausse des taux d'intérêt: vers des arbitrages massifs des ménages?', https://groupebpce.com/etudes-economiques/rendez-vous-epargne-placements-de-janvier-2023

Buti, M. and P. Pohl (2014). 'Lacklustre Investment in the Eurozone: Is there a Puzzle?', Centre for Economic Policy Research, https://cepr.org/voxeu/columns/lacklustre-investment-eurozone-there-puzzle

CEPII (2015). 'L'économie mondiale 2016', *La Découverte*, https://doi.org/10.3917/dec.cepii.2015.01

Chelsky, J., C. Morel, and K. Mabruk (2013). 'Investment Financing in the Wake of the Crisis: The Role of Multilateral Development Banks', *Economic Premise*, World Bank, June, 121

Cingolani, M. (2017). 'Investissement publics nécessaires -le rôle potentiel des banques publiques', CIRIEC, n°2017/07, https://www.ciriec.uliege.be/wp-content/uploads/2018/03/WP2017-07.pdf

Cusset, P. and Trannoy, A. (2023). 'Alimentation, logement, transport : sur qui l'inflation pèse-t-elle le plus?'. *La note d'analyse de France Stratégie*, 119: 1–11. https://www.cairn.info/revue-la-note-d-analyse-2023-4-page-1.htm#:~:text=Globalement%2C%20le%20panier%20a%20augment%C3%A9,le%20transport%20(11%20%25)

De La Rosière, J. (2022). 'Ending the Reign of Financial Illusion: For Real Growth', Odile Jacob

—— D. Cahen, and E. Krief (2023). 'Macroeconomic Scoreboard', Eurofi, April, https://www.eurofi.net/wp-content/uploads/2023/04/macroeconomic-scoreboard_stockholm_april-2023.pdf

Demaria, S. and S. Rigot (2016). 'Normes comptables et prudentielles des intermédiaires financiers au regard de l'investissement à long terme', 6th états généraux de la recherche, Autorité des Normes Comptables, 12 décembre

EIB (2014). 'European Finance Strategic Investment', factsheet

—— (2021). 'Report to the European Parliament and the Council on 2021 EIB Group Financing and Investment Operations under EFSI', 2021-efsi-report-to-the-ep-and-council.pdf

—— (2023). Investment Report 2022/2023

Engels, F. (1975). *Socialism: Utopian and Scientific*, Peking, 1st edn

European Commission (2021). https://investeu.europa.eu/about-investeu_en

European Long-Term Investors Association (2023). 'Ukraine Measures', https://www.eltia.eu/images/2023.02.17_-_ELTI_Ukraine_measures.pdf

ELTI, NEFI, AECM, (2020). 'Overview of Measures against the Economic Impact of the Coronavirus (COVID-19) Outbreak', https://www.eltia.eu/

images/2020.06.17_-_ELTI_NEFI__AECM_-_Coronavirus_COVID-19_Support_Measures. pdf

INSEE (2022). https://www.insee.fr/fr/statistiques/fichier/2830286/econ-gen-poids-dette-pub-ue-2.xlsx

Griffith-Jones, S., and N. Naqvi. (2020). 'Industrial policy and risk sharing in public development banks: Lessons for the post-COVID response from the EIB and EFSI', July / Global Economic Governance Programme 143

Jaillet, P. (2012). 'Investissement à long terme : enjeux pour la croissance, la stabilité monétaire et financière', *Revue d'économie financière*, 108.4: 169-88

Jamet, J. F. (2008). 'L'Europe face à la crise financière', Fondation Robert Schuman, https://www.robert-schuman.eu/fr/questions-d-europe/0089-l-europe-face-a-la-crise-financiere

Keynes, J. M (1936). The general theory of employment interest and money, Vol VII, Cambridge University Press

Le Moigne, M., Saraceno, F. et Villemot Sébastien (2015). 'Le plan Juncker peut-il nous sortir de l'ornière ?', *Revue de l'OFCE*, 144.8: 357–86

Li, B. (2023). 'Scaling up Climate Finance for Emerging Markets and Developing Economies', https://www.imf.org/en/News/Articles/2023/02/28/ sp022823-scaling-up-climate-finance-for-emerging-markets-and-developing-economies

Marodon, R., X. Jiajun, and Ru Xinshun (2021). Mapping 500+ Development banks, Agence Française de Développement, https://www.afd.fr/en/ressources/ mapping-500-development-banks

McKinsey Global Institute (2021). 'The Rise and Rise of the Global Balance Sheet', www. mckinsey.com/~/media/mckinsey/industries/financial%20services/our%20insights/ the%20rise%20and%20rise%20of%20the%20global%20balance%20sheet%20how%20 productively%20are%20we%20using%20our%20wealth/mgi-the-rise-and-rise-of-the-global-balance-sheet-full-report-vf.pdf

Meltzer, J. P. (2016). 'Financing Low Carbon, Climate Resilient Infrastructure: The Role of Climate Finance and Green Financial Systems', 21 September, http://dx.doi.org/10.2139/ ssrn.2841918

Monnet, J. (1978). 'Memoirs', trans. by R. Mayne. Garden City: Doubleday & Company

OCDE, (2016). 'Coopération pour le développement 2016 : Investir dans les Objectifs de développement durable, choisir l'avenir', Éditions OCDE, Paris, https://doi.org/10.1787/dcr-2016-fr

Panagiotis, A., H. Eivind Friis, and W. Wright (2022). *A New Vision for EU capital Markets*, Report, New Financial, 2022, https://newfinancial.org/wp-content/ uploads/2022/02/2022.01-A-New-Vision-for-EU-Capital-Markets-New-Financial.pdf

Pisani-Ferry, J. et al. (2023). 'Les incidences économiques de l'action pour le climat', Rapport à la Première Ministre, France Stratégie, mai

Potier, J. P. (2015). 'Joseph A. Schumpeter et la conjoncture économique des années 1930-1940. Dépression, stagnation ou signes avant-coureurs du déclin du capitalisme?', *Revue économique*, 66.5: 993–1019

Prodi R., C. Sautter et al. (2018). 'Boosting Investment in Social infrastructure in Europe', European Commission, Discussion Paper, 74, https://www.eltia.eu/activities/ high-level-task-force-on-social-infrastructure

White House (2022). 'Economic Report to the President', Chapter 3 https://www.whitehouse.gov/wp-content/uploads/2022/04/Chapter-3-new.pdf

Zylberberg, L. (2020). ' Les institutions financières publiques ne doivent pas être les albatros de la relance ', *Confrontations Europe*, n°130, Sept.-Nov. 2020

—— (2018). 'Les financement européens au service des territoires,' *Revue d'économie financière*, 132.4: 59–71

8. Making Green Public Investments a Reality in the EU Fiscal Framework and the EU Budget

Atanas Pekanov and Margit Schratzenstaller

Additional green public investment at the Member-State level will be needed to address the climate emergency as a central priority in the EU. This chapter discusses two paths to enable increased green public investments in the EU: through possible amendments to the current EU fiscal framework or through funding from the EU budget. The Commission's proposal from November 2022 regarding orientations for a reform of the EU-governance framework widens the leeway for debt-financed public investment. However, existing green public investment needs are not considered sufficiently. Therefore, we discuss several options to enable the flexibility of national budgets to ensure a level of green public investment which—together with private resources—is sufficient to close the existing green investment gaps. In addition, the use of the lever the EU budget theoretically offers to contribute to green public investment in the EU needs to be intensified. At about 1% of EU GNI (1.7% of EU GNI including NGEU) the overall volume of the EU budget is limited. The more important are steps to strengthen spending in policies that create EU value added, inter alia green public investment.

8.1 Introduction

The European Green Deal (EGD), the EU's 'new growth strategy' that was adopted in 2019 with the aim of making the EU climate neutral by 2050, requires massive investment in the decarbonisation of the economies of the EU.[1] Geopolitical developments with the Russian invasion in Ukraine highlight the need to speed up the clean-energy transition and the strengthening of Europe's energy independence. The 'Fit for 55' Package launched by the European Commission in mid-2021 aims at

---

1   We are indebted to Cornelia Schobert for careful research assistance.

https://doi.org/10.11647/OBP.0386.08

realising the ramped-up ambition in the EU's climate targets. These important goals will require significant public investment in the coming years.

Public investment encompasses investment in projects associated with long-term positive externalities so that the long-term social rate of return of such investment exceeds the private rate of return. In the case of green public investments (GPI), these positive externalities result from the reduction of environmental damage and of energy dependence and benefit society as a whole. Certain investment projects display specific characteristics which may make them unattractive to private investors. Infrastructure networks, which represent a considerable share of green investment have various properties that particularly deter private investors. These include indivisibilities over long lifespans, high fixed and sunk costs, and asset specifics—a range that implies high risks and thus impairs the ability and/or willingness of private investors to undertake them. Natural monopoly situations, which are relevant for many infrastructural networks, may also require public involvement. Specifically related to the issue at hand is that the green transition requires the development and implementation of innovative, often risky and untested, green technologies. In addition, in face of rising interest rates, which decrease the profitability of such investments by increasing the cost of financing them, private investors may be reluctant to undertake such investments (Bertram et al. 2022). Overall, therefore, the state has an important role to play in the green transition through co-financing, private-public partnerships, and state guarantees, but also through public investment (European Investment Bank 2021; Delgado-Téllez et al. 2022). A certain share of the necessary green investment, therefore, will need to be redirected from Member States' budgets to complement private investment or will need to be funded under the common EU budget.

Analogously to public investment in general, an argument can be made for at least partially financing GPI, which creates long-term benefits for future generations, by public debt, instead of solely relying on tax increases or shifts within the expenditure structure. These long-term benefits include the positive environmental externalities but may also consist of long-term productivity-enhancing effects that have been observed in relation to certain public-investment projects (Fournier 2016; European Fiscal Board 2019). According to the 'pay-as-you-use' principle (Musgrave 1939), debt service for debt-financed public investment with long-term benefits accruing to the next generation(s) can be seen as an option to make them contribute adequately to the provision of such public investment. From this perspective, debt financing of public investment provides for a fair intergenerational distribution (Yakita 1994; Balassone and Franco 2000), reducing incentives for de- or under-investment today which would harm future generations (Bertram et al. 2022). Green investment—like investment in general—adds to the stock of assets, warranting deficit financing (Corti et al. 2022).

Projections of the 'green investment gap', that is, the additional spending that needs to be undertaken to meet the 2030 climate targets, have been adapted several times during the last years due to rising climate ambitions. In 2019, prior to the increase of the

2030 emission reduction target from 40% to 55% compared to 1990 levels through the EGD, the European Commission (2019) estimated the green investment gap at €260bn per year. To achieve the EGD objectives, the European Commission (2021) doubled its estimate for the green investment gap and indicates additional necessary investments for the current decade of €520bn per year (3.7% of 2019 GDP) compared to the previous decade. Hereby, an annual amount of €390bn is required to decarbonise the economy and, particularly, the energy sector; another €130bn per year needs to be invested to achieve other environmental objectives. The sheer size of this green investment gap implies that a significant part of the funding for the increased investment will have to come from the EU level and from EU Member States in addition to private investors (Claeys and Tagliapietra 2020; European Commission 2022a).

This chapter discusses two paths to enable increased green public investments—through possible amendments to the current EU fiscal framework or through funding from the EU budget.[2]

8.2 Fiscal Framework

National budgetary decisions in EU Member States (MS) are managed under a common European fiscal framework known as the Stability and Growth Pact (SGP), and a coordination mechanism known as the European Semester. The SGP has been revised multiple times since its establishment in 1997 to address some of its previous shortcomings.[3] The rules have often been criticised as being too pro-cyclical, that is, not restricting debt enough in bad times, and not providing enough fiscal space in good times (see, for example, Bénassy-Quéré et al. 2018, or Ubide 2019). The various amendments introduced over time have made the European fiscal framework better suited to steering macroeconomic policy, but they also rendered the fiscal rules overly complex and non-transparent (Friis et al. 2022).

The SGP has, however, also been criticised for its lack of flexibility to enable public investments via higher deficits when they were most needed from a macroeconomic standpoint. In reaction, the European Commission published a Communication (2015) on the use of flexibility clauses and their interpretation, focusing on a more flexible application of the SGP rules by taking into account exceptional circumstances, structural reforms and other relevant factors, as well as investments. The investment clause in the SGP is a way to enable more investment, especially in times of economic downturn. The Communication enabled a reinterpretation of the existing fiscal rules, without the need to explicitly change them or take legislative action. In the current version, for the investment clause to be invoked, however, a strict set of conditions

---

2   The part of this chapter that relates to fiscal rules is a summary version of a longer study prepared for the European Parliament (Pekanov and Schratzenstaller 2023).
3   See Pekanov and Schratzenstaller (2020) for an overview of major changes to the EU fiscal framework.

needs to be met.[4] Although the investment exemption clause has been assessed as a positive change to the SGP, the strict conditions have made it very difficult to be invoked and so far, only two countries (Italy and Finland) have made use of it.

Partly because of the pro-cyclical character of fiscal rules, public investment has suffered in the aftermath of the GFC and has markedly declined as a share of current primary expenditures in many Member States—especially those which are more indebted (Figure 8.1 and Figure 8.2). The period of fiscal consolidation has contributed to this general weakness of public investment (Storm and Naastepad 2016; Darvas and Wolff 2021). Public investment often experiences considerable reductions during downturns, as it is easier to reduce without significant political costs in comparison to current expenditures, government transfers, or other programmes. Particularly in aging societies, public support for preserving current expenditures may be higher than for future-oriented investment (Darvas and Wolff 2021).

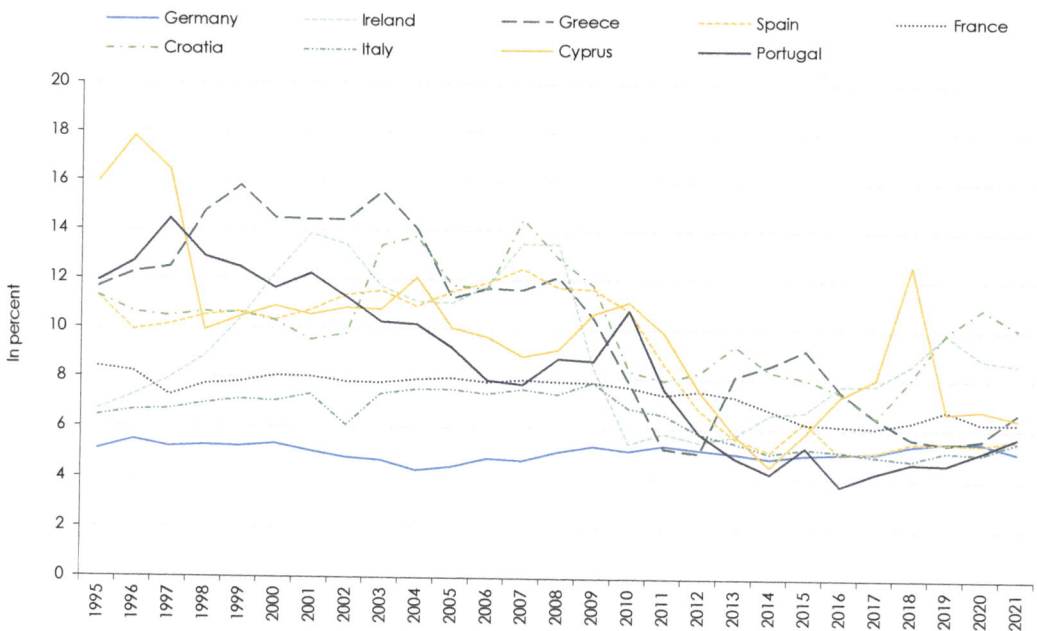

Fig. 8.1 Gross Fixed Capital Formation as a Share of Primary Expenditure in Selected Member States.
Note: Primary expenditure = Total general government expenditures minus property income.
Source: Eurostat.

---

4   These conditions can be found at https://ec.europa.eu/commission/presscorner/detail/en/ MEMO_15_3221

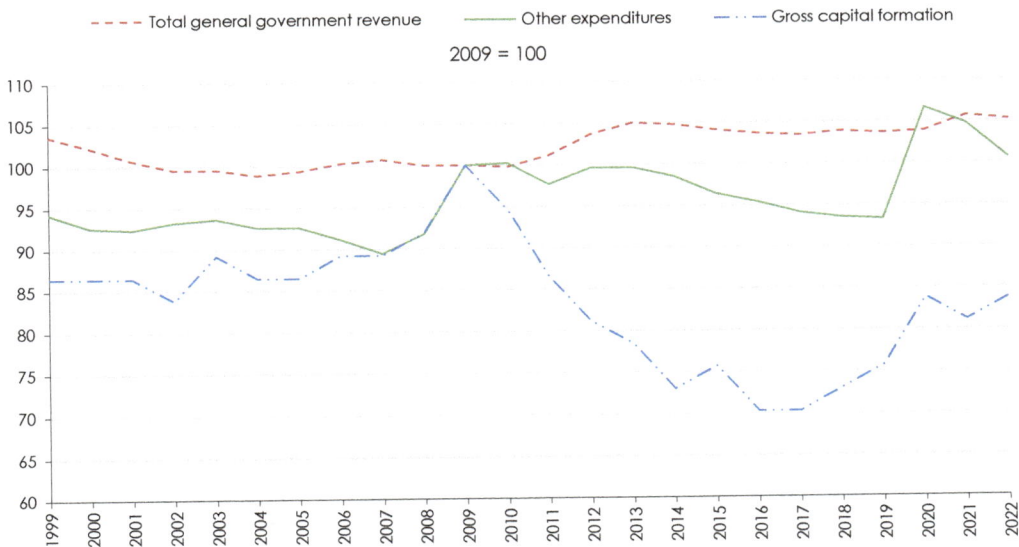

Fig. 8.2 Euro Area General Government Revenue, Investment, and Other Expenditures, in % of GDP.
Source: Eurostat. Other expenditures = Total general government expenditure minus gross capital formation.

8.3 Options to Support GPI in the EU Fiscal Framework

In light of the substantial resources required to finance the necessary green transition discussed above, additional public investments by Member States (MS) or within the EU budget will need to be mobilised throughout the next decade. The current fiscal framework of the EU does not provide enough flexibility for MS to react adequately to these challenges by increasing debt-financed green public investment (GPI). Thus, amendments within the fiscal framework may be necessary.

On 9 November 2022, the Commission (2022b) issued a 'Communication on orientations for a reform of the EU economic governance framework'. It focuses on three main pillars. First, the Commission suggests an expenditure rule: net primary expenditures (that is, total expenditures excluding interest and unemployment payments as well as additional expenditure covered by tax increases) shall serve as the only indicator to gauge compliance with the debt and deficit criteria. The expenditure path shall be determined by the Commission based on a debt-sustainability analysis. The second pillar relates to the national medium-term fiscal-structural plans to be submitted by Member States, detailing the measures to comply with the expenditure path. Thirdly, the Communication states that the 60% of GDP debt criterion shall remain. While it does not give concrete time frames about when this level must be achieved, it does assert, as an indicative objective, that the 3% of GDP deficit criterion shall be monitored and sanctioned more strictly in the future.

Altogether, the proposal adds a substantial element of country-specific flexibility and reinforces the long-term orientation of the EU fiscal framework, while at the same time reducing its complexity. The Commission's communication proposes differentiated adjustment speeds for different MS, according to their debt levels, to give more credibility to the imposition of medium-term targets, which might otherwise seem unrealistic. Moreover, debt-financed public investment can be considered explicitly, albeit not in the form of a golden rule which would exempt public investment permanently from deficit and debt statistics: rather, the time period allowed to return to a path of decreasing debt ratios can be prolonged from four to seven years if MS submit national medium-term fiscal-structural plans including public investment endorsed by the Commission and adopted by the Council. While the Commission Communication explicitly mentions that national medium-term fiscal structural plans (which can include investment proposals) should, in particular, 'address common EU priorities, including the National Energy and Climate Plans (aligned with the targets of the EU Climate Law...', GPI is not accounted for separately in the Commission's proposal. More generally, the evaluation of national medium-term fiscal-structural plans can be subjective or can lead to political negotiations, thus politicising the process and making it more complicated for the Commission to reach an agreement with individual MS and, in turn, potentially slowing down the implementation of necessary GPI.

Against this background, we discuss below four approaches for a reform of the fiscal rules better accommodating for the existing GPI requirements:

- A GPI-exemption clause complementing the current SGP flexibility clauses would be relatively easy to implement and not require Treaty changes. It would, however, further complicate an already complex set of fiscal rules and would not ensure that MS indeed invest the necessary amount towards greening their economies.

- With a golden rule for GPI the respective deficit accrued would not be counted towards deficit and debt statistics relevant for EU fiscal rules. While this would also complicate the fiscal framework further, a 'green golden rule' would incentivise governments to transform as much as possible from their spending towards GPI.

- A third approach would be for the European Commission to estimate and the Council to recommend country-specific benchmark shares of government expenditures in each country to be dedicated to GPI.

- An EU Climate Fund (CF) financed by common EU debt could offer MS loans to MS at favourable interest rates to finance GPI.

8.3.1 GPI Exemption Clause in the SGP

A straightforward approach would be to add a GPI definition to the existing investment-exemption clause of the SGP to enable short-run deviations from deficit targets and Medium-Term Objectives (MTO). It would help to frontload GPI, especially if the temporary exemption was extended over a longer time period. The clause can be applied to MS that can present verifiable plans for GPI reforms under consideration, with sufficient proof of their long-term benefits in terms of environmental sustainability, economic growth, and productivity. This would need to be accompanied by a set of specific deadlines and ways to control their implementation. The plans would require clear evidence that the investment in question will help improve environmental sustainability. This evidence could rest on the EU taxonomy for sustainable activities. The exemption could be granted after a thorough process of proving that the investments in question would indeed contribute to climate neutrality and/or further environmental goals, in a way similar to proving that investments will have a 'positive, direct and verifiable long-term effect on growth and on the sustainability of public finance' in the existing investment clause. The legal implementation would include changing or using a new Communication and then embedding the changes in the Code of Conduct of the SGP.

Pros:

- The GPI-exemption clause would be easy to implement even in the current EU fiscal framework if there is a clear definition of which public investment is to be counted as green. It will help to frontload GPI, especially if the temporary exemption can be extended over a longer period of time.

- It would not require a legal change but only an amendment within the flexibility clause of the SGP to include GPI as a separately defined condition for activating it. The process, conditions, recommendations, and the coordination can be embedded easily into the European Semester.

Cons/Potential Problems:

- If the envisaged GPI is only eligible after a thorough review of the project in question, this might imply that most investment is realised slowly, and projects would be implemented with a significant time lag.

- The GPI-exemption clause would not necessarily incentivise national governments to undertake the investment necessary to close their green investment gaps; it would only enable it.

- It would add further to the complexity and uncertainty of the fiscal rules. The three existing escape clauses of the SGP have introduced opacity.

- Exemption clauses are short-term in nature, applying under exceptional circumstances and for selected projects; they, therefore, are of limited use considering the longer-term substantial GPI needs, which will be the normal state in the foreseeable future (Bénassy-Quéré 2022).

- A GPI-exemption clause similar to the current clause would be insufficient in size, as it allows only a maximum deviation of 0.5% of GDP initially, which is to be corrected in the following four years.

8.3.2 Introduction of a 'Green Investment Golden Rule'

A second option would be to embed a green investment golden rule in the current fiscal framework. A golden rule for investment has been discussed and proposed as a way to improve the European fiscal rules framework for a long time.[10] A classical golden investment rule is based on a classification of government spending into two types—current expenditure versus capital expenditure (that is, public investment). The golden investment rule would allow deficit-financed public investment to not be counted for deficit and debt statistics, while current expenditures need to be balanced or fulfil some maximum deficit target (for example, the existing one of 3%). A more targeted golden rule could focus on GPI only. Such a green golden rule would be even more effective in mobilising resources for the green transition by having a strong incentivising effect for governments to transform as much of their public investment as possible into GPI. A green golden rule would also allow MS to not count their additional co-financing on EU projects (above their national commitment) to their deficit statistics, thus incentivising them to undertake additional investment in in such green projects.

Pros:

- A green golden rule will be effective to incentivise Member States to transform and mobilise large parts of their expenditures towards GPI.

- A green golden rule is a permanent provision enabling the implementation of longer-term GPI strategies most MS will need in the current decade and beyond.

- It will also protect GPI during cyclical downturns when public investments are easier to reduce or postpone to a later period. This should ensure that long-term investments to fight climate change will not suffer from fiscal tightening.

Cons/Potential Problems:

- A green golden rule may require significant legal changes towards the Fiscal Compact and the expenditure benchmark.

- It would increase the complexity and administrative burden.

- It could create inefficient shifts away from green expenditure which has an investment character but is not counted as green investment (for example, green qualifications) towards GPI which is eligible but possibly less efficient (Bénassy-Quéré 2022).

Compared to the Commission's proposal, a green golden rule would specifically focus on GPI and not on public investment in general, so that its scope would on the one hand be narrower. On the other hand, a green golden rule would create larger leeway for GPI, as the 3% of GDP deficit limit would be disregarded, as well as the impact of GPI on the debt ratio. The green golden rule would be a permanent provision, thus accommodating for the existing long-term GPI needs.

8.3.3 A Benchmark for GPI as a Share of Government Expenditures

The third approach would be for the European Commission to recommend a benchmark for each MS as a share of government expenditures that should be committed towards GPI (for example, a certain percentage of overall government public investment/expenditure). This benchmark share would be based on an estimated country-specific green investment gap. The share would therefore not have to be uniform across MS: Some MS perform better in terms of environmental sustainability already; furthermore, the green (public) investment gap differs between MS (Delgado-Téllez et al. 2022). If calculated in relation to government expenditures, which vary considerably between MS in terms of GDP, the shares in such an approach would not constitute an excessive breach in MS fiscal-policy sovereignty, as each would not prescribe the size of government spending but, rather, only direct a part of its composition. The difference between this and the previous two options is that the European Commission would pro-actively recommend to MS (in a top-down approach) that a certain share of their expenditures should be in the form of GPI.

The progress of MS could then be operationalised following the precedent of the Six-pack reform by introducing a definition of a necessary speed at which MS should close their GPI gaps. The Commission would evaluate whether this happens at a 'satisfactory pace'. The efficiency of such proactive guidance by the European Commission on how much MS should spend on greening their economy will depend on the implementation process. However, the history of fiscal rules and monitoring of recommended reforms in the EU brings a mixed picture of how effective the compliance by Member States can be. Although sanctions can be applied by the Council if there are breaches to the SGP and the Macro-Economic Imbalance Procedure (MIP), they were never applied in practice and the existing enforcement regime has been weak.

Pros:

- Legally a benchmark share for GPI would be easy to introduce within the European Semester, by enriching it with GPI goals and adequate indicators.[5]

---

5   Similarly, the EU Greening Initiative has made first attempts at reaching such goals without the need to change other EU legislature, including the SGP. See: https://ec.europa.eu/environment/integration/green_semester/about_en.htm

Cons/Potential Problems:

- Achieving the goal of mobilising significant GPI in MS will be very much dependent on the implementation of the GPI-benchmark share. If it is implemented as a soft law with the European Commission only issuing recommendations to MS about the share of GPI they should invest in, it runs the risk of being ineffective, similar to the Country Specific Recommendations (CSR).

A GPI-benchmark share could rather easily be integrated in the Commission proposal of a net-expenditure path, by excluding GPI spending from net expenditures. Alternatively, the medium-term fiscal-structural plans submitted by MS could foresee a pre-determined share of GPI in their public investment—similar to the mechanism behind the implementation of the national Recovery and Resilience Plans (NRRP)—requiring a minimum share of green spending financed through the Recovery and Resilience Facility (RRF) of 37%.

8.3.4 An EU Climate Fund

In the State of the Union address in September 2022, Commission President Ursula von der Leyen proposed an EU Sovereignty Fund (SF). One option for the financing of such an EU SF—following the example of the EU Recovery and Resilience Fund (RRF)—would be to take up debt on capital markets, making use of the EU's credit rating which grants low interest rates for common EU debt. MS could then apply for loans at these favourable interest rates to finance GPI. Those MS facing relatively high interest rates for public debt would be given the opportunity to debt finance strategically important green infrastructure projects at favourable interest rates. An option with a more limited scope focused on GPI would be to establish an EU Climate Fund (CF), which would fund specific investment projects targeting the green transition and climate change. Such an EU CF would have the advantage vis-à-vis an EU SF to provide incentives for MS to direct their investment activities toward GPI.

The granting of EU CF loans could be based on a combined bottom-up/top-down approach. MS could either apply for loans based on national strategic GPI plans. Alternatively, the Commission could identify strategic green infrastructure projects and actively approach the affected MS with strategic GPI proposals, including also a funding proposal. The Commission proposals could focus on cross-border GPI projects which would be neglected in a bottom-up approach, as experiences with the RRF show. The handling of CF loans, including the drafting of proposals, their assessment, approval, and monitoring, could build upon RRF experiences and the institutional and procedural provisions established to implement national recovery and resilience plans. Similar to the RRF, the assessment of MS GPI plans could be based on the EU Taxonomy; in addition, they could be screened by an independent European Fiscal Agency (Garicano 2022). CF loans could also top up specific industrial projects in the area of green investment supported through Important Projects of Common European Interest (IPCEI) funding, as proposed by Commissioner Thierry Breton in the context of an EU SF (European Commission 2022c).

Of course, CF and RRF investment plans should be coordinated. An EU CF could then act as a permanent successor institution of the temporary RRF, which will phase out in 2026. The CF would not constitute a reform of the existing fiscal rules framework. Depending on its scope and volume, it could either complement or substitute a reform of fiscal rules aiming to further GPI based on one of the three reform options sketched above.

Pros:

- An EU CF would alleviate the burden of interest payments associated with additional public debt to finance GPI particularly for those MS facing relatively high interest rates.

- It could be used to finance strategically important cross-border GPI projects, particularly in the areas of railway and energy-supply infrastructure, which are underfunded based on purely national decision-making and budgets.

- It could make use of already-existing EU and national RRF implementation structures.

- It would avoid making EU fiscal rules even more complex (Bénassy-Quéré 2022).

- An EU CF could help to mitigate a subsidy race within the EU by coordinating MS GPI policies to some extent.

Cons/Potential Problems:

- An EU CF would be rather unattractive for those MS enjoying favourable interest rates for their national debt. To avoid dealing with administratively burdensome application, implementation, and monitoring procedures accompanied by the Commission and the Council, they may prefer to directly incur debt on capital markets for their GPI projects.

Although the recent Commission proposal explicitly aims to increase the leeway for public investment, the CF could act as a complement to further widen the space for national GPI. It would account for the fact that the investment gap is probably biggest regarding green investment, although this is not explicitly acknowledged and considered in the Commission's proposal.

Table 8.1 summarises the four options to further GPI in the EU fiscal framework and evaluates them based on several criteria.

Table 8.1 Summary Evaluation of Options for Amending the Current Fiscal Framework to Better Accommodate for GPI

Proposal	Ensures the Necessary Investment	Complexity and Administrative Burden	Legal/Institutional Changes Needed	Further Comments
Options for a GPI-Friendly Fiscal-Rules Framework				
Golden Rule for GPI	Incentivises MS to make the maximum amount of GPI possible Allows longer-term and more substantial deviation from deficit targets	Significant increase in complexity and administrative burden	Changes to the Fiscal Compact/Six-pack Reform	Would create larger leeway for GPI than the Commission proposal Could be integrated in the Commission proposal
Exemption Clause for GPI	Enables but does not ensure Member States will make sufficient GPI Allows only limited temporary deviation from deficit targets	Medium increase in complexity and administrative burden	New Communication on the flexibility clause and amendment to the Code of Conduct of the SGP	Would create considerably lower leeway for GPI than the Commission proposal

Proposal	Ensures the Necessary Investment	Complexity and Administrative Burden	Legal/Institutional Changes Needed	Further Comments
(Binding) Share of GPI as a Percentage of Current Expenditure	Incentivises GPI but risks non-compliance	Medium increase in complexity and administrative burden	Changes to the European Semester	Low political feasibility (if binding) or low compliance (if only with a recommendatory character) Could be easily integrated in the expenditure path proposed by the Commission to increase leeway for GPI; alternatively, binding GPI shares in public investment proposed in national fiscal-structural plans could be foreseen
EU Climate Fund	Incentivises particularly MS facing high interest rates to make debt-financed GPI Incentivises cross-border GPI	Neutral with regard to the EU fiscal framework	New legal proposal also based on amendment of ORD New Communication on counting CF GPI towards fiscal rules Changes to the European Semester	Incentives differ across MS depending on country-specific interest rates for public debt Could act as a complement to the EU proposal to particularly support (cross-border) GPI

Source: Authors' elaboration

8.4 Green Public Investment in the EU Budget

The EU budget plays a pivotal role in the EU's green-investment strategy. As the first of the various measures included in the European Green Deal, the European Commission launched the investment pillar in January 2020: The European Green Deal Investment Plan aims to make available and leverage the necessary funding for the green transition during the ten-year-period 2021 to 2030 in the public and private sectors.[6] At least €1 trillion of sustainable investment should be mobilised through the Multi-Annual Financial Framework (MFF) and by leveraging additional public and private financing. Hereby, about €500bn should stem directly from the EU budget (assuming a sustained level of ambition regarding climate spending for the years post-MFF 2021–2027). These figures rest on an initially envisaged climate mainstreaming goal of 25% for the MFF, according to which 25% of MFF 2021–2027 expenditures (up from 20% during the MFF 2014–2020) should contribute to climate goals.

Additionally, in 2020, the temporary COVID-19 recovery plan Next Generation EU (NGEU) was agreed with an overall volume of €750bn[7] (€390bn in grants and €360bn in loans for Member States), with the Recovery and Resilience Facility (RRF) as its most important instrument amounting to a volume of €672.5bn (€312.5bn in grants and €360bn in loans). Thus, in the current decade, the contribution from the EU budget to green-investment needs in the EU rests on two pillars: the MFF 2021–2027 (and its post–2027 successor) and NGEU.

In light of the COVID-19 crisis, the climate-mainstreaming goal was increased to 30% for the overall EU budget, amounting to a volume of up to €1,824.5bn, that is, the MFF 2021–2027 which comprises total spending of €1,074bn and NGEU with a total volume of €750bn. Overall, this would imply climate-related spending of at least 30% of an overall volume of €1,824.5bn, that is, about €550bn.

However, there is reason to assume that the lever the EU budget offers to reinforce green investment in the EU is used insufficiently on the one hand and that its potential is overstated on the other hand.

First of all, the climate-mainstreaming goal does not distinguish between different types of expenditure and, therefore, also includes spending that—strictly speaking—cannot be categorised as public investment. One example is the direct payments to farmers within the common agricultural policy (CAP) that are counted against the climate target if they provide incentives for climate- and environment-friendly farming practices. Interpreting the total of climate-related spending as green investment, therefore, considerably exaggerates the respective contribution of the EU budget.

Related is the problem that, despite some improvements in the climate-spending tracking methodology, it can be assumed that there is still a considerable share of spending marked as climate-relevant but which can be doubted (Levarlet et al. 2022).

---

6   See D'Alfonso (2020) for an overview.
7   All figures in 2018 prices.

This can be illustrated using, again, the example of the Common Agricultural Policy (CAP). The climate-related performance of the CAP has been strongly criticised by the European Court of Auditors (2021) for the MFF 2014–2020 as it contributed little to a reduction of agricultural emissions. Another example is cohesion policy, the climate contribution of which in such key areas as rail infrastructure or electricity is also overstated (European Court of Auditors 2022). Further, for the current MFF, the tracking methodology is still too focused on an input-oriented *ex ante* assessment, while *ex post* evaluations and results, and particularly the specific contribution of interventions to the EU climate targets, are not given sufficient attention (European Court of Auditors 2022).

An improvement compared to the preceding MFF 2014–2020 is the implementation of the Do No Significant Harm (DNSH) principle in the EU budget, which precludes spending with a significant negative impact on the environment. Nevertheless, several exceptions to the DNSH principle can be found in the EU budget. For example, the RRF regulation prohibits investments in nuclear energy but not in natural gas. These do not count against the climate-mainstreaming goal, but they are eligible for financing under the RRF (Levarlet et al. 2022). Another example is the CAP regulations that do not explicitly mention the DNSH principle. They include several provisions precluding environmentally harmful spending, but these are rather vague.

The funding available via the RRF is an important element of the contribution of the EU budget to the required green investment in the EU during the next few years. However, it must be acknowledged that its full potential might not be used. While the foreseen grants to Member States have been allocated completely, this is not the case for the available loans. Under the first national Recovery and Resilience Plans (NRRPs), about 43% of available loans have been allocated to seven Member States. Under the revised NRRPs, another 33% of available loans have been requested by ten Member States under the REPowerEU chapter but have not yet been granted (European Commission 2023a). Were these loan requests assessed positively by the Commission and approved by the Council, close to 76% of available loans would be disbursed. One shortcoming of the RRF is that the funded projects are almost exclusively domestic projects, while cross-border projects with a real European added value based on EU spill-over effects do not play a role (Andersen 2021). Moreover, the RRF is a temporary instrument limited to the period 2021 to 2026. After its termination, green investment through the EU budget will fall back to the much lower MFF level. In addition, there is some degree of uncertainty regarding the level of ambition regarding green investment in the post–2027 MFF.

Against this background, several conclusions can be drawn regarding needs and directions for reforms to make the EU budget future-proof in the sense that it delivers a significant contribution towards a sustainable Europe. Some of these reforms could already be initiated within the upcoming MFF mid-term review.

First of all, the green-investment component of the EU budget needs to be strengthened. This requires a shift of expenditures towards green investment with a real EU added value which would not have been carried out by national governments.

Such green investment projects (could) play a particularly strong role in research and innovation programmes; in the Connecting Europe Facility (CEF), which invests in interconnected trans-European networks in the fields of transport, energy, and digital services; and in cohesion policy. Funding for research and investment as well as the CEF, which at 7.1%[8] (up from 6% in the 2014–2020 MFF) and 1.7% (up from 1.6% in the 2014–2020 MFF), respectively, currently makes up a rather modest share of overall MFF spending during the 2021–2027 period; this should be reinforced. Cohesion funds, which reach almost 31% of overall MFF expenditures, should be restructured towards green cross-border investment projects. The proposals made by the Commission in its midterm review of the MFF published in June 2023, however, do not put a specific focus on reinforcing green investment (European Commission 2023b).

Moreover, the climate-mainstreaming target, that is, the envisaged share of climate-related spending in overall spending, needs to be aligned to the EU's climate targets. At the same time, the quality of climate-related spending needs to be ensured and improved. For this purpose, the current climate-accounting methodology should be developed further. Additional steps are also required to strengthen the performance framework for the EU budget, to complement the still-dominant input-oriented perspective with a result-oriented perspective. Not least, the DNSH principle needs to be implemented more strictly, based on clear and transparent criteria and without exceptions.

8.5 Conclusions

Additional green public investment at the Member-State level, at least partially debt-financed, will be needed to address the climate emergency as a central priority in the EU beyond the current policy cycle. The overall budgetary and fiscal EU framework needs to ensure these goals of higher green public investments are achieved. The Commission's proposal from November 2022 regarding orientations for a reform of the EU-governance framework widens the leeway for debt-financed public investment. However, existing green public investment needs are not considered sufficiently. Therefore, options (2), (3), or (4) discussed above should be followed through to enable the flexibility of national budgets to ensure a level of green public investment which—together with private resources—is sufficient to close the existing green-investment gaps.

In addition, the use of the lever the EU budget theoretically offers to contribute to green public investment in the EU needs to be intensified. At about 1% of EU GNI (1.7% of EU GNI including NGEU), the overall volume of the EU budget is limited. Steps must be taken to strengthen spending in policies that create EU value added, inter alia green public investment.

Any reform of EU fiscal rules accommodating GPI as well as reforms within the EU budget should be embedded in a broader mix of measures supporting the green

---

8   Horizon Europe.

transition in general and green private investment in particular. Here, carbon pricing, environmental taxation in general (including the repeal of the substantial fossil-fuel subsidies, which would increase fiscal space for GPI in MS), and environmental regulations are of particular importance; so, too, are long-term policy commitments providing investment security (Lenaerts et al. 2022). In any case, the upcoming reform of the EU fiscal framework as well as the upcoming MFF mid-term review and the post–2027 MFF need to account for the massive GPI needs confronting all EU MS, and they need to be better coordinated with the current initiatives to realise the EGD.

References

Andersen, T. (2021). 'Economic Policy Responses to the Coronavirus Crisis—Stabilization and Insurance'. *CESifo Forum*, 22(01), 14–19, https://www.cesifo.org/de/publikationen/2021/aufsatz-zeitschrift/economic-policy-responses-coronavirus-crisis-stabilization

Balassone, F., and D. Franco (2000). 'Public Investment, the Stability Pact and the "Golden Rule"'. *Fiscal Studies*, 21(2), 207–29

Bénassy-Quéré, A. (2022). 'How to Ensure that European Fiscal Rules Meet Investment'. *VoxEU Column, VoxEU CEPR Debate*, https://cepr.org/voxeu/columns/how-ensure-european-fiscal-rules-meet-investment

——, M. Brunnermeier, H. Enderlein, et al. (2018). 'Reconciling Risk Sharing with Market Discipline: A Constructive Approach to Euro Area Reform'. *CEPR Policy Insight*, 91, https://cepr.org/publications/policy-insight-91-reconciling-risk-sharing-market-discipline-constructive-approach

Bertram, L., J. Hafele, et al. (2022). 'New Fiscal Rules for the EU — Design Choices Matter'. ZOE Institute for Future-fit Economies, https://zoe-institut.de/en/publication/new-fiscal-rules-for-the-eu-design-choices-matter/

Claeys, G., and S. Tagliapietra (2020). 'A Trillion Reasons to Scrutinise the Green Deal Investment Plan'. *Bruegel Blog*, 15 January, https://www.bruegel.org/blog-post/trillion-reasons-scrutinise-green-deal-investment-plan

Cohen-Setton, J. and S. Vallée (2021). 'Measuring the European Fiscal Stance After COVID-19 from National and European Budget Plans'. *CESifo Forum*, 22(01), 26–36, https://www.cesifo.org/DocDL/CESifo-Forum-2021-1-cohen-setton-vall%C3%A9e-NGEU-january.pdf

Corti, F., C. Alcidi, et al. (2022). 'A Qualified Treatment for Green and Social Investments within a Revised EU Fiscal Framework'. *CEPS Research Report*, RR2022-02, https://cdn.ceps.eu/wp-content/uploads/2022/05/RR2022-02_Green-and-social-investments.pdf

D'Alfonso, A. (2020). 'European Green Deal Investment Plan. Main Elements and Possible Impact of the Coronavirus Pandemic'. *Briefing, European Parliamentary Research Service*, PE 649.371, https://www.europarl.europa.eu/RegData/etudes/BRIE/2020/649371/EPRS_BRI(2020)649371_EN.pdf

Darvas, Z. and G. B. Wolff (2021). 'A Green Fiscal Pact: Climate Investment in Times of Budget Consolidation'. *Bruegel Policy Brief*, https://www.bruegel.org/policy-brief/green-fiscal-pact-climate-investment-times-budget-consolidation

Delgado-Téllez, M., M. Ferdinandusse, and C. Nerlich (2022). 'Fiscal Policies to Mitigate Climate Change in the Euro Area'. *ECB Economic Bulletin Articles*, 6, https://www.ecb.europa.eu/pub/economic-bulletin/articles/2022/html/ecb.ebart202206_01~8324008da7.en.html

European Commission (2015). 'Making the Best Use of the Flexibility within the Existing Rules of the Stability and Growth Pact'. COM (2015), 12 Final, https://eur-lex.europa.eu/legal-content/EN/TXT/?uri=CELEX%3A52015DC0012&qid=1699363177272

—— (2019). 'United in Delivering the Energy Union and Climate Action: Setting the Foundations for a Successful Clean Energy Transition'. COM (2019), 285 Final, https://eur-lex.europa.eu/legal-content/EN/TXT/?uri=CELEX%3A52019DC0285&qid=1699363088364

—— (2021). 'The EU Economy After COVID-19: Implications for Economic Governance'. COM (2021), 662 Final, https://eur-lex.europa.eu/legal-content/EN/TXT/?uri=CELEX%3A52021DC0662

—— (2022a). 'Towards a Green, Digital and Resilient Economy. Our European Growth Model'. COM (2022), 83 Final, https://eur-lex.europa.eu/legal-content/EN/TXT/PDF/?uri=CELEX:52022DC0083

—— (2022b). 'Communication on Orientations for a Reform of the EU Economic Governance Framework'. COM (2022), 583 Final, https://eur-lex.europa.eu/legal-content/EN/TXT/PDF/?uri=CELEX:52022DC0583&from=EN

—— (2022c). 'A European Sovereignty Fund for an Industry "Made in Europe"'. Blog of Commissioner Thierry Breton, 15 September 2022, https://ec.europa.eu/commission/presscorner/detail/en/STATEMENT_22_5543

—— (2023a). 'Report from the Commission to the European Parliament and the Council on the Implementation of the Recovery and Resilience Facility: Moving Forward'. COM (2023), 545 Final/2, https://commission.europa.eu/system/files/2023-09/COM_2023_545_1_EN_0.pdf

—— (2023b). 'Proposal for a Council Regulation Amending Regulation (EU, Euratom) 2020/2093 Laying Down the Multiannual Financial Framework for the Years 2021 to 2027'. COM(2023), 337 Final, https://commission.europa.eu/system/files/2023-06/COM_2023_337_1_EN_ACT_part1_v3.pdf

European Court of Auditors (2021). 'Common Agricultural Policy and Climate—Half of EU Climate Spending but Farm Emissions are not Decreasing'. *Special Report*, 16, https://www.eca.europa.eu/Lists/ECADocuments/SR21_16/SR_CAP-and-Climate_EN.pdf

—— (2022). 'Climate Spending in the 2014–2020 EU Budget—Not as High as Reported'. *Special Report*, 9, https://www.eca.europa.eu/lists/ecadocuments/sr22_09/sr_climate-mainstreaming_en.pdf

European Fiscal Board (2019). 'Assessment of EU Fiscal Rules—With a Focus on the Six and Two-Pack Legislation', https://commission.europa.eu/system/files/2019-09/2019-09-10-assessment-of-eu-fiscal-rules_en.pdf

European Investment Bank (2021). 'EIB Investment Report 2020/2021: Building a Smart and Green Europe in the COVID-19 Era', https://www.eib.org/attachments/efs/economic_investment_report_2020_2021_en.pdf

Fournier, J.-M. (2016). 'The Positive Effect of Public Investment on Potential Growth'. OECD Economic Department Working Paper, 1347, https://doi.org/10.1787/15e400d4-en

Friis, J. W., R. Torre, and M. Buti (2022). 'How to Make the EU Fiscal Framework Fit for the Challenges of this Decade'. *VoxEU*, CEPR Policy Portal, https://cepr.org/voxeu/columns/how-make-eu-fiscal-framework-fit-challenges-decade

Garicano, L. (2022). 'Combining Environmental and Fiscal Sustainability: A New Climate Facility, an Expenditure Rule, and an Independent Fiscal Agency'. *VoxEU Column*, VoxEU CEPR Debate, https://cepr.org/voxeu/columns/combining-environmental-and-fiscal-sustainability-new-climate-facility-expenditure

Lenaerts, K., S. Tagliapietra, and G. B. Wolff (2022). 'The Global Quest for Green Growth: An Economic Policy Perspective'. *Sustainability*, 14(5555), https://doi.org/10.3390/su14095555

Levarlet, F., M. Alessandrini, et. al (2022). 'Climate Mainstreaming in the EU Budget: 2022 Update'. European Parliament, https://www.europarl.europa.eu/RegData/etudes/STUD/2022/732007/IPOL_STU(2022)732007_EN.pdf

Musgrave, R. A. (1939). 'The Nature of Budgetary Balance and the Case for the Capital Budget'. *American Economic Review*, 29(2), 260–71

Pekanov, A., and M. Schratzenstaller (2020). 'The Role of Fiscal Rules in Relation with the Green Economy'. *Committee on Economic and Monetary Affairs, European Parliament*, https://www.europarl.europa.eu/RegData/etudes/STUD/2020/614524/IPOL_STU(2020)614524_EN.pdf

—— (2023). 'A Targeted Golden Rule for Public Investments? A Comparative Analysis of Possible Accounting Methods in the Context of the Review of the Stability and Growth Pact'. Economic Governance and EMU Scrutiny Unit, European Parliament, https://www.europarl.europa.eu/RegData/etudes/IDAN/2023/733760/IPOL_IDA(2023)733760_EN.pdf

Storm, S. and C. W. M. Naastepad (2016). 'Myths, Mix-ups, and Mishandlings: Understanding the Eurozone Crisis'. *International Journal of Political Economy*, 45(1), 46–71, https://doi.org/10.1080/08911916.2016.1159084

Ubide, Á. (2019). 'Fiscal Policy at the Zero Lower Bound'. *Intereconomics: Review of European Economic Policy*, 54(5), 279–85, https://doi.org/10.1007/s10272-019-0839-7

Yakita, A. (1994). 'Public Investment Criterion with Distorted Capital Markets in an Overlapping Generations Economy'. *Journal of Macroeconomics*, 16(4), 715–28, https://doi.org/10.1016/0164-0704(94)90009-4

9. Financing Climate Investment in the EU: the Role of Monetary and Financial Policies

Yannis Dafermos and Maria Nikolaidi

The climate crisis requires an unprecedented transformation of the EU fiscal, industrial, trade, and regulatory policy frameworks. However, this transformation needs to be supported by the greening of the EU monetary and financial policies. This would facilitate the financing of the large amount of investment in climate mitigation and adaptation that is needed in the coming years. In this chapter, we present a set of tools that central banks, financial regulators, and financial supervisors can employ to advance the EU decarbonisation and climate resilience targets. We highlight that these tools should be used in a context of a concrete 'sticks and carrots' policy mix framework that moves beyond market-based approaches.

9.1 Introduction

The EU needs to urgently increase its investment in climate mitigation and adaptation. Climate mitigation investments in renewables, energy efficiency, and green technologies are essential for achieving the EU 2050 net-zero target. Climate adaptation investments in flood defences, climate-smart agriculture, water management, early-warning systems, and climate-resilient transport are necessary for limiting the adverse effects of increasing global warming on EU economies and societies.

Fiscal, industrial, trade, and regulatory policies have a prominent role to play in scaling up climate investment and reducing carbon-intensive investment. The combined use of carbon taxes, green subsidies, green public investment, and regulations about carbon-intensive goods/assets is a prerequisite for achieving climate targets. However, monetary and financial policy tools also have a crucial role to play in shifting investment from 'dirty' projects towards green projects and facilitating the financing of the additional investment that is necessary to decarbonise EU economies and increase climate resilience.

https://doi.org/10.11647/OBP.0386.09

In this chapter, we analyse two categories of monetary/financial- tools that can be used to support climate investment in Europe: (i) central banking tools and (ii) financial regulation/supervision tools.[1] Table 9.1 provides an overview of selected monetary/ financial policy tools and their potential climate calibrations. In the rest of the chapter, we analyse these tools in detail and discuss how they can be applied in the EU.

Table 9.1 Selected Monetary/Financial Tools for Greening Public and Private Investment

Category	Monetary/financial tool	Climate calibration
Central banking	Collateral frameworks	Lower haircuts for green (public and private) assets; higher haircuts and exclusion for dirty private assets
	Asset purchases	Tilting of purchases towards greener (public and private) assets; exclusion of dirty private assets
	Refinancing operations	Lower refinancing rates for banks with a high representation of green loans on their balance sheet; higher rates for banks with many dirty loans on their balance sheet
Financial regulation/supervision	Capital requirements	Lower capital requirements for green loans; higher capital requirements for dirty loans; one-for-one fossil-based rule
	Credit controls	Dirty credit ceilings; green credit floors
	Mandatory disclosures	Prudential climate transition and resilience plans on how banks intend to align their financial investments with net zero and climate resilience targets

Note: In the transactions between financial institutions, the 'haircut' captures the difference between the market value of the asset that is used as collateral and the value of the loan that can be obtained against this asset. The lower the haircut, the higher the loan that the borrower can receive for a given value of the collateral.
Source: Authors' elaboration.

---

1   Due to space constraints, our list of monetary/financial tools is not comprehensive. For example, we have not explicitly analysed tools related to shadow banking; on such tools, see Gabor et al. (2019) and Kedward et al. (2022). We have also not explicitly analysed the role of public banking.

9.2 Central Banking Tools

There are three main policy tools that central banks can use to support decarbonisation and climate adaptation. All these tools require approaches that identify how strong or weak is the climate performance of specific financial assets (for example, bonds or loans). Climate performance can be captured by metrics that reflect (i) the emissions profile of borrowers both in the past and the future, (ii) the activities that borrowers engage in (if they are environmentally harmful or if they contribute to mitigation/ adaptation based on taxonomies of activities), and (iii) the association of specific financial instruments with climate mitigation/adaptation projects (for example, green bonds).[2]

The first tool is the greening of collateral frameworks. Central bank collateral frameworks identify the types of financial assets that commercial banks can use to get access to central bank liquidity (Dafermos et al. 2022). In general, the assets that are included in collateral frameworks experience higher demand in the financial markets. This tends to reduce the interest rates of these assets and, thus, the cost of borrowing for their issuers (see, for example, Nguyen 2020; Pelizzon et al. 2020). In addition, the demand for financial assets is generally higher for those assets that are assigned a lower haircut in collateral frameworks. Therefore, central banks' decisions about which assets to include in collateral frameworks (and what haircuts to assign to them) affect the cost of borrowing for issuers of securities.

The greening of collateral frameworks can be associated with several types of assets. First, the greening can be applied to non-financial corporate bonds. This is particularly important because existing collateral frameworks typically suffer from a carbon bias in the sense that bonds related to carbon-intensive activities of companies are over-represented in these frameworks (see Dafermos et al. (2021) for the case of the Eurosystem collateral framework).[3] Increasing the haircuts for bonds issued by companies with weak climate performance and reducing the haircuts for green corporate bonds and bonds issued by strong climate performers can help the decarbonisation of the corporate bond markets and can financially support investments in climate mitigation and adaptation.

Second, green bonds issued by governments and national or supranational public banks can receive preferential treatment in central banks' collateral frameworks. Over the last years, a growing number of European governments have been issuing green sovereign bonds (see Figure 9.1). Poland and France were the first governments that did so in 2016 and 2017. Since then, many other EU governments have also issued green

---

2   For more details, see, for example, Dafermos et al. (2023).

3   This over-representation is primarily related to the fact that companies that engage in carbon-intensive activities tend to have a high representation in the bond market (to some extent because of their large size) and they typically receive good credit ratings.

bonds for the financing of specific green projects.[4] Many green bonds have also been issued by national and supranational public investment banks, such as the European Investment Bank and KfW. Making these bonds eligible in central bank collateral frameworks with relatively low haircuts can help reduce the cost that governments and public banks face when they invest in climate mitigation and adaptation.

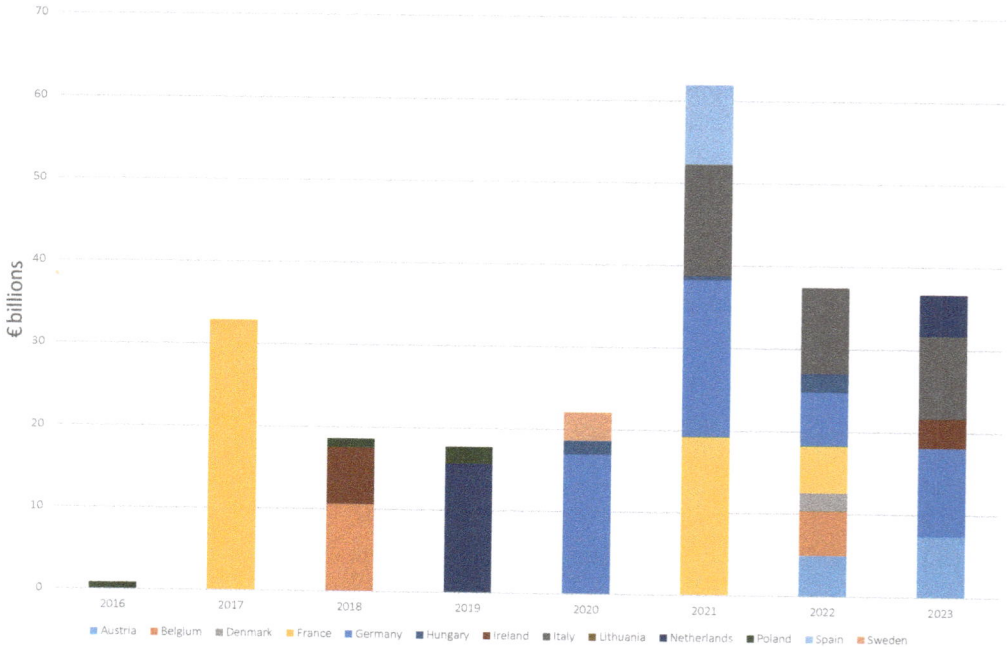

Fig. 9.1 Green Sovereign Bonds, Issued Amounts in EU countries, 2016–2023 (in €bn).
Note: The 2023 data include bonds issued as of October 2023.
Source: Refinitiv Eikon

Third, central banks can incorporate climate criteria into the eligibility and haircuts associated with asset-backed securities and covered bonds issued by financial institutions. This would prompt financial institutions to green the loans that they provide to households and firms. However, the data requirements for the greening of this component of collateral frameworks are generally higher than what is the case with public and non-financial corporate bonds.

The second tool that central banks can use to support climate mitigation and adaptation is the greening of asset purchases. As part of their unconventional policies, the European Central Bank (ECB) and other EU central banks have bought several types of assets, including securities issued by governments, public banks, non-financial corporations, and financial institutions. Central banks can tilt these purchases based

---

4   There is some evidence for the existence of a 'sovereign greenium': green sovereign bonds enjoy a lower yield relative to similar conventional sovereign bonds (see Ando et al. 2023).

on climate criteria. In other words, they can buy more bonds with a stronger climate performance and less bonds characterised by a weaker climate performance. During the current period, one in which central banks are shrinking their balance sheets as a response to high inflation, tilting implies (i) the purchase of greener assets for reinvestments that central banks conduct due to maturing securities and (ii) the active selling of carbon-intensive bonds of non-financial corporations and their partial replacement with greener assets.

The third tool that central banks can use is the greening of their refinancing operations. Through refinancing operations, commercial banks get access to short-term and long-term liquidity. The terms under which they get access to this liquidity can have implications for their credit provision decisions. To make refinancing operations greener, central banks can reduce the interest rates for banks that have a relatively high proportion of green loans on their balance sheets and set higher refinancing rates for banks that provide too many dirty loans.[5] This would help the decarbonisation of both corporate and mortgage loans.[6]

All these tools can be applied by European central banks. Importantly, the ECB has already attempted to decarbonise its corporate bond purchases as part of its climate action plan. In October 2022, it started applying climate criteria to the corporate bonds bought as part of its reinvestments (ECB 2022b).[7] However, the ECB stopped the majority of its reinvestments in July 2023, effectively terminating the decarbonisation of its corporate-bond purchases (ECB 2023). To continue the decarbonisation of its asset purchases, the ECB can start selling bonds issued by companies with a weak climate performance, replacing them with bonds that are conducive to climate mitigation and adaptation (see Dafermos et al. 2023). The ECB can also consider supporting more actively green bonds issued by EU governments and public banks.[8]

The ECB has considered greening its collateral framework in its climate action plan (ECB 2022a). However, it has not yet taken any concrete actions and, in December 2022, it announced that it does not intend to incorporate climate considerations into the haircuts of its collateral framework.[9] Given the fact that the Eurosystem collateral

---

5   Green refinancing schemes have been adopted, for example, by the Bangladesh Bank, the People's Bank of China (PBoC) and the Bank of Japan. In 2009, the Bangladesh Bank established a refinancing scheme to support specific green projects (see Khairunnessa et al. 2021). In 2021, the PBoC launched the Carbon Emission Reduction Facility which offers low-interest loans to financial institutions that help firms decarbonise their operations (see PBoC 2021). In the same year, the Bank of Japan introduced a green loans scheme, providing zero-interest financing to lenders supporting climate-related projects (see Shirai 2022).

6   For a proposal on how to green the ECB's Targeted Longer-term Refinancing Operations (TLTROs), see van't Klooster and van Tilburg (2020) and van't Klooster (2022). For the carbon content of TLTRO III, see Colesanti Senni et al. (2023).

7   As of July 2023, the entire Eurosystem corporate bond portfolio was about €385 billion. Reinvestments were a small proportion of this portfolio (less than 10% on an annual basis).

8   This should not, however, change the ECB's purchases of non-green sovereign bonds.

9   The rationale that the ECB used to support this decision was that the existing haircuts schedule is sufficiently protective against climate risks. See ECB (2022c).

framework is a permanent central-banking tool, its greening is particularly important and the ECB should revisit its decision to postpone the incorporation of climate issues into the collateral framework. Moreover, the ECB and other EU central banks could design the greening of their refinancing operations. This is particularly important in the current environment of high interest rates. Green refinancing operations can help keep the interest rate on green loans and mortgages relatively low, encouraging green investments which often have high upfront costs and, thus, require external finance more than traditional investments.[10]

9.3 Financial Regulation/Supervision Tools

Currently, a significant amount of the financing that is provided to companies by EU banks supports dirty activities. For example, BNP Paribas, Deutsche Bank, and ING collectively provided more than $300bn of fossil fuel-related loans during the period 2016 to 2022 (Figure 9.2). Redirecting bank flows from such dirty activities towards green ones is, therefore, significant for greening assets related to buildings, manufacturing, power, and transport in the private sector. The greening of bank credit is also important since the private non-financial sector in the EU still relies significantly on bank loans for the financing of their activities. For example, more than 60% of the external finance for non-financial corporations in the euro area comes from bank loans (see Holm-Hadulla 2022), with this being more prominent in the case of Small and Medium-sized Enterprises (SMEs) (ECB 2021). On top of it, banks need to green the mortgages they provide to households. This would support residential investment for the decarbonisation of the housing stock in Europe, which, in many countries, is very energy inefficient and relies too much on fossil fuels for heating.

---

10   See Bloomberg (2023).

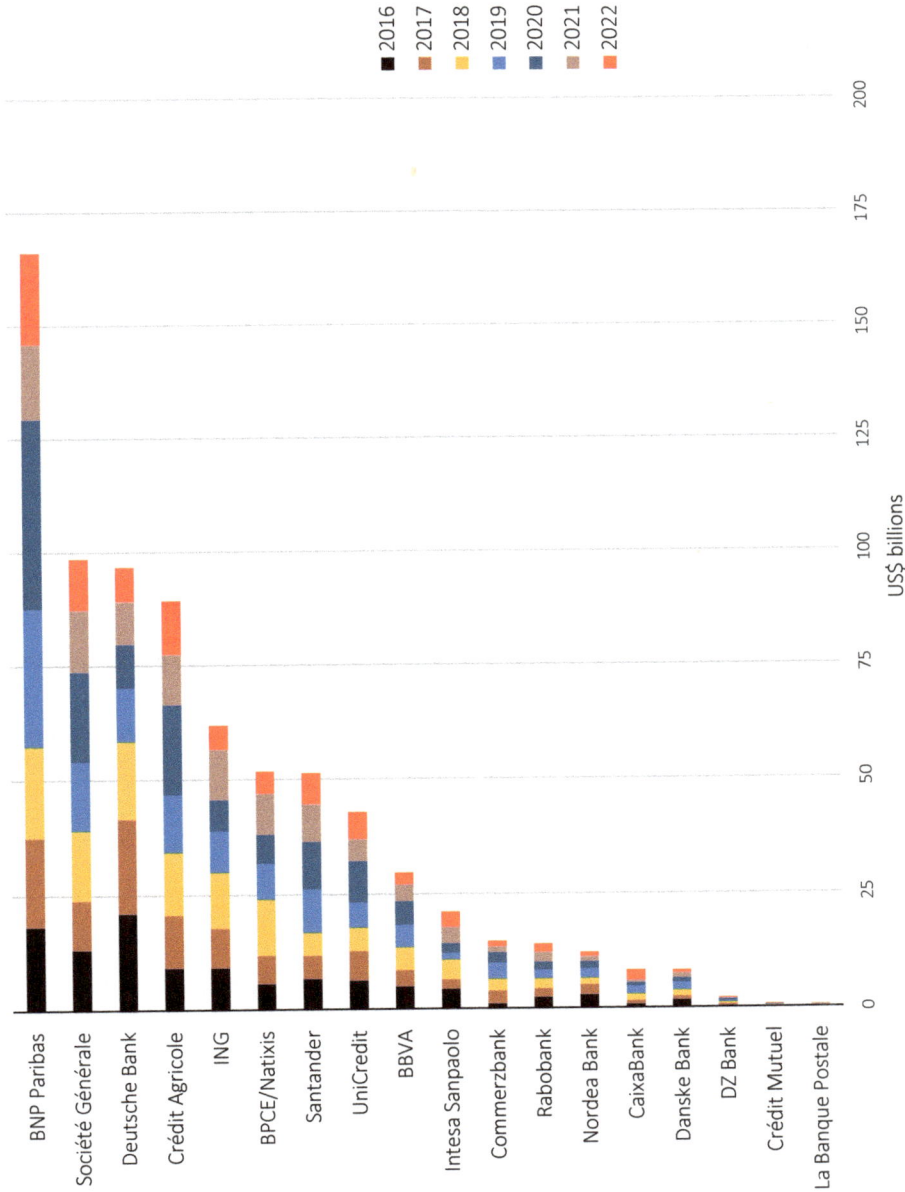

Fig. 9.2 Bank Financing of Fossil Fuels, EU, 2016–2022 (in US$bn).

Note: Fossil fuels include tar sands oil, Arctic oil and gas, fracked oil and gas, liquefied natural gas, ultra coal power, and coal mining.

Source: Rainforest Action Network (RAN), https://www.ran.org/

Apart from the greening of refinancing operations, a wide range of financial tools can be used to make bank financing climate-aligned. First of all, there are several tools related to capital requirements. One example is the green-differentiated capital requirements that can take the form of a green supporting factor, whereby the capital requirements against green loans are reduced, and/or a dirty penalising factor, whereby the capital requirements against dirty loans increase (Dafermos and Nikolaidi 2021; 2022). Such requirements can increase the lending interest rate and reduce credit availability for dirty loans compared to green loans. In the EU, a specific form of a green-supporting factor has been applied in Hungary (see MNB 2019; 2021). Magyar Nemzeti Bank (MNB) has lowered capital requirements that are linked to energy-efficient properties for the period 2020–2024 (see also CBI 2020). A specific case of a dirty-penalising factor is the one-for-one fossil-based rule. This rule suggests that banks should hold one euro of capital for each euro of loan that they provide to finance a fossil-fuel project (Philipponnat 2020). This would make fossil financing extremely expensive for banks.

However, climate-adjusted capital requirements might not lead to a significant reallocation of credit. A more direct way of achieving a green reallocation is the use of credit controls (Kedward et al. 2022). These can take the form of dirty credit ceilings that put a cap on the amount of credit that banks provide to borrowers with a poor climate performance. They can also take the form of green credit floors that make it compulsory for banks to allocate a specific proportion of their credit to green projects/borrowers with a strong climate performance.[11]

Generally speaking, EU financial regulators are reluctant to use the above-mentioned tools. As far as capital requirements are concerned, an issue that is often raised by financial regulators is that these adjustments in requirements are not risk-based. Thus, regulators are willing to consider climate adjustments in requirements only if it can be proved that green credit is less risky than dirty credit. Although the latter might be true, this way of looking at risks is narrow and micro-based. From a macroprudential perspective, any tool that decarbonises the financial system and supports climate adaptation finance can reduce climate-related systemic risks. There are at least three reasons for that. First, a decarbonised financial system can be more resilient to shocks related to future climate policies, such as carbon taxes and environmental regulation, which can disproportionately affect borrowers with a high climate footprint. Second, the active support of green credit and the discouragement of dirty credit can be conducive to lower EU emissions and, thus, lower global warming. This, in turn, can make the global financial system less exposed to physical risks associated with climate-related events and physical phenomena linked to the gradual increase in temperature (such as the rise in sea level). Third, any financial regulation that supports climate adaptation can make the EU economies less climate vulnerable. This, in turn, can reduce the financial fragility of the banking sector.

---

11   Green credit floors have been used, for instance, by the Bangladesh Bank and the Reserve Bank of India (see Baer et al. 2021).

Therefore, EU regulators need to be more open to the idea of using some forms of climate credit controls. Although credit controls have become an unfashionable tool in Europe over the last decades, the severity of the climate crisis and the failure of markets to address this crisis suggests that a rethinking of credit controls is necessary. Climate credit controls can be successful under two conditions. First, the definition of what is 'green' and what is 'dirty' should not be sector-based. It should, instead, rely on micro-based metrics about the climate performance of borrowers. Second, the evaluation of credit risk should continue to take place, including the evaluation of climate-related financial risks. This evaluation should be reflected in capital requirements. This would mean that only 'green' borrowers with relatively low risks would benefit from climate credit controls.

Financial supervision also has a useful role to play in supporting climate investments in the EU. One tool that financial supervisors can use is the climate transition and resilience plans which can take the form of mandatory disclosures about how banks intend to align their financial investments with the EU net zero and climate resilience targets.[12] Financial supervisors can ask banks to submit these plans within a certain time horizon and, if they find them unsatisfactory, they can apply penalties to banks, for example by asking them to hold more capital.

9.4 Conclusions

Monetary and financial tools can play a significant supportive role in achieving the EU targets for climate investment. Central banks, governments, and financial authorities across Europe can select among the tools that we included in our toolbox based on their national needs and mandates. But, to successfully do so, they need to move beyond conventional economic thinking that typically opposes the use of policies that are considered too interventionist from a market perspective. Instead, EU public institutions and governments should adopt a systems-based economic thinking that permits a more holistic understanding of the interactions between climate, economic, financial, and social systems. From a political economy perspective, this thinking suggests that market-based approaches that rely on derisking (Gabor 2023) are unlikely to succeed. Instead, a concrete 'sticks and carrots' policy mix is necessary whereby monetary/financial policy tools are implemented in conjunction with other climate fiscal, trade, and regulation policies that incentivise green investments and penalise dirty spending. EU authorities and governments also need to apply such a policy mix in a way that is consistent with global climate justice issues. Green investments are often associated with green extractivist practices that harm ecosystems and communities in the Global South (Dafermos 2023). The EU has a historical responsibility to achieve a quick decarbonisation without increasing its exploitation of the Global South.

12　For a comprehensive discussion of net zero transition plans, see Dikau et al. (2022).

References

Ando, S., C. Fu, F. Roch, and U. Wiriadinata (2023). 'How Large is the Sovereign Greenium?', IMF Working Paper 23, https://www.imf.org/en/Publications/WP/Issues/2023/04/07/How-Large-is-the-Sovereign-Greenium-530332

Baer, M., E. Campiglio, and J. Deyris (2021). 'It Takes Two to Dance: Institutional Dynamics and Climate-related Financial Policies', *Ecological Economics*, 190, 107210, https://doi.org/10.1016/j.ecolecon.2021.107210

Bloomberg (2023). 'Europe Faces an Inflation-regime Reckoning over Climate Goals', 17 June 2023, https://www.bloomberg.com/news/articles/2023-06-17/europe-faces-an-inflation-regime-reckoning-over-climate-goals?leadSource=uverify%20wall

Colesanti Senni, C., M. S. Pagliari, and J. van't Klooster (2023). 'The CO2 Content of the TLTRO III Scheme and its Greening', Grantham Research Institute on Climate Change and the Environment Working Paper 398, https://www.lse.ac.uk/granthaminstitute/publication/the-co2-content-of-the-tltro-iii-scheme-and-its-greening/

Climate Bonds Initiative (2020). 'How the Hungarian Central Bank could Help Solve the Energy Efficiency Puzzle: MNB Goes for Green on Housing Loans, 7 January 2020, https://www.climatebonds.net/2020/01/how-hungarian-central-bank-could-help-solve-energy-efficiency-puzzle-mnb-goes-green-housing

Dafermos, Y. (2023). 'Towards a Climate Just Financial System', SOAS Department of Economics Working Paper 259, https://eprints.soas.ac.uk/39680/

—— and M. Nikolaidi (2021). 'How can Green Differentiated Capital Requirements Affect Climate Risks? A Dynamic Macrofinancial Analysis', *Journal of Financial Stability*, 54, 100871, https://doi.org/10.1016/j.jfs.2021.100871

—— and M. Nikolaidi (2022). 'Greening Capital Requirements', INSPIRE Central Banking Toolbox—Policy Briefing 8. Grantham Research Institute on Climate Change and the Environment, London School of Economics and Political Science

——, D. Gabor, et al. (2021). 'Greening the Eurosystem Collateral Framework: How to Decarbonise the ECB's Monetary Policy', New Economics Foundation, https://neweconomics.org/2021/03/greening-the-eurosystem-collateral-framework

——, D. Gabor, et al. (2022). 'Greening Collateral Frameworks', INSPIRE Central Banking Toolbox—Policy Briefing 7. Grantham Research Institute on Climate Change and the Environment, London School of Economics and Political Science, https://www.lse.ac.uk/granthaminstitute/publication/greening-capital-requirements/

——, D. Gabor, et al. (2023). 'Broken Promises: The ECB's Widening Paris Gap', SOAS University of London; University of Greenwich; University of the West of England; Greenpeace, https://www.inspiregreenfinance.org/publications/greening-collateral-frameworks/

Dikau, S., N. Robins, et al. (2022). 'Net Zero Transition Plans: A Supervisory Playbook for Prudential Authorities'. Grantham Research Institute on Climate Change and the Environment and Centre for Climate Change Economics and Policy, London School of Economics and Political Science, https://www.lse.ac.uk/granthaminstitute/publication/net-zero-transition-plans-a-supervisory-playbook-for-prudential-authorities/

ECB (2021). 'Survey on the Access to Finance of Enterprises (SAFE)', ECB Surveys, https://www.ecb.europa.eu/stats/ecb_surveys/safe/html/ecb.safe202111~0380b0c0a2.en.html#toc8

ECB (2022a). 'ECB Takes Further Steps to Incorporate Climate Change into its Monetary Policy Operations', ECB Press Release, 4 July 2022, https://www.ecb.europa.eu/press/pr/date/2022/html/ecb.pr220704~4f48a72462.en.html

—— (2022b). 'ECB Provides Details on how it Aims to Decarbonise its Corporate Bond Holdings', ECB Press Release, 19 September 2022, https://www.ecb.europa.eu/press/pr/date/2022/html/ecb.pr220919~fae53c59bd.en.html

—— (2022c). 'ECB Reviews its Risk Control Framework for Credit Operations', ECB Press Release, 20 December 2022, https://www.ecb.europa.eu/press/pr/date/2022/html/ecb.pr221220_1~ca6ca2cc09.mt.html

—— (2023). 'Monetary Policy Decisions', ECB Press Release, 4 May 2023, https://www.ecb.europa.eu/press/pr/date/2023/html/ecb.mp230504~cdfd11a697.en.html

Gabor, D. (2023). 'The (European) Derisking State', *SocArXiv*, Center for Open Science, https://doi.org/10.31235/osf.io/hpbj2

——, Y. Dafermos, et al. (2019). 'Finance and Climate Change: a Progressive Green Finance Strategy for the UK', Report of the Independent Panel Commissioned by Shadow Chancellor of the Exchequer John McDonnell MP, https://labour.org.uk/wp-content/uploads/2019/11/12851_19-Finance-and-Climate-Change-Report.pdf

Holm-Hadulla, F., A. Musso, G. Nicoletti and M. Tujula (2022). 'Firm Debt Financing Structures and the Transmission of Shocks in the Euro Area', *ECB Economic Bulletin*, 4/2022, https://www.ecb.europa.eu/pub/economic-bulletin/articles/2022/html/ecb.ebart202204_02~b35a8321b7.en.html

Kedward, K., D. Gabor, and J. Ryan-Collins (2022). 'A Modern Credit Guidance Regime for the Green Transition', SUERF Policy Note 294, https://www.suerf.org/policynotes/59121/a-modern-credit-guidance-regime-for-the-green-transition

Khairunnessa, F., D.A. Vazquez-Brust, and N. Yakovleva. 'A Review of the Recent Developments of Green Banking in Bangladesh', *Sustainability*, 13, 1904, https://doi.org/10.3390/su13041904

Magyar Nemzeti Bank [MNB] (2019). 'MNB Introduces a Green Preferential Capital Requirement Programme'. Press Release, December, https://www.mnb.hu/en/pressroom/press-releases/press-releases-2019/mnb-introduces-a-green-preferential-capital-requirement-programme

—— (2021). 'Notice on the criteria for the Preferential Green Capital Requirement Treatment for housing loans'. February, https://www.mnb.hu/letoltes/notice-preferential-green-capital-requirement.pdf

Nguyen, M. (2020). 'Collateral Haircuts and Bond Yields in the European Government Bond Markets', *International Review of Financial Analysis*, 69, 101467, https://doi.org/10.1016/j.irfa.2020.101467

People's Bank of China [PBoC] (2021). 'PBOC Officials Answer Press Questions on the Launch of Carbon Emission Reduction Facility', http://www.pbc.gov.cn/en/3688006/3995557/4385447/index.html

Philipponnat, T. (2020). 'Breaking the Climate-Finance Doom Loop'. Finance Watch, June, https://www.finance-watch.org/publication/breaking-the-climate-finance-doom-loop/

Pelizzon, L., M. Riedel, et al. (2020). 'Collateral Eligibility of Corporate Debt in the Eurosystem'. SAFE Working Paper 275. Leibniz Institute for Financial Research, https://safe-frankfurt.de/publications/working-papers/details/publicationname/collateral-eligibility-of-corporate-debt-in-the-eurosystem-950.html

Shirai, S. (2022). 'Japan's Green Lending Scheme Presents Opportunities and Challenges', Green Central Banking, 2 August 2022, https://greencentralbanking.com/2022/08/02/japan-green-lending-scheme-sayuri-shirai/

van't Klooster, J. (2022). 'The European Central Bank's Strategy, Environmental Policy and the New Inflation: A Case for Interest Rate Differentiation', Grantham Research Institute on Climate Change and the Environment and Centre for Climate Change Economics and Policy, London School of Economics and Political Science, https://www.lse.ac.uk/granthaminstitute/publication/the-european-central-banks-strategy-environmental-policy-and-the-new-inflation/

——— and R. van Tilburg (2020). 'Targeting a Sustainable Recovery with Green TLTROs', Positive Money Europe, September, https://www.positivemoney.eu/2020/09/green-tltros/

10. In Search of Lost Time: An Ensemble of Policies to Restore Fiscal Progressivity and Address the Climate Challenge

Demetrio Guzzardi, Elisa Palagi, Tommaso Faccio, and Andrea Roventini

The European Union needs to raise significant resources to finance a just green transition. At the same time, there is a widespread fiscal regressivity in many EU countries. Indeed, recent empirical evidence shows that the tax systems of many EU members are characterised by low degrees of progressivity, with high-income groups paying lower effective tax rates vis-à-vis middle- and low-income classes. In order to jointly tackle such issues, we propose an ensemble of tax policies at the EU level that are grounded on recent proposals advanced in the literature. This fiscal reform includes a wealth tax targeting the top 1% of wealth holders, a tax on unrealised capital gains, and an increase of the minimum corporate tax. Our first estimates suggest that these measures can generate substantial yearly revenues in the order of 1.9%–2.9% of EU GDP. Such resources can contribute to the funding of the additional climate mitigation and adaptation policies required to tackle the climate emergency, while reducing inequality, thus contributing to put EU economies on sustainable and inclusive growth pathways.

10.1 Introduction

The last decades have witnessed trends of increasing income and wealth inequality in most countries of the European Union (EU), accompanied by sluggish growth (Piketty 2014; Blanchet et al. 2022; Guzzardi et al. 2023; Blanchet and Martínez-Toledano 2023). Such concentration of income and wealth is favoured by inequitable tax systems (Roine et al. 2009; Rubolino and Waldenström 2020). Indeed, not only have top income-tax rates progressively fallen but the globalised economic system has also allowed for the existence of several loopholes at the disposal of multinationals and billionaires to move

https://doi.org/10.11647/OBP.0386.10

their capital and elude taxation (Zucman 2014). This has resulted in an international race to the bottom, which has further reduced tax rates for corporate and personal income.

At the same time, the tall societal challenges of climate change require large amounts of resources to finance mitigation and adaptation policies. Indeed, the European Union has committed to the ambitious goals to cut its greenhouse-gas (GHG) emissions by at least 55% by 2030. Moreover, the costs of climate-change impacts and mitigation policies are unequally distributed across the population (Markkanen and Anger-Kraavi 2019; Taconet et al. 2020), disproportionately hitting those in the bottom part of the income distribution. At the same time, the most affluent individuals are responsible for the bulk of the emissions in high-income countries (Chancel 2022). Therefore, inequality and climate change need to be jointly addressed.

In this chapter, we first assess how taxation has evolved over the recent decades in developed countries and how it has impacted inequality trends. What emerges is that the degree of progressivity of tax systems has decreased so much that in the USA and in EU countries for which evidence exists, the richest part of society pays lower effective tax rates than the rest of the population. The tax system of the USA and of many EU countries has thus become 'regressive'.

We then present some policy proposals advanced in the literature to restore the progressivity of the tax systems. More specifically, we consider a package of fiscal interventions that can be introduced in the European Union, namely an EU-wide wealth tax, a taxation scheme for unrealised capital gains, and different tools to increase corporate taxation. We discuss how the potential issues related to their implementation can be addressed. Our first estimates show that the proposed tax reform could considerably boost EU tax revenues in the order of 1.9% – 2.9% of EU GDP in 2022. Moreover, our tax reform would reduce income and wealth inequality as each of the proposed measures is able to increase fiscal revenues by taxing the richest individuals of the income distribution without affecting the rest of the population.

By restoring the lost progressivity of their fiscal system, EU governments could reap the necessary resources needed to tackle the climate emergency. We find that the revenues generated by our fiscal package can finance the EU mitigation and adaptation policies while increasing the fiscal burden for the top part of the income distribution, which is responsible for most of EU GHG emissions (Chancel 2022).

The rest of the chapter is organised as follows: Section 10.2 considers recent empirical evidence regarding the progressivity of the tax system in various countries. Section 10.3 examines three primary proposals at the European level to reinstate the lost progressivity of the fiscal system and to fund policies for a fair green transition. These proposals include a wealth tax focused on the wealthiest individuals (Section 10.3.1), a capital-gains tax (Section 10.3.2), and a minimum corporate tax (Section 10.3.3). Section 10.4 discusses how the additional resources collected at the EU level can finance a fair transition towards a greener economy, and, lastly, Section 10.5 concludes the discussion.

10.2 Recent Worrying Trends in Tax Progressivity

Tax progressivity has been decreasing since the 1980s in most regions of the world, although with country specificities. Such a trend is largely due to lower taxes at higher income levels (Peter et al. 2010), and this is particularly the case for advanced countries (Bozio et al. 2018; Saez and Zucman 2019b; Bruil et al. 2022; Guzzardi et al. 2023). In the USA, Saez and Zucman (2019b) estimate tax incidence on the whole income distribution and find that the effective tax rate (obtained by jointly considering different categories of taxes) was steeply progressive in the 1950s but, by 2018, has turned into a flat tax over the income distribution with regressive rates for the richest 0.01%. Figure 10.1 depicts average tax rates for different income groups in the United States. It strikingly shows the freefall in progressivity at the top of the income distribution, with the top 400 of income earners decreasing their tax rate from around 70% in 1950 to just above 20% in 1980. Moreover, Figure 10.1 shows that the regressivity at the very top of the distribution is a recent phenomenon stemming from specific policy choices.

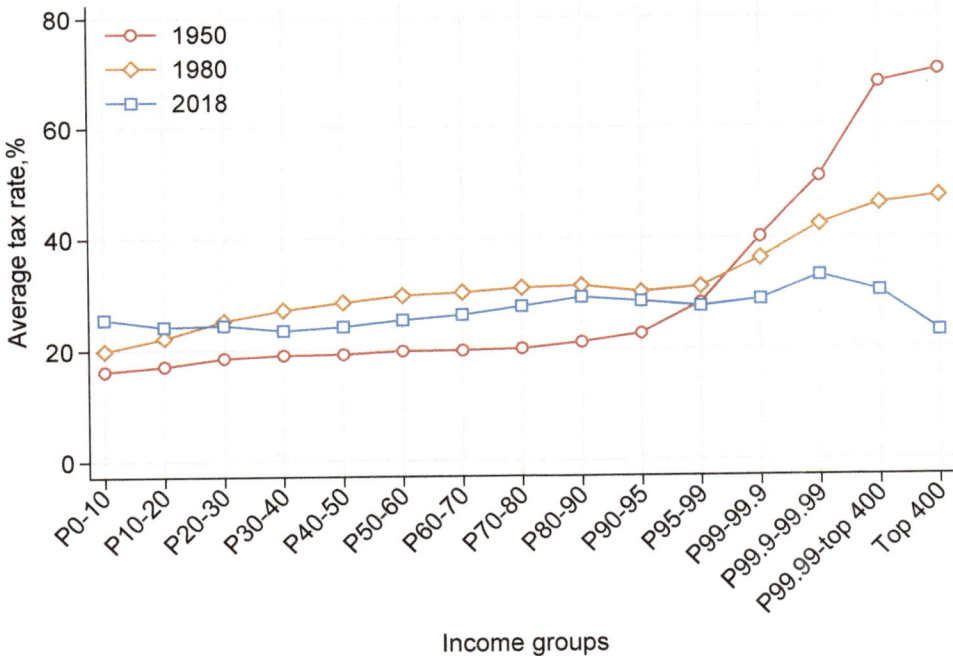

Fig. 10.1 Average Tax Rates by Income Group in the United States.
Note: P0-10 on the x-axis stands for the income group from percentile 0 to percentile 10. Analogously for other income groups.
Source: Data are from Saez and Zucman (2020).

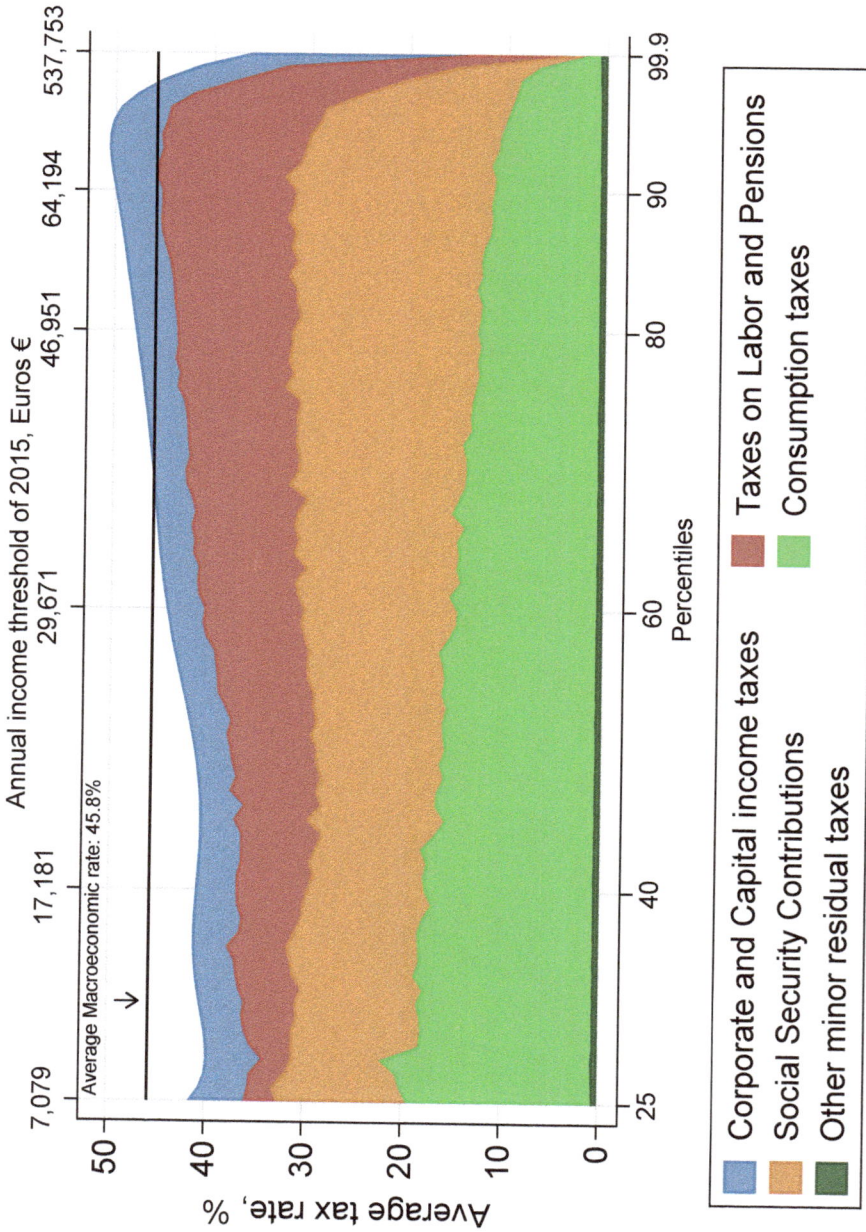

Fig. 10.2 Average Tax Rate by Income Percentiles in Italy, 2015.
Source: Data are from Guzzardi et al. (2022).

Both in France (Bozio et al. 2018) and in the Netherlands (Bruil et al. 2022), there is evidence for a regressive tax system at the top of the income distribution, with the top 1% paying lower effective tax rates than individuals at lower percentiles. In Italy, this regressivity starts at the 95th percentile (Guzzardi et al. 2023), with overall tax rates estimated to fall from a peak of 50% to 35% for the richest individuals (see Figure 10.2).

These results are driven by the composition of income and the related degree of progressivity of taxes on different incomes. First, capital incomes are more heavily concentrated at the top of the distribution, and these are mainly taxed at flat rates. Second, consumption taxes have a regressive impact as they are paid in higher proportions at the bottom and middle of the distribution. Third, the progressivity of the personal income tax is not progressive enough to compensate for flat components of the fiscal system that empirically result as regressive. Indeed, in the case of Italy, Figure 10.2 shows that, although taxes on labour and pensions are mostly progressive, flat consumption taxes are de facto regressive, as propensities to consume are higher at the bottom of the income distribution, in line with empirical findings on consumption (Dynan et al. 2004; Jappelli and Pistaferri 2014; Saez and Zucman 2016; Bunn et al. 2018).

The aforementioned trends are the result of decades of regressive tax reforms. First, the personal income tax, the main source of progressivity in the tax system, has been continuously revised by decreasing the number of tax brackets (Fitoussi and Saraceno 2010) and by reducing top marginal tax rates (Piketty 2014; Piketty et al. 2014), as shown in Figure 10.3 for ten high-income countries. This trend has not been reversed even if recent research contributions have shown that higher top marginal tax rates are desirable. Indeed, in an optimal taxation framework, the top tax rate in the USA and UK could exceed 80% without harming growth, while maximizing government tax revenues (Piketty et al. 2014).[1] This reinforces the evidence on the Laffer curve, which finds a revenue-maximizing tax rate around 70% (Trabandt and Uhlig 2011).

Second, taxation has increasingly shifted from capital to labour. Several countries have introduced the Dual Income Taxation (DIT) system. DIT imposes a lower and less progressive (often flat) tax rate on capital incomes while keeping progressive taxes on labour (an example is the case of Nordic countries in the beginning of the 1990s, see Sørensen 1994; Iacono and Palagi 2022). Furthermore, globalisation has increasingly provided corporations with opportunities to move their profits to countries with lower tax rates (Zucman 2014), thereby incentivizing an international race to the bottom for corporate taxation.

---

1 See also a related *VoxEU* column: Taxing the 1%: Why the top tax rate could be over 80%" 8-12-2011 by Saez, E., S. Stantcheva, and T. Piketty, available at https://cepr.org/voxeu/columns/taxing-1-why-top-tax-rate-could-be-over-80

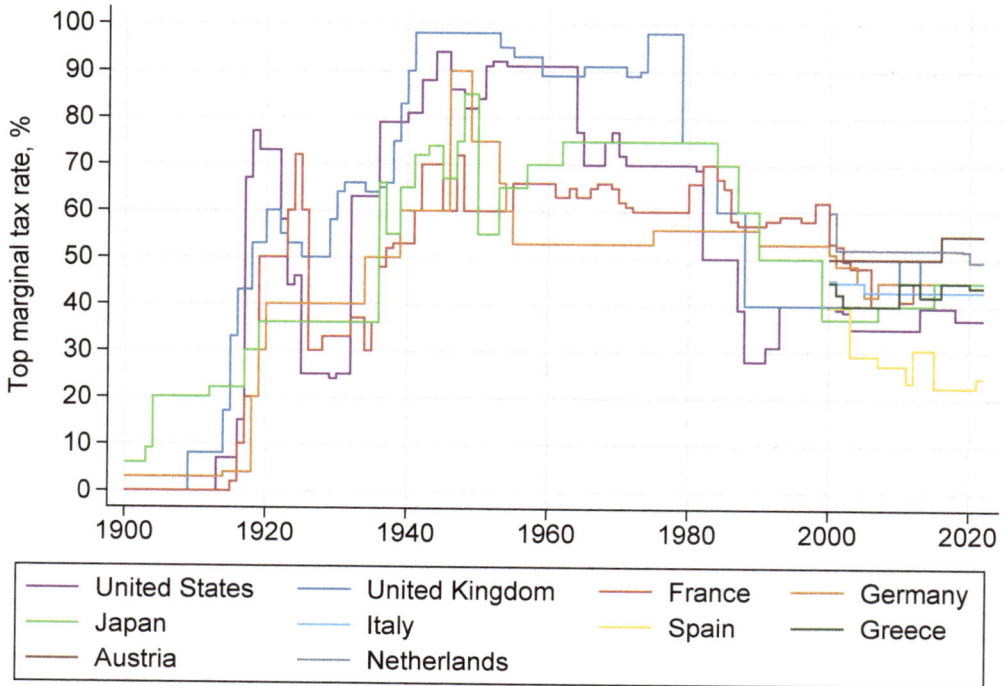

Fig. 10.3 Top Marginal Tax Rates over Time.
Source: Data covering the period before 2000 are from Piketty (2014) and Chancel et al. (2017).
Post-2000 data are taken from the OECD Tax Database: dataset Table I.7.

What have been the economic impacts of the falling progressivity of the tax system? Lower progressivity has certainly been a major contributor to rising inequality trends, especially by boosting top-income shares (Roine et al. 2009; Jaumotte and Osorio Buitron 2020). Indeed, the tax reforms implemented in Western countries during the 1980s and early 1990s have particularly fattened income shares for the richest 1%, with top marginal tax-rate cuts accounting for a large part of the impact (Rubolino and Waldenström 2020).

One could argue that increasing levels of inequality are not a problem because, by spurring growth, they trickle down to the whole income distribution. However, burgeoning evidence shows unequivocally that this is not the case. Hope and Limberg (2022) find that tax cuts do not trigger higher levels of economic activity that percolate to the poor and middle classes. Instead, tax cuts lead to higher income growth for the rich. Shifting the focus from households to firms does not alter the general conclusion. With a meta-analysis of the existing literature, Gechert and Heimberger (2022) show that corporate-tax cuts also do not boost economic growth. On the opposite side, recent studies find that lower levels of inequality are associated with longer growth spells and that redistribution does not harm growth (Dabla-Norris et al. 2015; Berg et al. 2018). Moreover, lower inequality is also associated with higher wellbeing and improved health conditions (Pickett and Wilkinson 2010). Therefore, the evidence seems to point more towards 'trickle-up' mechanisms (Palagi et al. 2023), with income growth at the bottom of the distribution benefiting also richer strands of society.

If lowering top tax rates does not spur growth (while increasing inequality), it certainly increases the risk of mounting public deficits due to the introduction of flat taxes. One emblematic episode highlighting the public financial risks generated by a flattening of the tax system is the steep rise in the cost of government debt that followed the announcement by Liz Truss's government in the UK of a massive tax cut, including a reduction of the top income-tax rate (see, for example, the analysis by the Institute for Fiscal Studies, Adam et al. 2002). Indeed, even major institutions such as the International Monetary Fund have recently advocated for policies restoring the degree of progressivity, by taxing the rich, as a way to increase revenues in countries with large debt stocks (IMF 2020). Such policy guidelines align with the previously mentioned theoretical work indicating that relatively high top-tax rates have a large revenue potential (Trabandt and Uhlig 2011; Diamond and Saez 2011; Piketty et al. 2014).

The evidence presented in this section clearly shows that recent decades have been characterised by a sequence of policies decreasing tax progressivity. Such policies have exacerbated inequality without spurring growth or employment. Moreover, lower progressivity has implied significant losses in terms of tax revenues for government spending, thus reinforcing adverse impacts on disparities, possibly defunding pre-distribution policies (for example, health and education). In the next section we will analyse some major policy proposals that could allow the restoration of higher levels of tax progressivity.

10.3 Turning the Tide: Policy Tools to Increase Tax Progressivity

In this section we will discuss some main proposals advanced nowadays to restore the progressivity of the tax system. We will first focus on the personal and household dimension by surveying the state of the art about wealth taxation (Section 10.3.1) and capital gains taxation (Section 10.3.2). We will then consider corporate taxation (Section 10.3.3).

10.3.1 Wealth Tax

There is a blossoming research line on wealth taxation that tries to assess its impact and account for the challenges in its effective implementation. A wealth tax mainly levied on the richest part of the wealth distribution (for example, the top 5%) could increase the progressivity of the overall tax system (see, for example, Guzzardi et al. (2022) for a simulation based on the Italian case). However, several key arguments against a wealth tax have already emerged.

One major concern is the issue of tax evasion. Wealth is, indeed, a mobile asset; even in the case of real estate, it can be relatively easy to sell and move investments to new locations. Individuals are able to sell their assets in a country with a wealth tax and move them out to avoid taxation. One potential solution to this problem would be to apply wealth taxes according to a person's residence, rather than the location of his or her wealth. Even in this case, wealthy individuals can choose to relocate and change their residence. This, in turn, may lead to a loss in total wealth for countries that introduce a wealth tax compared to neighbouring countries which do not tax assets. This scenario has been highlighted in a recent article from the *Guardian* that sheds light on the responses of Norwegian billionaires to a recent increase in the wealth tax (Neate 2023). Many billionaires, indeed, left the country to avoid the wealth tax.[2] However, at the time of writing, official data regarding the impact of these relocations on the total revenue generated by the Norwegian wealth tax are not yet accessible. On this topic, although there is a lack of comprehensive evidence taking into account the whole population and a large number of countries, the available empirical research shows that massive relocations of individuals between countries are rare (Kleven et al. 2020). In the case of France, the switch from the *Impôt de solidarité sur la fortune* (ISF) to the *Impôt sur la fortune immobilière* (IFI) had a negligible impact on the relocation of individuals abroad, although it affected the distribution of corporate dividends (Bach et al. 2021).[3] In any case, to minimize the risk of tax elusion, an EU-wide wealth tax common to all countries would be highly desirable, as proposed by Piketty (2021)[4] and Landais et al. (2020), as it would considerably discourage any potential relocation of assets or residence. Also, it would facilitate the introduction of common anti-avoidance rules, such as exit taxes.

Wealth taxes may also be avoided via portfolio adjustments through which individuals may reallocate their wealth towards assets that are not subject to taxation (see Duran-Cabré et al. 2019; Bastani and Waldenström 2020; Advani and Tarrant 2021; Saez and Zucman 2022b). Such an issue, however, is particularly relevant only when the legislation on wealth tax allows for many tax-exempt assets and different tax rates. This is what has happened in Spain, where Duran-Cabré et al. (2019) find that higher tax rates have induced individuals to make significant shifts in their portfolios to reduce the taxable wealth without affecting savings and minimally affecting total net wealth. As suggested by Saez and Zucman (2019a), the solution to this issue is relatively straightforward: the tax base needs to include all net wealth, thus ruling out any opportunity for portfolio adjustments to enable tax avoidance. This implies that a wealth tax levied on total net wealth is preferable to fragmented property taxes. Nevertheless, evasion may still occur if wealth has to be self-reported as is the case in Switzerland, where 'half of the apparent

---

2   However, some experts argue that the billionaires' relocations could be attributed instead to a response to modifications in the fiscal treatment of capital gains taxes (Advani et al. 2023).
3   Individuals can relocate their assets within the same country; in Switzerland, tax payers tend to move from cantons with higher wealth taxes to those with lower marginal rates (Brülhart et al. 2022).
4   On the need for a wealth tax to fight climate change, see also Piketty (2022).

wealth accumulation following the tax cut' is explained by 'self-reporting of previously hidden assets' (Brülhart et al. 2022: p. 36). Reliance on third-party valuation, therefore, is crucial to ensure accurate reporting, improve the accuracy of net wealth assessments, and effectively implement wealth taxes, as extensively suggested by the OECD Tax Policy Studies (OECD 2018) and by several scholars (for a review, see Advani and Tarrant 2021).

The final problem concerns the presence of liquidity constraints that some individuals may face with a wealth tax. This is particularly relevant if non-income generating assets are part of the wealth that is taxed. However, this issue can be solved by allowing for deferred tax payments as suggested by OECD (2018). This would ensure that people with unexpected liquidity constraints could postpone their tax payment. Nevertheless, taxing wealth could also induce a more productive use of assets (Guvenen et al. 2023), as individuals would have a greater incentive to use their wealth to generate income to cover their tax obligations (or else to sell it). This would lead to a reallocation of wealth toward more productive activities, possibly increasing economic growth over time.

Having discussed the possible weaknesses related to the introduction of a wealth tax, we can quickly estimate the potential tax revenues stemming from such a plan in the European Union. In order to obtain estimates on a comprehensive wealth tax, we start from total private net wealth, including tax-exempt assets.[5] Using estimates of wealth distribution for the European Union from the World Inequality Database (WID. world; Bajard et al. 2021), we can make a first assessment of different types of wealth tax. For example, levying a 1% tax rate on the top 1%—who own at least €1.5 million in 2021 and hold 25% of total EU personal wealth—would generate approximately 0.6% of EU GDP each year (assuming a 15% evasion rate). In a more progressive scenario, wealth-tax revenues might increase dramatically: for example, a 2% marginal rate for the top 0.1% and an additional 3% marginal rate for the 300 billionaires resident in the EU (Forbes 2022 list) could generate an annual revenue of 1% of EU GDP (see the estimates provided by Landais et al. 2020; Kapeller et al. 2021; Krenek and Schratzenstaller 2022). How the tax revenues from wealth would be employed for alternative scopes and shared across EU states would be a political choice.

Overall, we believe that the different issues analysed in this section should not be viewed as a motivation to dismiss the introduction of an EU-level wealth tax, as there are effective ways to solve them. Therefore, an EU-level progressive wealth tax could be an effective solution for regaining the lost tax progressivity, while raising significant resources which could be used to tackle societal challenges such as climate change (see Section 10.4). Many European countries have already introduced the wealth tax into their fiscal system: Austria, Denmark, France, Finland, Norway, and

---

5   Indeed, a re-assessment of which assets should be subject to the tax (ideally all) would be useful when practically designing a wealth tax. One key mistake which was made on the eve of the introduction of the wealth tax in France in 1981 was not to have a comprehensive tax base and to allow for various exemptions (Verbit 1991).

Switzerland (Sandford 1988; OECD 2018). Moreover, a wealth tax on the richest 1% of the population would be backed by the majority of the population, as survey evidence shows political support for a wealth tax on millionaires (Fabre et al. 2023).

10.3.2 Capital Gains Tax

One of the main reasons for the increase in inequalities and for the regressivity of tax systems for the top income shares discussed in Section 10.2 stems from the relevant role of financial income in the earnings of the most affluent people. A well-tailored capital gains tax is an effective option for increasing the fiscal burden for the richest individuals in the income distribution, partially reversing the loss of progressivity of the tax system. However, despite such potential benefits, a reform of capital gains taxation is not sufficiently debated in the European Union.

How does a capital gains tax work? The tax is levied on the profits obtained from the sale of various assets, including stocks, real estate, business shares, artworks, etc. The tax is calculated by considering the difference between the purchase ('basis') price and the sale price of the asset. For instance, if a person buys a stock for €1,000 and sells it for €2,500, the resulting capital gain of €1,500 will be taxed. In principle, this form of taxation should not introduce biases in reporting, and it should be impossible to evade, as it would be triggered every time assets are transferred.

There are two main problems related to capital gains taxation in Europe. The first stems from the significant disparity in tax rates across EU countries. For instance, in Germany the capital gains tax is 0% for real estate, while a flat tax of 26.3% is levied on other types of property. In Spain, the capital gains tax is progressive, but the top marginal rate is 26%, well below the top one for labour income. In Italy, the flat capital gains tax is set at 26% (with a lower rate of 12.5% for certain assets). In France, it is 36.2%, but the rate shrinks with the possession time of the underlying asset. The Netherlands has a 0% capital gains tax on all types of assets. More broadly, the average rate of capital gains tax in 123 countries is 18% (Christensen et al. 2023). There is, then, an urgent need for proposals to align capital gains taxation with the one on labour, increasing the former to restore the progressivity of the tax system. As capital gains are primarily concentrated among the wealthiest segments of the population (Advani and Summers 2020), higher tax rates would have the most significant impact on the richest individuals, thereby reducing inequality.

The second problem arises when individuals are allowed to postpone their capital gains tax payments indefinitely by retaining the asset until their death and then transferring it as an inheritance or gift (Nanda and Parkes 2019). Many European countries—Austria, Estonia, Germany, Ireland, Italy, Luxembourg and Sweden (OECD 2021a)—adopt this kind of 'carry-over' rule, which transfers assets' basis value to inheritors. Especially in the case of the ultra-wealthy, such a rule can considerably reduce the potential tax revenues: subsequent generations can defer their capital gains indefinitely and, thus, avoid payment of the tax. The situation is even worse for the European countries where the law provides for a 'step-up in basis'—France, Hungary, Latvia, Lithuania, Portugal, Slovenia, and Spain (OECD 2021a)—which resets an asset's basis value to the level at the time of the death of the owner, thus drying up the possible revenue streams of the capital gains tax.[6] Uniform rules across EU countries are also required to fix the issue of indefinite postponing of capital gains realisation. A standardized EU rule that imposes the payment of capital gains taxes at the time of the owner's death would not only deter indefinite deferment and disincentivise asset- and individual-relocation to evade taxation, but it would also generate significant tax revenues. Such a taxation on unrealised capital gains would be particularly useful for increasing the effective tax rate paid by the very wealthy, who use their stock of wealth as collateral to finance their spending by borrowing (Eisinger et al. 2021).

How much revenue could a tax on unrealised capital gains generate? In the USA, a study by Oxfam (Christensen et al. 2023) shows that the potential revenues from a 20% one-off tax on unrealised capital gains for the five richest individuals in the period 2017–2022 would raise approximately $51bn. A similar exercise was conducted by Saez et al. (2021), who estimated that a one-time tax of approximately 40% on the accumulated stocks of unrealised capital gains of around a thousand USA billionaires would raise $1000bn. Such a tax could complement increased rates on realised capital gains, as proposed by Saez and Zucman (2021).

We performed similar calculations for the European Union. According to the *Forbes* (2022) list, there are about three hundred billionaires in the EU in 2022, a substantially lower number than in the USA. In line with the results of Saez et al. (2021), we conservatively assume that half of the wealth of EU is made of unrealised capital gains,[7] estimating €792bn of taxable wealth. Applying a tax rate of 26% as commonly done for realised capital gains in many countries, the total tax revenues would amount to €205bn. Moreover, with a higher tax rate of 40% aligned with those with such income, tax revenues could grow up to €316bn.

In order to implement such a proposal, one could introduce a permanent tax on unrealised capital gains over a five-year period (in line with Saez et al. 2021) for the richest individuals above a certain wealth threshold, possibly the top 1%. In this way one could wipe out the incentive to indefinitely postpone capital gains realisation and ensure a more stable source of revenue for the EU governments. Additionally, since capital gains would be considered realised every five years, any additional gains accrued in the following period would only be taxed on the incremental value, thus avoiding double taxation.[8]

---

6   A third category of countries, including Denmark and Finland, implements both a 'carry-over' rule or a 'step-up in basis' depending on the nature of assets.

7   Saez et al. (2021) find that, in the USA, the share of unrealised capital gains increases with wealth. We assume a constant share.

8   Double taxation has often been raised as a potential issue in the discussion of taxing capital gains and dividends at the same rates as other income sources. Notice, however, that double taxation is not

Based on such assumptions, we perform a basic simulation exercise using WID. world data (Bajard et al. 2021), focusing on the wealthiest 1% in the European Union, who own a total wealth of €16,600bn. We conservatively assume an average real wealth growth rate of 9.4%, half of that observed over the past 5 years. Moreover, we consider that only half of this growth is due to unrealised gains, obtaining a real appreciation of wealth equal to 4.7%. We find that €780bn of unrealised capital gains could be subject to the new tax, obtaining extra revenues of approximately €312bn, which would imply a yearly average of €62bn. Note that such a tax would amount to an annual average of merely 0.3% of the entire wealth of the top 1%.

The proposed capital gains tax should not be perceived as a radical fiscal policy. As the capital gains tax already exists in many EU countries, it only needs to be aligned with the marginal tax rates on labour income for those belonging to the top 1% of the wealth distribution. Moreover, the proposal is in tune with the Biden administration's plan to implement an annual tax on unrealised capital gains for the top 0.01% in the USA wealth distribution. The new capital gains tax could effectively increase revenues while reducing wealth inequality by ensuring that the ultra-wealthy pay their fair share of taxes.

10.3.3 Corporate Tax

Corporate taxation is a field of intervention that has recently regained attention. In October 2021 more than 130 countries signed an agreement to implement a 15% minimum tax on multinational profits (OECD 2021b). Although this is a significant first step, the proposal has raised several criticisms as it entails a low tax rate (Saez and Zucman 2022a), one far below effective rates paid by the majority of households in high-income countries (Bozio et al. 2018; Saez and Zucman 2019b; Guzzardi et al. 2023; Bruil et al. 2022). Moreover, low- and middle-income countries (LMICs) have criticized the measure as it will result in an inequitable transfer of revenues to high-income countries in which multinationals' headquarters are based (Chancel et al. 2023).

Despite such criticisms, the European Union would benefit from this measure. Indeed, many studies collected by the EU-Tax Observatory have estimated significant revenue losses at the EU level due to profit shifting. More specifically, profit shifting has cost the European Union yearly tax-revenue losses ranging from a minimum of €15bn (Janský and Palanský 2019) to a maximum of €40bn (Tørsløv et al. 2023), while Cobham and Janský (2018), Garcia-Bernardo and Janský (2022), and Álvarez-Martínez et al. (2022) estimate a total revenue loss of approximately €35bn per annum.

A minimum effective corporate tax is advantageous from at least two perspectives. First, it would promote fair competition. Currently, lower tax rates for multinational

---

uncommon in tax systems. For example, people are subject to VAT taxes on their consumption after having paid income taxes (Nanda and Parkes 2019).

enterprises (MNEs) compared to local firms create an unjust advantage for larger corporations. Second, implementing a global minimum-tax-rate rule would enhance income redistribution and progressivity, as corporate tax is a tax on corporate profits, a highly concentrated source of income and de facto a minimum tax on the affluent. By implementing this policy, governments can ensure that MNEs and wealthy individuals pay their fair share of taxes, promoting a more equitable distribution of income.

Research by the EU-Tax Observatory (Barake et al. 2021) shows that the introduction of a 15% minimum tax in the EU could generate additional revenues of €90bn (in 2022 euros); at 21%, it could provide €179bn; at 25%—the rate advocated by the Independent Commission for the Reform of International Corporate Taxation (ICRICT)—€255bn. The revenue potential is, therefore, significant. The EU Council has agreed to adopt the 15% global minimum effective tax rate in the European Union and the Directive that implements it will become effective from January 2024. Decisions on tax matters require unanimity in the EU council, giving countries that have historically attracted significant profits by offering MNEs low effective tax rates (for example, Ireland, Hungary, Poland, and Netherlands) a power to veto decisions. Moving to a higher rate could, therefore, be challenging, but it may occur if other countries (for example, in primis, the United States) increase their minimum tax rate above 15%, as this could induce EU members to follow to avoid to lose tax revenues.

Several proposals have been put forth that complement the 15% minimum tax on multinational profits. As corporate value is concentrated and boosted by market power, especially in high-tech sectors, Saez and Zucman (2022a) propose the institution of a 0.2% tax on corporations' stock shares for all publicly listed companies and large private companies headquartered in G20 countries. This measure would both have a high revenue potential, as it could raise 0.2% of world GDP each year, and be progressive, as stock ownership at present is highly unequally distributed. The authors also underline that liquidity would not be an issue as the tax could be paid in kind by issuing new stock.

A further corporate tax measure is to tax excess profits (Chancel et al. 2023). The high inflation, particularly as driven by energy prices, is going hand in hand with larger profits (see, for example, the evidence provided by the European Central Bank, Acre et al. 2023), while households especially at the bottom of national income distributions tend to be severely affected by increases in prices (Edelstein and Kilian 2009; Bruegel analysis by Claeys and Guetta-Jeanrenaud 2022). All these factors help to justify a tax on excess profits. Of course, the threat of profit shifting should be kept in mind while designing such a proposal (Hebous et al. 2022), which requires, as usual, harmonization among countries. In recent years, many countries have implemented windfall profit taxes, either independently, as in Italy or Spain, or in a coordinated manner within the EU. Indeed, in 2022, the Council of the European Union reached a consensus to apply an EU-wide windfall profit tax on fossil-fuel companies. The purpose of this tax is to generate funds to support households and businesses grappling with high-energy prices. Windfall profits are defined as profits surpassing 120% of the reference period, which is determined as the average profit from 2018–2021. These excess profits are subject to a minimum tax rate of 33%. Considering that windfall profits have been observed in sectors other than energy, such as pharmaceuticals, food, banking, and military, there is a great potential to expand the excess profit tax to such relevant industries on a permanent basis.

10.4 Tax Progressivity for a Just, Green Transition

Given the increasing level of inequality and the regressivity of the tax system in many countries (Section 10.2), increasing tax progressivity should be an objective for a well-functioning society. A more progressive tax system could also provide the European Union with relevant resources to tackle societal challenges (as also discussed in the 'Manifesto for the Democratization of Europe', see Piketty 2018). The revenue potential of introducing EU taxes on wealth and unrealised capital gains, as well as to raise the minimum corporate tax rate to 25% would amount to $472bn corresponding to 2.9% of EU GDP (see Table 10.1).

Table 10.1 Yearly Tax Revenue Estimates

	in billion €	in % of 2022 EU GDP
Wealth tax	155	1%
Capital gains tax	62	0.4%
Corporate tax (15%–25%)	90–255	0.5–1.5%
Totals (yearly)	307–472	1.9–2.9%

Note: Tax revenues are reported if additional to the current system. See Section 10.3 for details on the different measures. Recall that, although the unrealised capital gains tax is levied over a period of 5 years, we here report the corresponding yearly value (see Section 10.3.2). Also, note that we do not report additional revenues that could be raised through a comprehensive tax on windfall profits due to the lack of estimates (see Section 10.3.3).

Source: Authors' estimations for the wealth tax and capital gains tax are based on WID.world data; corporate-tax estimates are based on the EU Tax Observatory data collection https://www.taxobservatory.eu/repository/the-scale-of-corporate-tax-avoidance/

Although these are quick estimates and the actual implementation of such policies would require a careful thought on the different limitations, our analysis shows that there is huge potential of collecting additional resources to tackle urgent societal challenges. Once a political consensus is achieved, the best design of taxes to increase the progressivity becomes a technical matter. And such a consensus could be supported by large parts of the population who are in favour of a wealth tax on millionaires (and of using the proceeds to finance low-income countries and climate change policies, Fabre et al. 2023).

The most pressing societal challenge faced by the European Union is climate change, which calls for both mitigation policies to cut GHG emissions and adaptation strategies to protect EU citizens from the impact of global warming. Let us first consider the cost of mitigation policies, as well as their potential impact on inequality. With the 'Fit for 55' package, the European Union has committed to the ambitious goal of reducing EU emissions by at least 55% by 2030. Although decarbonization and the green transition entail new economic opportunities, they also come with costs. The IPCC's *Sixth Assessment Report* (2023) shows, indeed, a large gap in the average annual mitigation investment needs: the actual average flows need to double to reach the minimum levels required for mitigation policies, with the gap in Europe amounting to almost €230bn yearly at minimum.[9] Moreover, the impact of mitigation policies on inequality is asymmetric (Markkanen and Anger-Kraavi 2019; Taconet et al. 2020). Carbon taxes are indeed typically regressive, hitting more the poorest income classes, possibly triggering social protests as in the case of French *Gillets Jaunes*.

Even if Europe meets GHG emissions-reduction targets, the global temperature will increase by at least 1.5 degrees C, further strengthening the already sizeable impacts of climate change on production and inequality (Burke et al. 2015; Coronese et al. 2019; Diffenbaugh and Burke 2019; Palagi et al. 2022). This is why adaptation measures are urgently needed. In Europe, estimates of adaptation investment needs range between €35 and €200bn per year (see European Environment Agency 2023). Such a range of investment is extremely wide, as estimates depend both on the extent of implemented mitigation strategies and on the large uncertainty of climate impacts on our economies.[10] The cost of climate impacts are unevenly distributed across the income distribution as more affluent individuals have more resources to shield themselves from extreme natural events. Moreover, potential inequality issues could arise also between EU countries given that the Mediterranean region is a particularly fragile area in terms of expected damages from extreme climate events (Coronese et al. 2019; Palagi et al. 2022).

Our proposed reforms to increase the progressivity of the EU tax system could provide the required resources to finance both mitigation and adaptation policies, while reducing inequality. According to our estimations in Section 10.3.1, the EU wealth tax could provide resources to fill most of the EU mitigation financing gap. The rest of resources could be provided by the unrealised capital gains tax and the 25% EU corporate tax which could finance also EU adaptation needs. Finally, the residual revenues could be channelled to middle- and low-income countries via the loss and damage fund created during the COP27 in Sharm el-Sheikh.[11]

---

9   For further details, see Figure 4.6 in the IPCC's synthesis report (2023).

10   For similar estimates referring to high-income countries see Stern and Stiglitz (2023). They find that adaptation and resilience spending must increase from $52bn in 2019 to a target of $327bn in 2030 in order to be consistent with a pathway to net-zero emissions by 2050.

11   Chancel et al. (2023) show that a 1.5% global wealth tax on individuals with net wealth over 100 million would be sufficient to cover the estimated adaptation funding needs of middle- and low-income countries.

To conclude, as climate change and inequality are two self-reinforcing phenomena, with climate change disproportionately affecting the poor (Diffenbaugh and Burke 2019; Palagi et al. 2022), and the global richest being responsible for the bulk of emissions (Chancel 2022), the introduction of a progressive tax system appears a timely and necessary action on the EU climate-policy agenda.

10.5 Conclusions

In this chapter, we have provided evidence on the evolution and distribution of the fiscal burden in advanced countries focusing on the European Union. The evidence shows that the degree of progressivity of tax systems has sunk so much in recent decades that the richest income classes are paying lower effective tax rates than bottom- and middle-income groups. This lost progressivity is enlarging disparities with no discernible effect on growth or employment.

We have then discussed how to restore some degree of the lost progressivity by passing an EU-wide tax reform encompassing a wealth tax levied on the richest 1% of the population, a tax on unrealised capital gains, and a substantial increase of the minimum tax on corporate profits. Our first estimates show that the revenues generated by such fiscal intervention are substantial. More specifically, an EU wealth tax could generate resources amounting to 1% of EU GDP. A tax on unrealised capital gains over the past 5 years would allow the EU to collect almost 2% of its GDP (0.4% yearly). Finally, an EU-level minimum corporate tax ranging between 15% and 25% could generate additional revenues corresponding to 0.5% and 1.5% of EU GDP.

Such a fresh flow of resources could be employed to finance both the mitigation and adaptation policies required to tackle the climate emergency. In this way, our package of fiscal interventions would allow EU countries to jointly reduce inequality, increase the fairness of their tax system, cut greenhouse-gas emissions, and dampen the social impact of extreme climate events. The proposed tax reform could then contribute to putting EU economies on a sustainable and inclusive pathway.

This work is just the first step in designing a fairer and climate-friendly tax system for the European Union. A complete assessment of the impact and revenue potential of the fiscal policy tools considered here require additional work. First, an extensive sensitivity analysis must be carried out on the estimated revenues, by varying the underlying assumptions. Second, additional analyses must be performed to assess the possible capital outflow triggered by EU-level fiscal policies. Nevertheless, given the regressivity of the current EU fiscal systems, our general conclusions robustly hold: there is ample space to impose higher taxes for those belonging to the top 1% of the EU wealth distribution.

References

Arce, O., E. Hahn, and G. Koester (2023). How tit-for-tat inflation can make everyone poorer. The ECB Blog 30-03-2023 https://www.ecb.europa.eu/press/blog/date/2023/html/ecb.blog.230330~00e522ecb5.en.html

Adam S., I. Delestre, C. Emmerson, P. Johnson, R. Joyce, I. Stockton, T. Waters, X. Xu, B. Zaranko (2022). 'Mini-Budget Response', Institute for Fiscal Studies, 23 September, https://ifs.org.uk/articles/mini-budget-response

Advani, A., E. Chamberlain, A. Summers (2023). 'Wealth Tax: the Debate Continues'. *Tax Journal*, 3 September, https://www.taxjournal.com/articles/wealth-tax-the-debate-continues

Advani, A. and A. Summers (2020). 'Capital Gains and UK Inequality'. World Inequality Lab Working Papers (2020/09)

Advani, A. and H. Tarrant (2021). 'Behavioural Responses to a Wealth Tax'. Fiscal Studies 42(3–4), 509–37, https://doi.org/10.47445/105

Álvarez-Martínez, M. T., S. Barrios, D. d'Andria, M. Gesualdo, G. Nicodème, and J. Pycroft (2022). 'How Large is the Corporate Tax Base Erosion and Profit Shifting? A General Equilibrium approach'. *Economic Systems Research*, 34(2): 167–98, https://doi.org/10.2139/ssrn.3144296

Bach, L., A. Bozio, A. Guillouzouic, and C. Malgouyres (2021). 'Évaluer les effets de l'impôt sur la fortune et de sa suppression sur le tissu productif'. Institut des politiques publiques (IPP), *Rapport IPP*, n°36, Octobre 2021

Bajard, F., L. Chancel, R. Moshrif, and T. Piketty (2021). 'Global Wealth Inequality on wid.world: Estimates and Imputations'. *World Inequality Lab*, Technical Note N° 2021/16.

Barake, M., T. Neef, P.-E. Chouc, and G. Zucman (2021). 'Revenue Effects of the Global Minimum Tax: Country-by-Country Estimates'. Note, EU-Tax Observatory

Bastani, S. and D. Waldenström (2020). 'How Should Capital be Taxed?' *Journal of Economic Surveys*, 34(4): 812–46, https://doi.org/10.1111/joes.12380

Berg, A., J. D. Ostry, C. G. Tsangarides, and Y. Yakhshilikov (2018). 'Redistribution, Inequality, and Growth: New Evidence'. *Journal of Economic Growth*, 23: 259–305, https://doi.org/10.35188/unu-wider/2020/874-0

Blanchet, T., L. Chancel, and A. Gethin (2022). 'Why is Europe More Equal than the United States?'. *American Economic Journal: Applied Economics*, 14(4): 480–518, https://doi.org/10.1257/app.20200703

Blanchet, T. and C. Martínez-Toledano (2023). 'Wealth Inequality Dynamics in Europe and the United States: Understanding the Determinants'. *Journal of Monetary Economics*, 133: 25–43, https://doi.org/10.1016/j.jmoneco.2022.11.010

Bozio, A., B. Garbinti, J. Goupille-Lebret, M. Guillot, and T. Piketty (2018). 'Inequality and Redistribution in France, 1990–2018: Evidence from Post-Tax Distributional National Accounts (DINA)'. *World Inequality Lab Working Papers*, 2018/10

Bruil, A., C. van Essen, W. Leenders, A. Lejour, J. Möhlmann, and S. Rabaté (2022). 'Inequality and Redistribution in the Netherlands'. Technical Report, *CPB Discussion Paper*.

Brülhart, M., J. Gruber, M. Krapf, and K. Schmidheiny (2022). 'Behavioral Responses to Wealth Taxes: Evidence from Switzerland'. *American Economic Journal: Economic Policy*, 14(4): 111–50, https://doi.org/10.1257/pol.20200258

Bunn, P., J. Le Roux, K. Reinold, and P. Surico (2018). 'The Consumption Response to Positive and Negative Income Shocks'. *Journal of Monetary Economics*, 96: 1–15, https://doi.org/10.1016/j.jmoneco.2017.11.007

Burke, M., S. M. Hsiang, and E. Miguel (2015). 'Global Non-Linear Effect of Temperature on Economic Production'. *Nature* 527(7577): 235–39, https://doi.org/10.1038/nature15725

Chancel, L. (2022). 'Global Carbon Inequality over 1990–2019'. *Nature Sustainability* 5(11): 931–38, https://doi.org/10.1038/s41893-022-00955-z

——, P. Bothe, and T. Voituriez (2023). 'Climate Inequality Report: Fair Taxes for a Sustainable Future in the Global South'. Technical Report, World Inequality Lab

Chancel, L., R. Clarke, and A. Gethin (2017). 'World Inequality Report 2018: Technical Notes for Figures and Tables'. *WID*. World Technical Note, series 8, 152

Christensen, M. B., C. Hallum, A. Maitland, Q. Parrinello, and C. Putaturo (2023). 'Survival of the Richest: How we Must Tax the Super-Rich Now to Fight Inequality'. *Oxfam International*, https://doi.org/10.21201/2023.621477

Claeys G., L. Guetta-Jeanrenaud (2022). 'Who is Suffering Most from Rising Inflation?'. *Bruegel* 1 February, https://www.bruegel.org/blog-post/who-suffering-most-rising-inflation#:~:text=Specific%20goods%20increase%20inflation%20inequality,and%20their%20relative%20importance%20smaller

Cobham, A. and P. Janský (2018). 'Global Distribution of Revenue Loss from Corporate Tax Avoidance: Re-Estimation and Country Results'. *Journal of International Development*, 30(2): 206–32, https://doi.org/10.1002/jid.3348

Coronese, M., F. Lamperti, K. Keller, F. Chiaromonte, and A. Roventini (2019). 'Evidence for Sharp Increase in the Economic Damages of Extreme Natural Disasters'. *Proceedings of the National Academy of Sciences*, 116(43): 21450–55, https://doi.org/10.1073/pnas.1907826116

Dabla-Norris, M. E., M. K. Kochhar, M. N. Suphaphiphat, M. F. Ricka, and M. E. Tsounta (2015). 'Causes and Consequences of Income Inequality: A Global Perspective'. International Monetary Fund

Diamond, P. and E. Saez (2011). 'The Case for a Progressive Tax: From Basic Research to Policy Recommendation'. *Journal of Economic Perspectives*, 25(4): 165–90, https://doi.org/10.1257/jep.25.4.165

Diffenbaugh, N. S. and M. Burke (2019). 'Global Warming has Increased Global Economic Inequality'. *Proceedings of the National Academy of Sciences*, 116(20): 9808–9813, https://doi.org/10.1073/pnas.1816020116

Duran-Cabré, J. M., A. Esteller-Moré, and M. Mas-Montserrat (2019). 'Behavioural Responses to the (Re)introduction of Wealth Taxes: Evidence from Spain'. *IEB Working Paper*, https://doi.org/10.2139/ssrn.3393016

Dynan, K. E., J. Skynner, and S. P. Zeldes (2004). 'Do the Rich Save More?' *Journal of Political Economy*, 112(2), https://doi.org/10.1086/381475

Edelstein, P. and L. Kilian (2009). 'How Sensitive are Consumer Expenditures to Retail Energy Prices?'. *Journal of Monetary Economics* 56(6): 766–79, https://doi.org/10.1016/j.jmoneco.2009.06.001

Eisinger, J., J. Ernsthausen, and P. Kiel (2021, Jun). 'The Secret IRS Files: Trove of Never-Before-Seen Records Reveal how the Wealthiest Avoid Income Tax'. ProPublica

European Environment Agency (2023). 'Assessing the Costs and Benefits of Climate Change Adaptation'. *European Environment Agency Briefing*, 3 March, https://www.eea.europa.eu/publications/assesing-the-costs-and-benefits-of

Fabre, A., T. Douenne, and L. Mattauch (2023). 'International Attitudes Toward Global Policies'. *Working Paper*, 2023/08, WIL: World Inequality Lab

Fitoussi, J.-P. and F. Saraceno (2010). 'Inequality and Macroeconomic Performance'. *Document de travail de l'OFCE*, 2010–13

Forbes (2022). 'Forbes Billionaires 2022: The Richest People in the World'.

International Monetary Fund Research Department (2020). *World Economic Outlook, October 2020: A Long and Difficult Ascent*. International Monetary Fund, 177, https://doi.org/10.5089/9781513561868.081

Garcia-Bernardo, J. and P. Janský (2022). 'Profit Shifting of Multinational Corporations Worldwide'. arXiv preprint. *arXiv*, 2201.08444, https://dx.doi.org/10.2139/ssrn.4435224

Gechert, S. and P. Heimberger (2022). 'Do Corporate Tax Cuts Boost Economic Growth?' *European Economic Review*, 147, 104157, https://doi.org/10.1016/j.euroecorev.2022.104157

Guvenen, F., G. Kambourov, B. Kuruscu, S. Ocampo, and D. Chen (2023). 'Use it or Lose it: Efficiency and Redistributional Effects of Wealth Taxation'. *Quarterly Journal of Economics*, 138(2): 835–94, https://doi.org/10.1093/qje/qjac047

Guzzardi, D., E. Palagi, A. Roventini, and A. Santoro (2022). 'Reconstructing Income Inequality in Italy: New Evidence and Tax Policy Implications from Distributional National Accounts'. *Working Paper Series* 2022/06, Laboratory of Economics and Management (LEM), Scuola Superiore Sant'Anna, Pisa, Italy

—— (2023). 'Reconstructing Income Inequality in Italy: New Evidence and Tax System Implications from Distributional National Accounts'. Forthcoming, *Journal of the European Economic Association*

Hebous, S., D. Prihardini, and N. Vernon (2022). 'Excess Profit Taxes: Historical Perspective and Contemporary Relevance'. *IMF Working Paper*, https://doi.org/10.5089/9798400221729.001

Hope, D. and J. Limberg (2022). 'The Economic Consequences of Major Tax Cuts for the Rich'. *SocioEconomic Review* 20(2): 539–59, https://doi.org/10.1093/ser/mwab061

Iacono, R. and E. Palagi (2022). 'Still the Lands of Equality? Heterogeneity of Income Composition in the Nordics, 1975–2016'. *BE Journal of Economic Analysis & Policy* 22(2): 221–68, https://doi.org/10.1515/bejeap-2021-0165

IPCC (2023). 'Climate Change 2023: Synthesis Report'. Contribution of Working Groups I, II and III to the Sixth Assessment Report of the Intergovernmental Panel on Climate Change [Core Writing Team, H. Lee and J. Romero (eds.)]. IPCC, Geneva, Switzerland, 184 pp., https://doi.org/10.59327/ipcc/ar6-9789291691647

Janský, P. and M. Palanský (2019). 'Estimating the Scale of Profit Shifting and Tax Revenue Losses Related to Foreign Direct Investment'. *International Tax and Public Finance*, 26: 1048–103, https://doi.org/10.1007/s10797-019-09547-8

Jappelli, T. and L. Pistaferri (2014). 'Fiscal Policy and MPC Heterogeneity'. *American Economic Journal: Macroeconomics*, 6(4): 107–36, https://doi.org/10.1257/mac.6.4.107

Jaumotte, F. and C. Osorio Buitron (2020). 'Inequality: Traditional Drivers and the Role of Union Power'. *Oxford Economic Papers*, 72(1): 25–58, https://doi.org/10.1093/oep/gpz024

Kapeller, J., S. Leitch, and R. Wildauer (2021). 'A European Wealth Tax for a Fair and Green Recovery'. Technical report, *ICAE Working Paper Series*, http://hdl.handle.net/10419/246862

Kleven, H., C. Landais, M. Munoz, and S. Stantcheva (2020). 'Taxation and Migration: Evidence and Policy Implications'. *Journal of Economic Perspectives*, 34(2): 119–42, https://doi.org/10.1257/jep.34.2.119

Krenek, Alexander and Margit Schratzenstaller (2022). 'A Harmonized Net Wealth Tax in the European Union'. *Jahrbücher für Nationalökonomie und Statistik*, 242(5–6): 629–68, https://doi.org/10.1515/jbnst-2021-0045

Landais, C., E. Saez, and G. Zucman (2020). 'A Progressive European Wealth Tax to Fund the European COVID'. *Europe in the Time of COVID-19*, 113

Markkanen, S. and A. Anger-Kraavi (2019). 'Social Impacts of Climate Change Mitigation Policies and their Implications for Inequality'. *Climate Policy* 19(7): 827–44, https://doi.org/10.1080/14693062.2019.1596873

Nanda, S. and H. Parkes (2019). 'Just Tax: Reforming the Taxation of Income from Wealth and Work'. Institute for Public Policy Research

Neate, R. (2023). 'Super-Rich Abandoning Norway at Record Rate as Wealth Tax Rises Slightly'. *Guardian*, 10 April, ttps://www.theguardian.com/world/2023/apr/10/super-rich-abandoning-norway-at-record-rate-as-wealth-tax-rises-slightly

OECD (2018). 'The Role and Design of Net Wealth Taxes in the OECD', *OECD Tax Policy Studies*, No. 26, OECD Publishing, Paris, https://doi.org/10.1787/9789264290303-en

—— (2021a). 'Inheritance Taxation in OECD Countries', *OECD Tax Policy Studies*, No. 28, OECD Publishing, Paris, https://doi.org/10.1787/e2879a7d-en

—— (2021b). 'Statement on a Two-Pillar Solution to Address the Tax Challenges Arising from the Digitalisation of the Economy', https://www.oecd.org/tax/beps/statement-on-a-two-pillar-solutionto-address-the-tax-challenges-arising-from-the-digitalisation-of-the-economy-july-2021.pdf.

Palagi, E., M. Coronese, F. Lamperti, and A. Roventini (2022). 'Climate Change and the Nonlinear Impact of Precipitation Anomalies on Income Inequality'. *Proceedings of the National Academy of Sciences*, 119(43), e2203595119, https://doi.org/10.1073/pnas.2203595119

Palagi, E., Napoletano, M., Roventini, A., and Gaffard, J. L. (2023). An agent-based model of trickle-up growth and income inequality. Economic Modelling, 129, 106535, https://doi.org/10.1016/j.econmod.2023.106535

Peter, K. S., S. Buttrick, and D. Duncan (2010). 'Global Reform of Personal Income Taxation, 1981–2005: Evidence from 189 Countries'. *National Tax Journal*, 63(3): 447–78, https://doi.org/10.17310/ntj.2010.3.03

Pickett, K. and R. Wilkinson (2010). *The Spirit Level: Why Equality is Better for Everyone*. Penguin UK.

Piketty, T. (2014). *Capital in the Twenty-First Century*. Harvard University Press Cambridge, MA, https://doi.org/10.4159/9780674369542

Piketty, T. (2018). 'Manifesto for the Democratisation of Europe'. *Le Monde,* 10 December, https://www.lemonde.fr/blog/piketty/2018/12/10/manifesto-for-the-democratisation-of-europe/

—— (2021). *Capital and Ideology.* Harvard University Press, https://doi.org/10.4159/9780674245075

—— (2022) 'It is Impossible to Seriously Fight Climate Change without a Profound Redistribution of Wealth'. *Le Monde,* 5 November, https://www.lemonde.fr/en/opinion/article/2022/11/05/thomas-piketty-it-is-impossible-to-seriously-fight-climate-change-without-a-profound-redistribution-of-wealth_6003038_23.html

——, E. Saez, and S. Stantcheva (2014). 'Optimal Taxation of Top Labor Incomes: A Tale of Three Elasticities'. *American Economic Journal: Economic Policy,* 6(1): 230–71, https://doi.org/10.1257/pol.6.1.230

Roine, J., J. Vlachos, and D. Waldenström (2009). 'The Long-Run Determinants of Inequality: What Can we Learn from Top Income Data?'. *Journal of Public Economics,* 93(7–8): 974–88, https://doi.org/10.1016/j.jpubeco.2009.04.003

Rubolino, E. and D. Waldenström (2020). 'Tax Progressivity and Top Incomes Evidence from Tax Reforms'. *Journal of Economic Inequality,* 18: 261–89, https://doi.org/10.1007/s10888-020-09445-8

Saez, E., S. Stancheva, and T. Piketty (2011). 'Taxing the 1%: Why the Top Tax Rate Could be Over 80%'. *VoxEu,* 8 December, https://cepr.org/voxeu/columns/taxing-1-why-top-tax-rate-could-be-over-80

Saez, E., D. Yagan, and G. Zucman (2021). *Capital Gains Withholding.* University of California Berkeley

Saez, E. and G. Zucman (2016). 'Wealth Inequality in the United States since 1913: Evidence from Capitalized Income Tax Data'. *Quarterly Journal of Economics,* 131(2): 519–78, https://doi.org/10.1093/qje/qjw004

—— (2019a). 'How would a Progressive Wealth Tax Work? Evidence from the Economics Literature'. Brookings Institution

—— (2019b). *The Triumph of Injustice: How the Rich Dodge Taxes and How to Make them Pay.* WW Norton & Company.

—— (2020). 'The Rise of Income and Wealth Inequality in America: Evidence from Distributional Macroeconomic Accounts'. *Journal of Economic Perspectives,* 34(4): 3–26, https://doi.org/10.3386/w27922

—— (2021). *How to Get $1 Trillion from 1000 Billionaires: Tax their Gains Now.* University of California Berkeley.

—— (2022a). 'A Wealth Tax on Corporations' Stock'. *Economic Policy,* 37(110): 213–27, https://doi.org/10.1093/epolic/eiac026

—— (2022b). 'Wealth Taxation: Lessons from History and Recent Developments', in *AEA Papers and Proceedings,* 112: 58–62. American Economic Association, https://doi.org/10.1257/pandp.20221055

Sandford, C. (1988). 'Taxation of Net Wealth, Capital Transfers and Capital Gains of Individuals', 19. Paris, France: Organisation for Economic Co-operation and Development

Sørensen, P. B. (1994). 'From the Global Income Tax to the Dual Income Tax: Recent Tax Reforms in the Nordic Countries'. *International Tax and Public Finance*, 1(1): 57–79, https://doi.org/10.1007/bf00874089

Stern, N. and J. E. Stiglitz (2023). 'Climate Change and Growth'. *Industrial and Corporate Change*, 32(2): 277–303, https://doi.org/10.1093/icc/dtad008

Taconet, N., A. Méjean, and C. Guivarch (2020). 'Influence of Climate Change Impacts and Mitigation Costs on Inequality between Countries'. *Climatic Change*, 160: 15–34, https://doi.org/10.1007/s10584-019-02637-w

Tørsløv, T., L. Wier, and G. Zucman (2023). 'The Missing Profits of Nations'. *Review of Economic Studies*, 90(3): 1499–534, https://doi.org/10.1093/restud/rdac049

Trabandt, M. and H. Uhlig (2011). 'The Laffer Curve Revisited'. *Journal of Monetary Economics*, 58(4), 305–27, https://doi.org/10.1016/j.jmoneco.2011.07.003

Verbit, G. P. (1991). 'France Tries a Wealth Tax'. *University of Pennsylvania Journal of International Business*, 12, 181

Zucman, G. (2014). 'Taxing Across Borders: Tracking Personal Wealth and Corporate Profits'. *Journal of Economic Perspectives*, 28(4): 121–48, https://doi.org/10.1257/jep.28.4.121

11. European Public Goods[1]

Marco Buti, Alessandro Coloccia, and Marcello Messori

A well-functioning economic union needs a permanent central fiscal capacity. Stepping up the supply of European Public Goods (EPGs) delivered and financed at EU level appears the most promising avenue. EPGs should meet a number of criteria at the intersection of the economic theory of public goods, the theory of fiscal federalism, and EU-specific institutional and political features. The green, digital, and social transition; the supply of critical raw materials; health; security; and defence define the areas where economic, institutional, and political coherence meet. Several issues still need to be addressed before EPGs could be launched at the appropriate scale. However, the ongoing mid-term review of the EU Multiannual Financial Framework provides an opportunity for bringing EPGs to the centre of the policy debate.

11.1 Introduction

European Public Goods (EPGs) allow the European Union (EU) to pursue projects implemented at a centralised level by means of common financing. EPGs have been revived recently in the context of the green and digital transition (see Fuest and Pisani-Ferry 2019). This renewed attention was prompted by the pandemic shock which convinced the EU Member States of the necessity to create a central fiscal tool, albeit of a temporary nature: Next Generation EU (NGEU) and its main component, the Recovery and Resilience Facility (RRF). Many observers believe that the RRF should be transformed into a permanent instrument, thereby creating a European Central Fiscal Capacity (CFC). However, despite its innovative scope, the RRF is mainly characterised by a national use of EU financial resources (transfers and loans), as the European Council negotiations led to a reduction in the share of EPGs (Papaconstantinou 2020). Therefore, making it permanent would be politically controversial as it would raise the concern that the EU is turning into a 'transfers union'. This risk would be mitigated by focussing on the production of EPGs (see Buti and Papacostantinou 2022; D'Apice and Pasimeni 2020).

---

[1] A slightly different version of this chapter has been previously published, with the same title, in *VoxEu*, 9 June 2023, pp. 1–8. Alessandro Coloccia speaks in his personal capacity

https://doi.org/10.11647/OBP.0386.11

EPGs are politically less contentious compared to other forms of CFC for at least two reasons. First, the EPGs weaken the *juste retour* (or 'net balance') narrative, according to which each EU country tends to subtract how much it contributed to the EU budget from how much it receives directly back. Second, the production of EPGs would lessen the tensions between alleged 'creditors' and 'debtors' and the consequent risks of opportunistic behaviours linked to transfers to national budgets. From a policy perspective, EPGs could help deliver the 'triple transition' (green, digital, and social) and promote the role of the EU in the international markets, thus helping to reconcile European domestic and global agendas. Furthermore, EPGs can play an important role in tackling the economic and political fallout of the Russian invasion of Ukraine.

Let us add that, even if the EPGs can be produced at a centralised European level by coalitions of private firms belonging to various Member States, these goods will usually require a public intervention and will mainly contribute to the implementation of public investments. In defining EPGs (see Section 11.2), we do not emphasise the relations between these goods and public investment because—in principle—property rights are not a crucial component of our classification. However, our analysis has two implications: first, that EPGs play a fundamental role in the construction of a new European industrial policy and, second, that this policy is required to overcome the current obsolete EU's production model and to build an innovative and competitive economy able to strengthen European competitiveness in international markets. The new EU's industrial policy should be characterised by incentives designed to support private investment and by reforms and regulations to improve the efficiency of various markets and the effectiveness of economic institutions. In any case, an important component of this policy should also be the activation of public investments.

This chapter is part of a long-standing research stream on EPGs that has addressed their implications for the Euro Area (EA) policy mix (Buti and Messori 2021a, 2022a), the role of the EU in global governance (Buti and Messori 2021b, 2022b), and the future of NGEU (Buti and Messori 2023). Against this background, in Sections 11.2 and 11.3, we put forward an operational definition of EPGs and outline a preliminary classification of these goods. In Section 11.4, we explain how EPGs could be delivered and financed. Section 11.5 concludes by going back to the centrality of public investments in the new EU's industrial policy.

11.2 Key Features of EPGs

The EPGs can be interpreted as a specific application of the concept of Global Public Goods that was utilised by Kindleberger (1973) and many other authors (see Buchholz and Sandler 2021) to extend the theoretical concept of pure public goods (see Samuelson 1954, 1955; Buchanan 1968) to the activities involved in the integration of international markets. This extension implies that the classical analysis of public goods has been grafted onto other strands of economic literature, namely the theory of fiscal federalism. It has also weakened some of the original features of the public goods concept. Being a specific version of global public goods, EPGs require a further operational definition. We thus define three broad rationales for that definition: (i) economic, (ii) institutional, and (iii) political.[2]

According to the economic rationale, a 'pure' public good is characterised by two main features: (i) its utilisation by an additional beneficiary has a marginal cost approaching zero (non-rivalrous), and (ii) the exclusion of a potential beneficiary is either impossible or very inefficient (non-excludable). These two features have an important implication: market mechanisms tend to supply an insufficient amount of 'pure' public goods because a profit-maximising producer of this type of goods would bear the full costs but could internalise only a portion of the benefits (see, for instance, Stiglitz 1986: chapter 1). Hence, the creation of an efficient amount of public goods requires a direct or indirect public intervention.

At the global level, an undersupply applies not only to 'pure' public goods, but also to goods that satisfy only one of the two criteria above or even just a weak formulation of (one of) these same criteria. In the former case, the economic literature refers to 'mixed' public goods, in the latter to 'impure' public goods. Hence, the three types of public goods share the crucial feature mentioned above: that of giving rise to market failures. This feature is strengthened by two related and key characteristics of public goods: the ability of these goods to generate economies of scale and spillovers (positive externalities). Being a specific version of global public goods, EPGs incorporate all of these features. Hence, for the purpose of this chapter, we define EPGs as 'pure', 'mixed', and 'impure' public goods that produce positive externalities mainly thanks to centralised public interventions.

As to the institutional rationale for identifying EPGs, two additional specificities emerge. First, the production and financing of a given good or service take place optimally at the EU level as the added value of this same good or service increases when it is the outcome of a joint design and a common effort of the EU members. This feature leads to the second institutional aspect of the EPGs: it is in the mutual interest of the Member States to exploit the cross-border dimension to prepare, support, and implement the production of these goods and services.

Finally, according to the political rationale, EPGs should benefit the EU as a political entity and not only as the sum of its individual Member States. EPGs should strengthen the cohesion across countries and buttress citizens' support towards European cooperation. We label these features as 'beyond subsidiarity' to emphasise their multiplicative effects. Finally, EPGs should be 'mission oriented' by supporting EU's strategic domestic and international political priorities.

The EPGs' economic, institutional, and political rationales analysed above are 'translated' in the seven features illustrated in Table 11.1.[3]

---

2   For a similar attempt of specifying EPGs criteria, see Thöne and Kreuter (2020).
3   It should be noted that our analysis of EPGs is focused on 'material' public goods (and services), that is, on those EPGs based on investment and production processes. Hence, we leave the crucial issue

Table 11.1 Main Features of EPGs

RATIONALE	FEATURE	EXPLANATION
Economic	Non rivalry and/or non excludability	The existence of these two qualities or even of one of them, also in a weak form, imply that an EPG would be either a 'pure', 'mixed', or 'impure' public good.
	Economies of scale and scope	Beyond a minimum level, the production cost of additional units of EPGs decreases (economies of scale); the same applies to the joint financing and production of EPGs (economies of scope).
	Positive externalities	The production and utilisation of the EPGs in a given sector or by a given number of EU Member States create positive spillovers to other sectors and other EU Member States. Combined with economies of scale and scope, these externalities entail positive multiplier effects at EU level.
Institutional	Mutual interest	EU Member States have a mutual interest in jointly designing, financing, and producing EPGs because the availability of these goods is beneficial to each of the participating countries and the production of these same goods at national level would be too costly or unfeasible.
	Cross-border dimension	The effective acquisition of EPGs requires the involvement of financial resources of several or all EU Member States. Nevertheless, any good financed by EU resources but nationally produced is not included in our definition of EPGs.
Political	Mission oriented	EPGs are key to pursue EU's strategic priorities in the economic or non-economic areas.
	Beyond subsidiarity	EPGs produce externalities that improve the efficiency and effectiveness not only at national level, but also for the EU as a whole. Hence, the impact of the EPGs cannot be reduced to an assessment of subsidiarity.

Source: Authors' elaboration.

of the allocation of knowledge as a global public good (on this, see Stiglitz 1999) in the background, and we neglect the EPGs arising from reforms and 'immaterial' outcomes (for example, a positive externality such as financial stability).

Table 11.2 A Classification of EPGs

AREAS	OBJECTIVE	RATIONALE			EXAMPLES
		Economic	Institutional	Political	
Digital Transition	Boosting innovation and reconciling EU domestic and global agenda	XX	XX	XX	Cross border digital connectivity infrastructure (for example, 5G, backbone networks, quantum communication infrastructures), Research and Development
Green Transition and Energy	Decreasing EU energy dependence and safeguarding EU's leading role towards climate change	XX	XX	XX	Cross-border energy projects (for example, electricity, smart grids, and CO_2 networks)
Social Transition	Rebalancing welfare state towards re-skilling of human resources	X	X	X	EU platform for skills acquisition and exchanges
Raw Materials	Reducing competi-tiveness gaps and increasing strategic autonomy	X	XX	X	Common purchase of critical raw materials
Security and Defence	Overcoming different strategic perspectives to ensure EU protection	X	XX	XX	Borders management, and handling of migration flows
Health	Protection against health catastrophes	X	X	XX	Procurement of vaccines, near-shoring of basic medical facilities, research and development

Source: Authors' elaboration.

11.3 Identifying EPGs

Based on the analysis in the previous section, in Table 11.2, we identify six priority areas: digital transition, 'green' transition and energy, social transition, raw materials, security and defence, and health.[4] For each area, we provide a subjective assessment of compliance with the three rationales mentioned above and we indicate some non-exhaustive examples of specific EPGs that meet their corresponding objectives.

The first four challenges pertain to the economic field: a) reaching climate neutrality to preserve EU's international leadership in terms of low environmental impact and 'circular economy'; b) reducing EU's technological gaps in relation to the USA and China and innovating the EU production model by means of a centralised industrial policy (see Buti and Messori 2023); c) improving education and re-skilling as necessary conditions to successfully pursue the double transition without weakening European social protection; and d) buttressing the EU open strategic autonomy as part of a renewed system of multilateral governance. These four challenges call for the supply of EPGs in areas such as digital transition (cross-border digital connectivity infrastructure), 'green' transition and renewable energy (cross-border energy projects), labour market and social transition (platforms for skills acquisitions), strategic raw materials required for innovative productions.

Additionally, the experience with COVID-19 calls for EU interventions in health such as the centralisation of the purchase of vaccines, the near-shoring of basic medical facilities, and the centralisation of innovative medical research. Finally, the war at the EU's eastern borders and the human drama affecting large parts of Africa and the Middle East point to the need of EPGs in the areas of defence and security. Examples are the inclusive management of migration flows and the protection of the EU's external borders.

In Table 11.2, we provide a subjective assessment of the compliance of the six areas with the economic, institutional, and political criteria identified in Table 11.1. A double cross (XX) denotes a high potential, and a single cross (X) denotes a satisfactory potential. Whilst most projects listed in this Table would qualify as EPGs according to our definition based on the number of crosses, the three areas which come out as critical for the supply of EPGs are the digital transition, 'green' transition and energy, and security and defence.

11.4 Financing and Delivering EPGs

To finance and deliver EPGs, it is necessary to put in place a permanent CFC because the common EU projects discussed above have a medium- to long-term dimension. The creation of a permanent CFC raises difficult legal and institutional questions that go beyond the scope of this chapter. According to Tosato (2021), the EU Treaties are

---

4   A partly similar classification was elaborated, before the pandemic, by Fuest and Pisani-Ferry (2019).

sufficiently flexible to include a 'recurrent' CFC as a tool of managing repeated external shocks. We, therefore, focus on the questions of how to finance and deliver these goods.

NGEU and the SURE programmes offer two different options for the financing of a temporary CFC. The former allows the European Commission to issue European bonds in the financial markets on behalf of the EU thanks to the guarantees offered by the headroom of the Own Resources ceiling. The latter entitles the European Commission to issue bonds backed by national guarantees that are offered by the EU Member States. However, these direct or indirect guarantees cannot work in the case of a permanent or recurrent CFC, as required by the production of EPGs. The extension of these guarantees to a very long (or even infinite) horizon would involve implicit and growing liabilities for national budgets that would impose binding constraints on national fiscal policies. Hence, the financing of EPGs requires that the central level be endowed with specific tax bases, or, in the EU jargon, new Own Resources. This task is fraught with difficulties as shown by the modest progress in the enlargement of the European taxation since the report by Monti et al (2016) was published. The proposals by the European Commission for a new corporate taxation basis (Business in Europe: Framework for Income Taxation (BEFIT)) offers an opportunity to define more robust new own resources.[5]

Even if it were possible to solve the problem of a centralised financing of the EPGs there would remain the issue of their effective delivery. A pragmatic idea would be to rely on the 'vehicles' offered by EU programmes, either new or already in place. In this respect, while the RRF and SURE cannot play a role as EPGs' vehicles because their projects are implemented at national level even if centrally financed, other EU programmes can serve the purpose of delivering EPGs. Some parts of the 'RePowerEU' support common initiatives at EU level; the same applies to a few NGEU programmes, such as 'Connecting Europe Facility', 'InvestEU', and 'Horizon'. European initiatives are also the core of the 'Innovation Fund' and the 'Hydrogen Bank'. Moreover, if reformed to allow financing via EU resources and devoted to genuine EU-wide projects, the 'Important Projects of Common European Interest (IPCEI)' would offer a very useful tool. Finally, it may be necessary to create other EU vehicles, such as the EU Sovereignty Fund put forward by the President of the European Commission in the State of the Union speech in September 2022, as a way to bring together under a unified and visible policy instrument the various separate vehicles mentioned above. In this sense, the recent European Commission proposal to revise the Multiannual Financial Framework 2021–2027 by creating a unified platform ('Strategic Technologies for Europe Platform' (STEP)) of various EU programmes may represent the start of a movement in that direction.

---

5   The lack of an independent sources of EU revenue to back the issuance of European bonds to finance NGEU may partly explain the recent underperformance of such bonds in financial markets.

11.5 Conclusions

A well-functioning economic union needs a permanent CFC. Amongst the various options for the creation of such a CFC, stepping up the supply of EPGs delivered and financed at EU level appears the most promising avenue. We have argued that EPGs should meet a number of criteria at the intersection of the economic theory of public goods, the theory of fiscal federalism, and the specific institutional and political features of the EU.

We have provided a preliminary conceptual framework that helps to define and select EPGs. In particular, we have listed a number of characteristics, under three main rationales: economic, institutional, and political. Against this background, we have identified six policy areas (digital transition, green transition and energy, social transition, raw materials, security and defence, and health) that respond to the main challenges that the EU is facing. We have listed a number of specific projects and suggested how they could be financed and delivered at EU level. Creating EPGs in these areas would help the EU economy tackle the growing innovation gap vis-à-vis the USA and China in digital activities and artificial intelligence, buttress its energy autonomy, and, thereby, shift the EU economy onto a more sustainable 'business model'.

In our view, the case for increasing the supply of EPGs is strong. However, so far, the debate on a EPGs and, more generally, on a CFC has not taken centre stage for at least two reasons. First, a large amount of resources remains to be spent following the successful implementation of the national recovery and resilience plans: it is hard to conceive of a permanent or recurrent CFC without the clear success of the RRF. Second, the European Commission has decided to strategically decouple the discussion on the reforms of the fiscal rules from that of the CFC, offering the rationale that it might be easier to agree on new fiscal rules without overburdening an already difficult discussion with further controversial elements. This decoupling is understandable in the short term, but, in the longer term, the credibility and success of a rules-based fiscal framework crucially depends on nesting a CFC into the new economic-governance model.

Today the conditions of supplying an adequate amount of EPGs are not yet fulfilled. However, this does not mean that the debate on EPGs should be postponed to an indefinite future. The impact of post-pandemic bottlenecks and the economic consequences of the Russian invasion of Ukraine have highlighted that the EU should implement a new production model to compete with the other main economic areas (namely, the USA and China) and to strengthen its international role. The shift to this new production model requires an innovative industrial policy in which the support of public investment at national level and the production of EPGs by means of EU public investment play a crucial role.

References

Buchholz, W. and T. Sandler (2021). 'Global public goods: A Survey', *Journal of Economic Literature*, 59(2), 488–545, https://doi.org/10.1257/jel.20191546

Buchanan, J. (1968). *The Demand and Supply of Public Goods*, Rand McNally: Chicago

Buti, M. and M. Messori (2021a). 'The Search for a Congruent Euro Area Policy Mix: Vertical Coordination Matters', *CEPR Policy Insight*, 113, https://cepr.org/voxeu/columns/search-congruent-euro-area-policy-mix-vertical-coordination-matters

—— (2021b). 'Towards a New International Economic Governance: The Possible Role of Europe', *STG Policy Papers*, 20, School of Transnational Governance, November, https://doi.org/10.2870/705939

—— (2022a). 'A Central Fiscal Capacity in the EU Policy Mix', *CEPR Discussion Paper*, DP17577, https://cepr.org/publications/dp17577

—— (2022b). 'The Role of Central Fiscal Capacity in Connecting the EU's Domestic and Global Agendas', *STG Policy Papers*, June, 13, EUI School of Transnational Governance, https://doi.org/10.2870/7197

—— (2023). 'Resetting the EU's Business Model after the Watershed', *EPC Discussion Paper*, 13 February, https://www.epc.eu/en/publications/Resetting-the-EUs-business-model-after-the-watershed~4e54bc

Buti, M. and G. Papacostantinou (2022). 'European Public Goods: How Can We Supply More', *VoxEU*, 31 January, https://cepr.org/voxeu/columns/european-public-goods-how-we-can-supply-more

D'Apice, P. and P. Pasimeni (2023). 'Financing EU Public Goods: Vertical Coherence between EU and National Budgets', EUI RSCAS, 2020/47, https://hdl.handle.net/1814/67861

Fuest, C. and J. Pisani-Ferry (2019). 'A Primer on Developing European Public Goods', *EconPol Policy Report*, 3, 16 November

Kindleberger, C.P. (1973). *The world in depression: 1929–1939*, Berkeley and Los Angeles: University of California Press.

Monti, M. et al. (2016). 'Future Financing of the EU. Final Report and Recommendations of the High-Level Group on Own Resources', Brussels, December, https://data.europa.eu/doi/10.2761/36070

Papaconstantinou, G. (2020), 'European Public Goods: Just a Buzzword or a New Departure?', in 'Realising European Added Value', *European Court of Auditors Journal*, 3, https://www.eca.europa.eu/Lists/ECADocuments/JOURNAL20_03/JOURNAL20_03.pdf

Samuelson, P.A. (1954). 'The Pure Theory of Public Expenditure', *Review of Economics and Statistics*, 36(4): 387–89

—— (1955). 'Diagrammatic Exposition of a Theory of Public Expenditure. *Review of Economics and Statistics*, 37(4): 350–56

Stiglitz, J. E. (1986). *Economics of the Public Sector*, New York: W.W. Norton & Co.

—— (1999). 'Knowledge as a Global Public Good', in *Global Public Goods: International Cooperation in the 21st Century*, ed. by I. Kaul, I. Grunberg, and M. Stern, Oxford: Oxford University Press, pp. 308–25

Thöne, M. and H. Kreuter (2020) 'European Public Goods: Their Contribution to a Strong Europe'. *Bertelsmann Stiftung Vision Europe Paper*, 3 September, https://www.bertelsmann-stiftung.de/fileadmin/files/BSt/Publikationen/GrauePublikationen/European_Public_Goods_Their_Contribution_to_a_Strong_Europe_EN.pdf

Tosato, G.L. (2021), 'Sulla fattibilità giuridica di una capacità fiscale della UE a Trattati costanti', *Astrid Rassegna*, 15

12. Options for a Permanent EU Sovereign Fund: Meeting the Climate-Investment Challenge and Promoting Macroeconomic Stability

Philipp Heimberger and Andreas Lichtenberger

This chapter argues that a new, permanent EU fiscal capacity can contribute to meeting the green-transition challenges and providing countercyclical macroeconomic stabilisation. While the Recovery and Resilience Fund (RRF) is not large enough to address the current challenges, its introduction was an essential step forward in providing an operational blueprint for a permanent EU investment fund. The reform of EU fiscal rules is set to provide insufficient scope for the additional public climate investment required to meet the climate targets. Furthermore, the EU sovereignty fund proposed by the European Commission in the form of the Strategic Technologies for Europe Platform (STEP) adds little new money, focuses on green-tech subsidies instead of public investment, and falls short of providing a realistic vision of meeting public investment

12.1 Introduction

The introduction of the Recovery and Resilience Facility (RRF) in the context of Next Generation EU during the COVID-19 pandemic is a major common fiscal policy tool, representing a temporary large-scale public-spending initiative financed by issuing EU bonds. The RRF contributes to macroeconomic stabilisation while addressing structural policy goals related to climate and digitisation by way of public investment and reforms (Alcidi and Gros 2020; Bankowski et al. 2021). However, the grants channelled to individual member countries based on the issuance of EU bonds will only be available up to the year 2026. Debate over whether the RRF should remain a one-off initiative is in full swing (Allemand et al. 2023). This chapter contributes by discussing selected options for designing a new, additional EU sovereign fund.

https://doi.org/10.11647/OBP.0386.12

12.2 Arguments for a New, Additional, EU Sovereign Fund

This section discusses three main reasons in favour of a new, additional, EU sovereign fund. First, the reform of EU fiscal rules is set to provide national governments with insufficient space for public investment, in particular for climate and energy. Second, the RRF is too small to meet the climate goals and will only provide funds up to the year 2026. Third, the European Union lacks a permanent sovereign fund to promote macroeconomic stabilisation during downswings.

The current institutional architecture of the European Economic and Monetary Union makes public investment for several Member States more difficult, especially when fiscal consolidation pressures increase during and after crises. A central problem with regard to the euro area's institutional architecture is that interest rate spreads worsen the financing conditions of some Member States to a greater extent (De Grauwe and Ji 2022). This may inhibit their investments in the aftermath of a crisis and, thereby, hinder these economies to a greater extent in reaching the EU climate and energy goals.

In the aftermath of the COVID-19 crisis and the energy crisis, fiscal consolidation pressures tend to put downward pressure on public investment, especially in countries with higher public-debt ratios and higher interest burdens. In the absence of political countermeasures at the European level, there is a risk that public investment will fall short of what is needed. Public investment can be cut more easily than other government spending components when the pressure to pursue fiscal consolidation increases (Jacques 2021). In an environment of higher long-term interest rates, undertaking public-investment projects becomes more difficult.

Overall, the EU fiscal rules exhibit a high degree of complexity (Blanchard et al. 2021). The rules have failed to prevent rising public-debt ratios, even as austerity programmes put downward pressure on public investment. Overall, the design of the EU fiscal rulebook prior to the COVID-19 pandemic, when the rules were suspended, contributed to procyclical fiscal policy; thus, fiscal policy tended to amplify economic developments rather than to counteract them (Heimberger and Kapeller 2017).

In principle, reform of EU fiscal rules could increase the scope for public investment at the national level (Dullien et al. 2022). However, with the reform of EU fiscal rules proposed by the European Commission, individual EU Member States would only be able to submit plans for investments and reforms if they are consistent with sustainable government finances in the medium term based on debt-sustainability analysis (Heimberger 2023). Governments can extend fiscal consolidation paths by up to three years if the Commission's technical analysis suggests that these investments are compatible with debt sustainability, if, that is, they are focused on reducing public debt ratios in the long run (European Commission 2023a). The general idea is that only selected public investment projects should be subject to reduced fiscal-consolidation pressures. However, broad exemptions of (climate) public investments in deficit and debt calculations (for example, Truger 2016) are not included.

The reform of EU fiscal rules will not provide sufficient scope for the needed climate and energy investments of the public sector; hence, national governments will find it hard to meet the investment requirements. A prior assessment report of the European Commission is key in providing numbers on essential climate investment dimensions (European Commission 2021). Existing studies estimate the need for additional annual investment for the green transition in a range between 1.75% and 6% of EU economic output per year, where about half of the funding should be provided by the public sector (Stöllinger 2023; Wildauer et al. 2020; Pollin 2020). We focus on a lower bound estimate and assume an equal division of the costs between the public and the private sector. This entails a need for additional annual public investment for climate and energy of at least 1% of the EU GDP (Heimberger and Lichtenberger 2023).

A large part of climate investments will have to be financed through public borrowing. On the one hand, the urgency of the climate crisis creates immediate pressure to act, which would overwhelm a private sector left to its own devices; on the other hand, future generations will benefit substantially from these investments and the associated net public-wealth creation.

The RRF was a major step towards a stronger common European investment policy. To mitigate pandemic-related economic impacts, European decision-makers agreed on Next Generation EU (NGEU) in summer 2020. The largest part of NGEU consists of the RRF, which has a total size of €723bn at 2022 prices. Of this, €385bn are available in the form of repayable loans and €338bn are grants that the individual Member States do not have to repay directly.

The RRF represents a large-scale temporary EU-wide investment initiative through the issuance of EU bonds. The EU Commission raises funds on financial markets on behalf of all Member States, and countries hit harder by the COVID-19 pandemic are eligible to receive more funds than those less affected. Each Member State is obliged to spend at least 37% of its RRF funds on climate investments. However, to achieve the EU climate target by 2030 (which calls for a 55% reduction in CO_2 emissions compared to 1990 levels), would require an expansion of public investment on the order of ten times the green-investment share of the RRF, equivalent to about €460bn per year (Cornago and Springford 2021).

While the RRF allows for important investments, the instrument will only be in place for the period from 2021 to 2026; from 2024 onward, grants will be gradually phased out (see Figure 12.1). As national governments undertake RRF investments at the same time, there are positive cross-border economic effects, which are stronger for high-export countries such as Germany and Austria than for many of those EU countries that receive more grants directly (Picek 2020; Pfeiffer et al. 2023). Therefore, an isolated focus on the allocation of subsidies to individual EU Member States falls short because it neglects these positive spillover effects of investments.

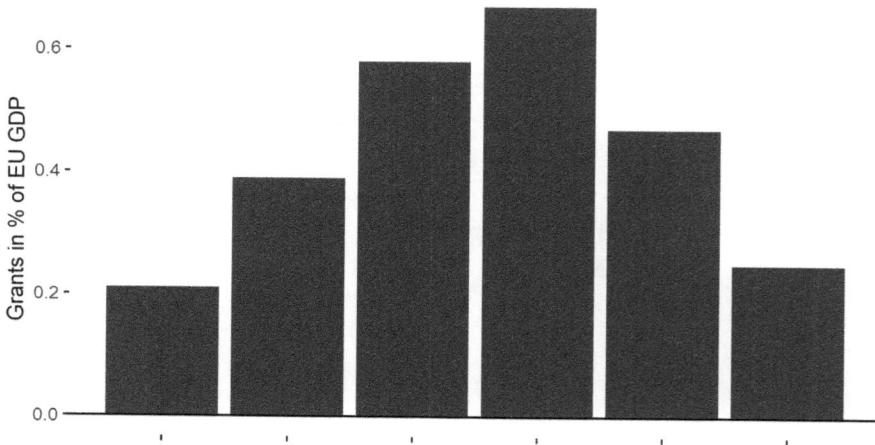

Fig. 12.1 RRF Grants for the Whole EU, 2021–2026.
Source: European Commission.

While the RRF represents an innovative European investment model, the instrument is still not nearly large enough to sufficiently address the investment requirements due to climate change and the energy crisis, especially since the grants only flow until 2026 and already diminish from 2024 onwards. In the absence of a successor sovereign fund, public-investment problems in Member States must, therefore, be expected to increase particularly after the year 2026.

When it comes to coping with existing investment requirements that go far beyond the RRF, a joint EU investment offensive is more promising than national initiatives. Individual initiatives are limited by pre-existing climate-change impacts, which are more prevalent in some EU countries than others, and by cross-border emissions that continue to occur (Arnold et al. 2022). In addition, coordinated investments also show stronger positive network effects in the area of new technologies. Coordinating investment efforts and securing their financing to achieve common goals is also more efficiently achieved at the EU level than at the nation-state level. A joint credit-financed effort with cost-sharing between generations also reduces pressure for tax increases in the present.

Tackling the climate and energy crisis is also relevant to ensure the political unity and, thus, the geopolitically strong position of the EU in the future. Other large economic blocs currently pursue aggressive industrial policies concerning green technologies to secure competitiveness and higher global market shares. In particular, the USA passed the Inflation Reduction Act (IRA) in August 2022. Through additional public spending via tax-credits and subsidies for energy-security and climate-change investment in the region of $370bn over the next 10 years, the IRA is not only supposed to help achieve reductions in greenhouse-gas emissions. It also intends to secure America's supremacy as the largest energy producer in the long term (Tucker and Malhotra 2022). The USA strives for international technology leadership, and additional climate spending is seen as an instrument to ensure that geopolitical ambitions can be met. In this context, the establishment of a sizeable EU investment fund could enhance the ability of the community of EU Member States to undertake strategic investment projects in climate and energy to mobilise private investments and promote the competitiveness in industries that are key for the future. This would enable European companies to properly compete with their peers in countries, such as the USA, where sovereign governments promote aggressive industrial policy based on sizeable additional public spending.

Furthermore, joint European decisions and initiatives require a distribution of economic burdens. Populations in EU countries are affected to different degrees by the consequences of the energy and climate crisis (Lenaerts et al. 2022). This makes policy implementations through coordination of nation-state initiatives increasingly difficult and requires joint EU solutions based on solidarity (Redeker and Jaeger 2022).

The European Economic and Monetary Union still lacks a permanent centralised fiscal capacity that contributes to cushioning macroeconomic shocks. When external shocks hit, such a facility would provide funding when national fiscal policies cannot respond adequately. Common monetary policy and domestic fiscal policy may be insufficient in responding to large common shocks; asymmetric impacts of a shock on different member countries may be impossible to address with domestic measures only (Misch and Rey 2022). As the next section will discuss, a European investment fund could provide stable funding for investments to avoid cuts during recessions, while a rainy-day fund could provide countercyclical funds, for example, via an unemployment re-insurance scheme.

12.3 Options for a New European Sovereign Fund

This section discusses three options for a new, additional, sovereign fund. First, a new, permanent investment fund based on the RRF model could provide funds so that individual member countries can make additional investments, in particular, related to climate and energy. Second, a new sovereign fund could focus on providing European public goods to emphasise the Pan-European dimension of investments. Third, a European 'rainy-day fund' could be introduced, which would finance expenditures during economic downturns in particularly affected countries by funds accumulated during boom periods. These options could be implemented individually or in combination.

12.3.1 A Permanent EU Investment Fund for Climate and Energy

RRF funds are disbursed gradually on the basis of evidence of investments and reforms implemented. In addition to meeting agreed milestones, investments and reforms must be consistent with long-term structural goals (such as climate neutrality). While using

RRF money for additional investments can have a substantial stabilising effect on the economy (Picek 2020), the programme's main purpose is to provide steady funding for investments and reforms over the period 2021–2026. The instrument is set up in a way that funds can flow regardless of swings in the business cycle.

A new, permanent EU Climate and Energy Investment Fund (CEIF), built on experience of the RRF, could support public investments that are tied to targets for achieving climate and energy goals (Heimberger and Lichtenberger 2023). The size of such a fund should allow for public investment of at least 1% of EU economic output annually to meet increased investment requirements even during periods of political and economic stress. An EU CEIF would help avoid procyclical cuts in public investment in the context of economic downswings, but it would not trigger transfers in reaction to negative shocks as in the case of a rainy-day fund.

An EU investment fund with green conditions would help achieve climate and energy targets. As funding criteria, the EU climate coefficient method, which already exists for green investments of the RRF funds, could be adapted (European Commission 2021). According to assumed contributions to the green transition, this method assigns weighting coefficients with regard to the eligibility of project expenditures. In the current situation, expenditures for projects to improve the energy efficiency of residential buildings or to expand solar-energy parks are weighted with a climate coefficient of 100%, while large companies' energy-efficiency projects only receive a climate coefficient of 40% and their digitisation initiatives attract 0%. Applying an adapted method could allow for a consistent pursuit of climate and energy goals that is also not threatened by deteriorations in the budget outlook. While loans taken out by individual countries have a direct impact on the national public debt ratio, grants financed via EU bonds would not pass through to the public debt ratio. This would make it easier for EU Member States to comply with reformed EU fiscal rules, which could then be enforced more strictly even after their prospective reform (European Commission 2023a). A permanent EU CEIF would also have the advantage that national green investments accepted by the European Commission and European Council could draw on a common taxonomy to determine which investments should be classified as 'green'.

In financing the permanent EU investment fund for climate and energy, the RRF could serve as a model. The European Commission would issue bonds on behalf of the EU to raise the investment funds in financial markets. Member states would not be individually liable for the EU bonds issued; the liability would remain with the EU, which would act in the financial markets backed by the guarantees of future contributions to the EU budget by EU Member States. The agreement on Next Generation EU provides for the establishment of new EU own resources that generate a revenue stream from which EU bonds can be serviced over a long period of time. A key advantage of repeating this financing method for the permanent EU investment fund would be that individual EU Member States' contributions to the EU budget would not need to be increased. Options for new EU own resources—such as Emission Trading System (ETS)-based resources, Carbon Border Adjustment Mechanism (CBAM)-based resources, and taxation reforms for financial goods, corporations, aviation, top earners, and wealth owners—have been discussed by Schratzenstaller et al. (2022). Some researchers also argue that an EU-wide wealth tax to finance green investments could result in tax revenue in the dimension of the annual investment gap, namely 1.5% of EU GDP annually, with other models generating between 3% and even 11% in additional tax revenue (Kapeller et al. 2023). Another option is not to service the EU bonds (entirely) with EU own resources but to allow the build-up of an EU debt stock.

A recent report published by the ECB (Abraham et al. 2023) that seriously engaged with public-investment needs for climate and energy also concluded that an 'EU Climate and Energy Security Fund providing €500bn by 2030 would be an effective and efficient option for addressing these climate and energy-related public investment needs' (Abraham et al. 2023: 4).

Establishing a permanent common fiscal capacity at the EU level could be an effective, low-cost and politically feasible initiative. Collectively providing funds through an EU investment fund along the lines of the RRF would be a more attractive investment option for many EU countries than if they had to borrow individually on their own (Cornago and Springford 2021). An EU CEIF would make it easier for governments to undertake additional green investments beyond existing public investment quotas while complying with EU fiscal rules. A reasoning similar to the multi-factor disbursement decision rule applied to the RRF could also be used in the case of the CEIF. Any concrete funds-allocation rule would have to pass a political negotiation process. However, for illustration purposes, we show what such a stylised funds allocation could look like. A satisfactory and sufficient criterion should at least bear in mind each Member State's needs for mitigation in the light of their respective financial abilities to cope with financing such a transition. Even though a lot more details could be considered, we here restrict ourselves to: (i) using the greenhouse-gas (GHG) emissions per capita for the variable that describes the need for change, since economies with very high GHG footprints require more structural change, (ii) accounting for the size of the country by including the current population count, and (iii) using the inverse of GDP per capita as a weight term that captures the degree to which financial support is needed. This implies that the share of the CEIF that should be attributed to each Member State i should be proportional to

$$CEIF_i = \frac{GHG_i}{pop_i} \, pop_i \left(\frac{GDP_i / pop_i}{\sum_i GDP_i / pop_i} \right)^{-1} = GHG_i \left(\frac{GDP_i / pop_i}{\sum_i GDP_i / pop_i} \right)^{-1}.$$

Figure 12.2 presents the results of such a distribution rule. The upper panel (A) shows the distribution of CEIF funds in absolute terms, which can be thought of as the share of the total annual investment funding volume of CEIF. If the CEIF allowed for investment of 1% of EU economic output per year (€146.5bn), large industrial countries like Poland (19.2% of the total investment funds), Germany (14.5%), Italy (9.6%), or Spain (8.4%) would receive the largest absolute grant amounts according to our allocation criteria. The lower panel (B) shows the amount of grants received by each country in relation to their own economic output. It can be seen that specifically Eastern Member States would receive relatively higher grants in comparison to their GDP, for example, Bulgaria (10.4%), Poland (4.9%), Romania (4.4%), and Latvia (3.4%), followed by Southern and Northern European countries.

The experience of debt-based financing at the EU level through the RRF can also be used to expand the thinking about financing options for an EU fiscal capacity. The introduction of a common European debt agency could circumvent the debt difficulties of individual countries, provide more funding space at lower funding costs, help to stabilise government-bond markets, and offer advantages in the issuance of assets considered particularly safe and liquid that, as such, would be in high demand (Saraceno et al. 2022). Institutional investors such as insurance companies and pension funds, show great demand for safe assets, the supply of which would be expanded by the increased and planned issuance of EU bonds over a longer period of time, thus contributing to the stability of financial markets (Alogoskoufis et al. 2020).

A) Distribution of CEIF funds in absolute terms

B) Distribution of CEIF funds in relative terms by country GDP

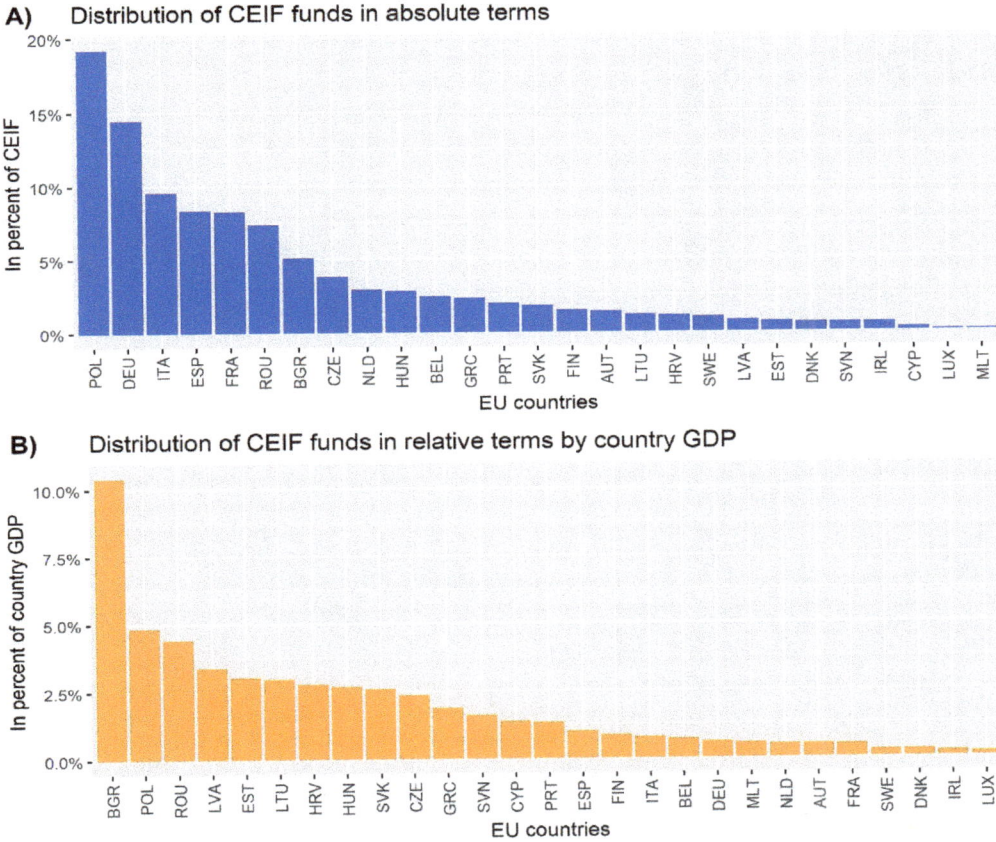

Fig. 12.2 Distribution of CEIF Funds in Absolute and in Relative Terms.
Note: Upper Panel (A) shows the percentage share of the CEIF that each EU Member State would receive based on absolute GHG emissions and the inverse of GDP per capita as disbursement criteria. Lower panel (B) shows the amount of the disbursement in relative terms based on the respective GDP (data based on 2021 values)
Source: Production-based GHG emissions in CO2 equivalents and population observations for 2021 adopted from Our World in Data; GDP at 2021 market prices and in € adopted from Eurostat.

12.3.2 European Public Goods: Focusing on the Pan-European Dimension

The boost from RRF funds is primarily attributed to national investment and reform projects, although the financing is based on issuing EU bonds. The option to implement a new long-term investment fund for climate and energy would also work by channelling funds to promote investment at the national level.

However, a new sovereign fund could also focus explicitly on genuinely European projects in the field of energy- and transport-system transformation to create common EU added value. EU public goods would benefit EU citizens across borders. For example, the improvement of transport and energy infrastructures is consistent with the shared necessity to decarbonize. Using the financing from an EU sovereign fund for European projects could contribute to overcoming the net-position thinking in EU Member States with regard to contributions to and transfers received from EU budgets (Bachtrögler-Unger et al. 2020).

Creel et al. (2020) propose investments in a European high-speed train system that could reduce CO2 emissions in the transport sector in the long term. In addition, in the area of energy and decarbonisation, they discuss the realisation of an integrated electricity grid for the transmission of 100% renewable energy and support for complementary battery and green-hydrogen projects. While a focus on Pan-European low-carbon transport and energy systems seems obvious in the context of pursuing ambitious climate and energy goals, other European projects could also be facilitated by an EU sovereign fund, such as security projects that enhance European autonomy in the context of the geopolitical struggle of the EU with China, Russia, and the USA.

12.3.3 A Rainy-Day Fund for Macroeconomic Stabilisation

The investment fund components discussed so far do not primarily focus on countercyclical stabilisation. Investments for climate and energy can be expected to have short-run and long-run impacts on the economy via fiscal multipliers (Fournier 2016). Furthermore, adaption investments for climate and energy are key to lessening future economic damage from climate change, thereby easing the pressure on national budgets in the long-run and making inaction economically unjustifiable (Zenios 2022; Steininger 2022). However, designing an investment fund with an emphasis on meeting long-run structural goals will not provide special countercyclical stabilisation properties during economic downswings.

For countercyclical purposes, a European 'Rainy-Day Fund' (RDF) could be introduced, which would finance expenditures during economic downturns in particularly affected countries by funds accumulated during boom periods (Lenarcic and Korhonen 2018; see Figure 12.3). A rainy-day fund would promote countercyclical macroeconomic stabilisation in future crises. For example, the IMF discusses a concept for the euro area wherein euro-area countries pay 0.35% of their economic output annually into a rainy-day fund to build up assets in good economic times that would be used to stabilise the region in the event of crises. The concept also includes mechanisms to avoid permanent fiscal transfers (Arnold et al. 2018). Rainy-day fund proposals include transfers triggered after negative shocks to economic activity (Furceri and Zdzienicka 2015), an investment-stabilization function that supports public investment especially during economic downturns (European Commission 2018), and unemployment re-insurance schemes (Dolls 2020).

Permanent EU fiscal capacity

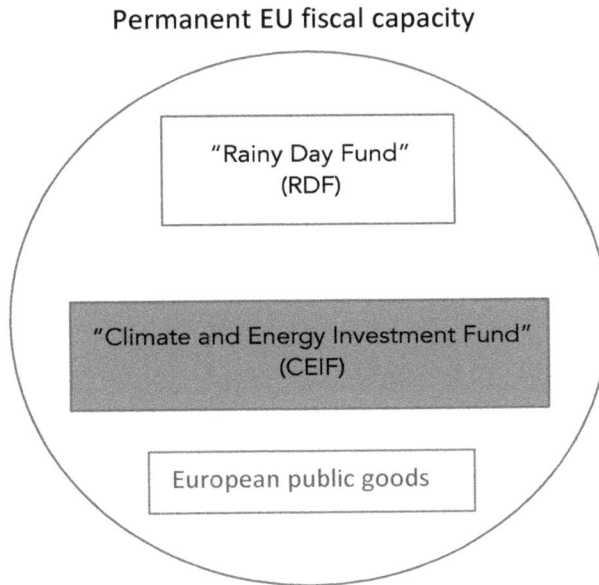

Fig. 12.3 Components of a Permanent EU Fiscal Capacity.
Source: Author's elaboration.

12.4 An EU Sovereignty Fund?

Prompted by USA green industrial-policy initiatives like the IRA, the EU is developing a policy response. On 20 June 2023, the European Commission announced the proposal of the 'Strategic Technologies for Europe Platform (STEP)' which shall take over the function of an EU sovereignty fund. The STEP is supposed to support the development of technologies in the field of digitalisation, decarbonisation, and biotech. Hence, its focus is on matching green-tech subsidies from the USA and China. Money flows will mostly be based on reshuffling existing funds. Instead of an injection of new cash, the policy draft reroutes money flows from existing budget positions with a €10bn top-up of Member States. Assuming multipliers between 1.3 and 10, the EC expects to mobilise a total volume of €160bn with €10bn of fresh money plus €50bn of redirected funds (see Table 12.1).

Table 12.1 EC Proposal for STEP

Program	Fresh Money	Adjustments	Multiplier	Headline number
InvestEU	3	7.5 (guaranteed)	10	75
Horizon (EIC)	0.5	2.13 (complemented)	~ 5	13
Innovation Fund	5		4*	20
European Defense Fund	1.5		1.33*	2
Subtotal	10			110
Cohesion fund reprioritizing**				14
Just Transition Fund**		6		6
RRF Resources for InvestEU products				30
Subtotal				50
Total				160

Note: * = Inferred; ** = Every 5% of programming towards STEP priorities leads to €18.9bn of [cohesion] resources made available, in addition to €6bn to be paid out from the Just Transition Fund
Source: Data from European Commission 2023b.

Besides assuming high multipliers and hardly adding any fresh money, the EU proposal of addressing a plethora of spending targets with €60bn, that is about 0.35% of current EU GDP, appears small. As outlined earlier, just to meet the EU climate goals an addition of at least 1% of EU GDP on an annual basis is considered necessary. Even assuming a crowding-in factor of 100% for all programmes, the total STEP spending volume would only amount to 0.7% of GDP.

12.5 Conclusions

This chapter has discussed selected options for a new, additional EU sovereign fund. A rainy-day fund for macroeconomic stabilisation in times of crisis could be combined with a long-term investment fund for climate and energy that provides public goods at the European and/or national level. However, the three options discussed in this chapter could also be implemented individually. A decision rule on the disbursement of funds could be based on multi-factor criteria as it was the case for the RRF. Similarly, the servicing of the debt for such a permanent sovereign fund could be ensured via new own EU resources or via allowing the build-up of an EU debt stock.

The debate on whether the EU needs a new, additional sovereign fund continues. The European Commission has tabled proposals for a European sovereignty fund. In their final proposal they reconcile their visions of a sovereign fund with the STEP. This programme, unfortunately, mostly reshuffles existing budgets and hardly adds new money; it does not even amount to half a percent of EU GPD in total. To keep alive at least the possibility of meeting the climate goals, European policymakers would need to do more.

References

Abraham, L., M. O'Connell, and I. Oleaga (2023). 'The Legal and Institutional Feasibility of an EU Climate and Energy Security Fund'. *ECB Occasional Paper*, 313, https://doi.org/10.2139/ssrn.4403664

Alcidi, C., and D. Gros (2020). 'Next Generation EU: A Large Common Response to the COVID-19 Crisis', *Intereconomics*, 55(4): 202–03, https://doi.org/10.1007/s10272-020-0900-6

Allemand, F., J. Creel, F. Saraceno, S. Levasseur, and N. Leron (2023). 'Making Next Generation EU a Permanent Tool. *FEPS*

Alogoskoufis, S., M. Giuzio, T. Kostka, A. Levels, L. Vivar, and M. Wedow (2020). 'How Could a Common Safe Asset Contribute to Financial Stability and Financial Integration in the Banking Union?' *Financial Integration and Structure in the Euro Area*, ECB-Publication, March

Arnold, N. G., B. Barkbu, H. E. Ture, H. Wang, and J. Yao (2018). 'A Central Fiscal Stabilization Capacity for the Euro Area'. *IMF Staff Discussion Note*, 18/03, https://doi.org/10.5089/9781484348178.006

Arnold, N., R. Balakrishnan, B. Barkbu, H. Davoodi, A. Lagerborg, W. Lam, P. Medas, J. Otten, L. Rabier, C. Roehler, A. Shahmoradi, M. Spector, S. Weber, J. Zettelmeyer (2022). 'Reforming the EU Fiscal Framework: Strengthening the Fiscal Rules and Institutions'. *IMF Departmental Papers*, 2022/014, https://doi.org/10.5089/9798400209888.087

Bachtrögler-Unger, J., M. Holzner, V. Kubekova, M. Schratzenstaller (2020). 'Overcoming Net Position Thinking in EU Member States', *ÖGFE Policy Brief*, July

Bankowsi, K., M. Ferdinandusse, S. Hauptmeier, P. Jacquinot, V. Valenta (2021). 'The Macroeconomic Impact of the Next Generation EU Instrument on the Euro Area', *ECB Occasional Paper*, 2021/255, https://doi.org/10.2139/ssrn.3797126

Cornago, E. and J. Springford (2021). 'Why the EU's Recovery Fund should be Permanent'. *Policy Brief*, July 14, Centre for European Reform (CER), https://www.cer.eu/publications/archive/policy-brief/2021/why-eus-recovery-fund

Creel, J., M. Holzner, F. Saraceno, A. Watt, J. Wittwer (2020). 'How to Spend It: A Proposal for a European COVID-19 Recovery Programme'. *WIIW Policy Report*, 38

De Grauwe, P. And Y. Ji (2022). 'The Fragility of the Eurozone: Has it Disappeared?', *Journal of International Money and Finance*, 120, 102546, https://doi.org/10.1016/j.jimonfin.2021.102546

Dolls, M. (2020). 'An Unemployment Re-Insurance Scheme for the Eurozone? Stabilizing and Redistributive Effects'. *CESifo Working Paper*, 8219, https://doi.org/10.2139/ssrn.3576297

Dullien, S., R. Repasi, C. Paety, A. Watt, S. Watzka (2022). 'Between High Ambition and Pragmatism: Proposals for a Reform of Fiscal Rules without Treaty Change', *IMK Study*, 77

European Commission (2018). 'Proposal for a Regulation of the European Parliament and of the Council on the Establishment of a European Investment Stabilization Function', COM(2018) 387 final

—— (2021). 'Next Generation EU: Green Bond Framework'. *Commission Staff Working Document*, https://ec.europa.eu/info/strategy/eu-budget/eu-borrower-investor-relations/legal-texts_en#nextgenerationeu-green-bond-framework

—— (2023a). 'Proposal for a Regulation of the European Parliament and of the Council on the Effective Coordination of Economic Policies and Multilateral Budgetary Surveillance and Repealing Council Regulation', 1466/97, COM(2023) 240 final

—— (2023b). 'EU Budget'. Press release, 20 June, https://ec.europa.eu/commission/presscorner/detail/en/ip_23_3364

Fournier, J. (2016). 'The Positive Effect of Public Investment on Potential Growth', *OECD Economics Department Working Papers*, 1347, OECD Publishing, Paris, https://doi.org/10.1787/15e400d4-en

Furceri, D. and A. Zdzienicka (2015). 'The Euro Area Crisis: Need for a Supranational Fiscal Risk Sharing Mechanism?'. *Open Economies Review*, 26(4): 683–710, https://doi.org/10.1007/s11079-015-9347-y

Heimberger, P. and J. Kapeller (2017). 'The Performativity of Potential Output: Pro-cyclicality and Path Dependency in Coordinating European Fiscal Policies'. *Review of International Political Economy*, 24(5), 904–28, https://doi.org/10.1080/09692290.2017.1363797

Heimberger, P. (2023). 'Debt Sustainability Analysis as an Anchor in EU Fiscal Rules: An Assessment of the European Commission's Reform Orientations', In-Depth Analysis Requested by the ECON Committee of the European Parliament, March

—— and A Lichtenberger (2023). 'RRF 2.0: A Permanent EU Investment Fund in the Context of the Energy Crisis, Climate Change and EU Fiscal Rules, *WIIW Policy Notes and Reports*, 63

Jacques, O. (2021). 'Austerity and the Path of Least Resistance: How Fiscal Consolidations Crowd out Long-Term Investments'. *Journal of European Public Policy*, 28(4): 551–70, https://doi.org/10.1080/13501763.2020.1737957

Kapeller, J., S. Leitch, and R. Wildauer (2023). 'Can a European Wealth Tax Close the Green Investment Gap?'. *Ecological Economics*, 209, 107849, https://doi.org/10.1016/j.ecolecon.2023.107849

Lenaerts, K., S. Tagliapietra, and G. Wolff (2022). 'How Can the European Union Adapt to Climate Change while Avoiding a New Fault Line?'. *Bruegel Policy Contribution*, 11/2022, https://doi.org/10.1007/s10272-022-1071-4

Lenarcic, A. and K. Korhonen (2018). 'A Case for a European Rainy Day Fund'. *ESM Discussion Paper Series*, 5, European Stability Mechanism (ESM)

Misch, F. and M. Rey (2022). 'The Case for a Loan-Based Euro Area Stability Fund'. *ESM Discussion Paper Series*, 20

Picek, O. (2020). 'Spillover Effects from Next Generation EU'. *Intereconomics*, 55: 325–31, https://doi.org/10.1007/s10272-020-0923-z

Pfeiffer, P., J. Vargaand, and J. in 't Veld (2023). 'Quantifying Spillovers of Coordinated Investment Stimulus in the EU'. *Macroeconics Dynamics*, 27(7): 1843–865, https://doi.org/10.1017/s1365100522000487

Redeker, N. and P. Jäger (2022). 'New Needs, New Prices, Same Money: Why the EU Must Raise its Game to Combat the War's Economic Fallout. *Jacques Delors Centre Policy Brief*, June

Saraceno, F., L. Gobbi, E. Belloni, C. A. Favero, and M. Amato (2022). 'Creating a Safe Asset without Debt Mutualisation: The Opportunity of a European Debt Agency'. *VoxEU*, 22 April, https://cepr.org/voxeu/columns/creating-safe-asset-without-debt-mutualisation-opportunity-european-debt-agency

Schratzenstaller, M., D. Nerudova, V. Solilova, M. Holzner, P. Heimberger, N. Korpar, A. Maucorps, and B. Moshammer (2022). 'New EU Own Resources: Possibilities and Limitations of Steering Effects and Sectoral Policy Co-Benefits'. Study Requested by the BUDG Committee of the European Parliament, March

Steininger, K. W. (2022). 'Foreseeability of Economic Damages Related to Inadequate Climate Mitigation and Adaptation', in *Climate Change, Responsibility and Liability*, June, pp. 93–102, https://doi.org/10.5771/9783748930990-93

Truger, A. (2016). 'Implementing the Golden Rule for Public Investment in Europe: Safeguarding Public Investment and Supporting the Recovery'. *Materialien zu Wirtschaft und Gesellschaft*, 138

Tucker, T., and S. Malhotra (2022). 'The Unprecedented Green Industrial Policy Wins in the Inflation Reduction Act', Roosevelt Institute, 5 August, https://rooseveltinstitute.org/2022/08/05/unprecedented-green-industrial-policy-wins-in-the-inflation-reduction-act/

Zenios, S. (2022). 'The Risks from Climate Change to Sovereign Debt', *Climatic Change*, 172, 30, https://doi.org/10.1007/s10584-022-03373-4

Contributor Biographies

Giovanni Barbieri is a Research Fellow at CRANEC (Centro di ricerche in analisi economica e sviluppo economico internazionale) at Università Cattolica del Sacro Cuore. He holds a PhD in Institutions and Policies. He was previously Adjunct Professor of History of International and Commercial Institutions at the University of Palermo (D.E.M.S., Italy), project researcher in the Kone Foundation Project 'Regional Challenges to Multilateralism' (Tampere University, Finland), and Visiting Scholar at 'Istituto Ciampi' in Florence (2022). His main expertise is in international political economy (IPE), in particular the problem of uneven development and the new challenges posed by rising countries to the current global governance scheme with particular reference to BRICS.

Eva Benages is a Research Technician at Ivie (Instituto Valenciano de Investigaciones Económicas) and Adjunct Professor at the Universitat de València. She graduated in Economics from the Universitat de València with special honors in 2004, holds a University Professional Specialization Diploma in Spanish Stock and Financial Markets (2003), and completed her postgraduate studies at the Universitat de València with a major in Economic Integration and Development (2007). She has participated in more than thirty national and international projects (EU KLEMS, PREDICT, SPINTAN, etc.) and is the co-author of numerous books, articles, and specialized reports. Her main fields of research are growth, productivity, capitalization, and public investment. ORCID: https://orcid.org/0000-0003-4511-7715

Andrea Brasili is a Senior Economist at the EIB (Luxembourg) interested in both micro (firm-level) data analysis and macroeconomic developments, particularly those related to fiscal policy. He received his PhD in Public Economics from the University of Pavia (Italy). Before joining the EIB, he worked in the private sector (in Italian banks and asset management companies) as a research economist, whilst still collaborating with academia.

Marco Buti is Tommaso Padoa-Schioppa Chair on economic and monetary integration at the European University Institute. Until May 2023, he was chief of staff of the Commissioner for the economy and, between 2008 and 2019, Director General for economic and financial affairs at the European Commission. He has written extensively on macroeconomic policy, global governance, and welfare-state reform.

Floriana Cerniglia is a full professor of Economics at Università Cattolica del Sacro Cuore (Milan) and Director of CRANEC (Centro di ricerche in analisi economica e sviluppo economico internazionale). She is the Co-Editor-in-Chief of *EconomiaPolitica, Journal of Analytical and Institutional Economics*. She received her PhD from the University of Warwick (UK) and her research interests are in Public Economics and in macroeconomic policies. She has published in leading international journals and she has coordinated and participated in a number of peer-reviewed research projects.

Alessandro Coloccia joined the European Commission in 2022 as a seconded expert from Cassa Depositi e Prestiti, the Italian National Promotional Institution. After having worked in the Cabinet of Commissioner for Economy, Paolo Gentiloni, he moved to Directorate-General for Economic and Financial Affairs (DG ECFIN). Previously, he worked for Cassa Depositi e Prestiti from 2019 to 2022 as a policy analyst in the European Affairs department. Alessandro started his career in 2018 as a policy officer in the Municipality of Paris. He holds a *cum laude* Bachelor of Arts degree in Social Sciences from University College Utrecht and a *cum laude* Master's degree in European Affairs from SciencesPo Paris.

Yanis Dafermos is a Reader in Economics at SOAS, University of London. He is also the Research and Knowledge Exchange Convenor of the SOAS Department of Economics, a Senior Fellow at the SOAS Centre for Sustainable Finance, and a Fellow at the Forum for Macroeconomics and Macroeconomic Policies (FMM). His research interests include financial macroeconomics, climate finance, ecological macroeconomics, climate-aligned development, and inequality. His work has been published in several peer-reviewed journals, such as the *Cambridge Journal of Economics, Ecological Economics, Environment and Planning A*, the *Journal of Financial Stability, Nature Climate Change,* and *New Political Economy*. He is a Committee member of the Post-Keynesian Economics Society (PKES), a Council member of the European Association for Evolutionary Political Economy (EAEPE), a member of the Editorial Board of Ecological Economics, and an Associate Editor of the Review of Evolutionary Political Economy. ORCID: https://orcid.org/0000-0002-8127-6249

Enzo Dia is Associate Professor of Economic Policy at the Università degli Studi di Milano-Bicocca and a Research Fellow at CRANEC (Centro di ricerche in analisi economica e sviluppo economico internazionale) at Università Cattolica del Sacro Cuore. He received his PhD from the University of Strathclyde (UK) and is a fellow of the Rimini Center for Economic Analysis. His research interests are in macroeconomics, banking, and institutional economics. He has published in leading international journals and he is Co-Editor of the *Journal of Macroeconomics*.

Tommaso Faccio is a lecturer in Accounting at Nottingham University Business School. He is a chartered accountant (ICAS) and his research interests include international tax, transfer pricing, tax treaties, and tax avoidance. Until July 2014, he was a Transfer Pricing

Senior Manager in the Deloitte LLP International Tax team and has significant experience advising multinationals on complex international tax issues, particularly in the area of Transfer Pricing and Permanent Establishment, first at Ernst and Young LLP and then at Deloitte LLP. Tommaso is a guest lecturer at the Berlin School of Economics and Law. ORCID: https://orcid.org/0000-0002-5801-1509

Demetrio Guzzardi is a PhD student in Economics at Scuola Superiore Sant'Anna in Pisa. He obtained his Master's degree in Economics from the Paris School of Economics and Sorbonne in Paris. Previously, he worked at the Economic Department of the OECD and the Directorate for Employment and Social Inclusion of the European Commission. He is also a Fellow of the World Inequality Lab (WIL) of the Paris School of Economics. His current research focuses on the estimation of income and wealth distribution, fiscal policies, and the possible role of climate change on shaping inequality. ORCID: https://orcid.org/0000-0001-5315-0756

Phillip Heimberger is Economist at the Vienna Institute for International Economic Studies (WIIW), where he leads the macro research group. He holds a PhD in economics from the Vienna University of Economics and Business. His main research interests are in macroeconomics, public finance, and international economics. His work focuses on the macroeconomic implications of fiscal policy and fiscal rules, the political economy of public debt, and the socio-economic impacts of economic globalisation. ORCID: https://orcid.org/0000-0001-9874-7345

Ekaterina Juergens completed her Master's degree in Economics at the University of Cologne and has been a PhD student at the at the University of Bamberg since May 2020. During her PhD, she works at the Macroeconomic Policy Institute (IMK) of the Hans-Böckler-Foundation in Düsseldorf where she is involved in research projects on government investment and fiscal policy. ORCID: https://orcid.org/0000-0003-1193-7950

Atanas Kolev is Principal Advisor at the Economics Department of the EIB. He has worked on a wide range of topics related to investment and investment financing at the firm-, sector-, and economy-wide levels. He has been an organiser and contributor to the annual economics conference of the EIB on topics like economic and social cohesion, investment in the energy sector, adaptation to climate change, public investment, and infrastructure investment. Atanas Kolev is currently a coordinator, reviewer, and economics editor for the EIB *Annual Investment Report*. He holds an Economics PhD from Universitat Autònoma de Barcelona.

Andreas Lichtenberger is Economist at the WIIW and a doctoral student at The New School in New York. He is interested in macroeconomic and fiscal policy analysis, ecological economics, inequality, and issues of economic development. In the past he worked as research and teaching assistant at The New School and Barnard College

/ Columbia University and gained professional experience at The World Bank, the Austrian Financial Market Authority (FMA), and in a development project in Ecuador. ORCID: https://orcid.org/0000-0001-7681-4914

Marcello Messori holds the Poste Italiane Chair in 'European Economy and European Economic Governance' at the Department of Economics and Finance, LUISS University (expiring at the end of November 2023). He is the coordinator of a group of advisers for the European Parliament and co-coordinator of the 'Gruppo Europa' at Astrid Foundation. He has been a visiting Professor at European Universities (Sciences-Po, Paris; Paris-X Nanterre; LATAPSES, Université de Nice) and a visiting scholar at several USA, Irish, and Australian Universities (mainly MIT and Stanford University). He has published more than two hundred and fifty works in Italian, English, French, and German. In recent years, his field of works has focused on the economic governance of the European Union, particularly its financial and economic policy problems. Messori has been the coordinator of national and international research groups, and he has been involved in various institutional activities. In this last respect, he has been president of the Italian Railways company and president of the Italian association of asset management (Assogestioni). Currently, he is president of Allianz Bank.

Maria Nikolaidi is an Associate Professor in Economics at the University of Greenwich. She is also a Fellow at the Forum for Macroeconomics and Macroeconomic Policies (FMM). Her research areas include macrofinancial policies, ecological macroeconomics, and financial fragility. Her work has been published in peer-reviewed journals, including the *Cambridge Journal of Economics, Ecological Economics*, the *Journal of Financial Stability*, the *Journal of Economic Surveys,* and *Structural Change and Economic Dynamics*. She has worked on research projects on ecological macroeconomic modelling, the greening of monetary policy, and the links between income distribution and growth. She is a member of the committee of the Post-Keynesian Economics Society (PKES) and a Trustee of the Foundation for European Economic Development (FEED). ORCID: https://orcid.org/0000-0002-8188-5482

Pier Carlo Padoan has been the Italian Minister of Economy and Finance and a Member of the Chamber of Deputies of the Italian Republic. Since April 2021, he has held the role of Chairman at UniCredit. He is Full Professor of Economics retired at the La Sapienza University of Rome. Currently, he is Vice President of Istituto Affari Internazionali, a board member of the Institute of International Finance, a member of the Luiss Institute for European Analysis and Policy, and a member of the BoD and Executive Committee of ABI. In 2021, Padoan was also appointed a member of the Board of Istituto Luigi Einaudi and of the Committee for Corporate Governance of Borsa Italiana. He is currently a member of the European Financial Services Round Table and of the Executive Committee of Assonime. In May 2022, he became Chairperson of the High Level Group on Financing Sustainability Transition, which is part of the High

Level Groups on EU Policy and Innovation. He has been Deputy Secretary General and Chief Economist of OECD and Executive Director of the International Monetary Fund. He has held academic positions at the University of Rome, College of Europe (Bruges and Warsaw); Université Libre de Bruxelles, University of Urbino; Universidad de la Plata; Chulalongkorn University; and the University of Tokyo.

Elisa Palagi is a Postdoctoral Researcher at the Institute of Economics at Scuola Superiore Sant'Anna in Pisa, Italy. She is also a Fellow of the World Inequality Lab (WIL) of the Paris School of Economics. She holds a PhD in Economics from Scuola Superiore Sant'Anna. Her research interests focus on economic inequality, in particular its relation with macroeconomic dynamics and climate change, both from an empirical and a theoretical point of view through the development of agent-based models. ORCID: https://orcid.org/0000-0002-9023-8308

Atanas Pekanov has been an economist at the Austrian Institute of Economic Research (WIFO) since 2017. He has also served as the Deputy Prime Minister for EU Funds of the Republic of Bulgaria in a number of technic governments (May – December 2021; August 2022 – May 2023) and was in charge of Cohesion Policy and the National Recovery and Resilience Plan. His main research interests are monetary and fiscal policy, EMU architecture, and cohesion policy in the EU. He previously worked at the European Central Bank and was selected twice as a scholarship holder of the Bulgarian National Bank (2015, 2019). He holds a Bachelor's degree in Economics from the Vienna University of Economics and Business and an M.Sc. in Economic Policy from the University College London. In 2019, Atanas won a Fulbright Scholarship and attended the Economics Department of Harvard University. He is currently also a lecturer and PhD candidate at the Vienna University of Economics and Business.

Francisco Perez is Professor Emeritus at the Universitat the València and Research Director of the Ivie. He graduated with special honours and received the National Graduation Award. He obtained his PhD in Economics at the Universitat de València, where he was Professor of Economics from 1986 to 2020. He has directed numerous studies on economic growth and international integration, competitiveness, regional economics, economics of education, and public finance. He is author of 89 books and over 200 book chapters and articles published in specialized journals, that have been quoted more than 7,600 times, reaching an H-index of 40. He has participated in over one hundred research projects, is a regular lecturer at many public and private institutions, and has participated in scientific meetings in over 50 universities and research centres in Europe and America. He is member of several academic associations, various boards of trustees and scientific councils of foundations dedicated to promoting research, and of the commission of experts for the economic reforms of Public Administrations. He has been an Eisenhower Fellow since 1998. In 2010, Perez was awarded the eighth Societat Catalana d'Economia Prize and, in 2016, he received the

Francesc de Vinatea distinction, the highest recognition from the Valencian Parliament. ORCID: https://orcid.org/0000-0003-4724-3598

Mathieu Plane is a Deputy Director of the Analysis and Forecasting Department at the OFCE Research Center in Economics, Sciences Po (Paris). He is in charge of economic forecasts for the French economy and works on economic policy issues. He teaches at Sciences Po, Paris and at the University of Paris Pantheon-Sorbonne. He was, in 2013–14, economic advisor to the Ministers of Economy, Industry, and the Digital Sector. He has recently published, in collaboration with other authors of OFCE, an analysis of fiscal measures and purchasing power in France in 2022 and 2023; *Under the Threat of Unemployment: Economic Outlook for the French Economy 2023–2024*, and *French Economy 2024* by Éditions La Découverte, Repères collection.

Debora Revoltella has been Director of the Economics Department of the European Investment Bank since April 2011. The department comprises thirty economists and provides economic analysis and studies to support the bank in defining its policies and strategies. Before joining the EIB, Debora worked for many years at CESEE, was head of the research department in COMIT, and later worked as Chief Economist for CESEE in UniCredit. Debora holds a PhD in Economics and has also worked as Adjunct Professor at Bocconi University. She is a member of the Steering Committees of the Vienna Initiative and CompNet, an alternate member of the Board of the Joint Vienna Institute, and a member of the boards of SUERF and the Euro 50 Group.

Katja Rietzler is Head of the Unit of Fiscal Policy at the Macroeconomic Policy Institute (IMK), part of the Hans-Böckler Foundation. She holds a PhD from the Freie Universität, Berlin. Her research focuses, among other topics, on fiscal issues of the municipalities, the German tax system, public-investment needs, and fiscal rules. In addition, she is responsible for the IMK's macroeconometric model. She regularly participates in parliamentary hearings as an expert on issues such as tax legislation, annual budgets, and the debt brake.

Andrea Roventini is a full professor of economics at the Institute of Economics of Scuola Superiore Sant'Anna and a research fellow at OFCE, Sciences Po (Paris). He holds a PhD in Economics and Management from Scuola Superiore Sant'Anna. His main research interests include complex system analysis, agent-based computational economics, business cycles, economic growth, and the effects of monetary, fiscal, technology, innovation, and climate-change policies. He is currently the unit leader and coordinator of the EEIST project (https://eeist.co.uk) financed by the UK's Department for Business, Energy and Industrial Strategy (BEIS) and the Children's Investment Fund Foundation (CIFF). He has been the principal investigator and consortium coordinator of the Horizon 2020 GROWINPRO project (http://www.growinpro.eu), and he has been involved in the projects IMPRESSIONS, DOLFINS, and ISIGrowth financed by the European Commission. He is editor of *Industrial and Corporate Chance – Macro*

Economics and Development and advisory editor of the *Journal of Evolutionary Economics*. ORCID: https://orcid.org/0000-0001-5518-3084

Francesco Saraceno is Deputy Department Director at OFCE, the research centre in economics at Sciences Po in Paris. He holds PhDs in Economics from Columbia University and the Sapienza University of Rome. His research focuses on the relationship between inequality, macroeconomic performance, and European macroeconomic policies. From 2000 to 2002, he was a member of the Council of Economic Advisors for the Italian Prime Minister's Office. He teaches international and European macroeconomics at Sciences Po, where he manages the Economics concentration of the Master's in European Affairs, and at Luiss in Rome. He is Academic Director of the Sciences Po-Northwestern European Affairs Program. He advises the International Labour Organisation (ILO) on macroeconomic policies for employment and participates in IMF training programmes on fiscal policy. ORCID: https://orcid.org/0000-0003-0121-4329

Jochen Schantz is Senior Economist at the European Investment Bank. After completing a PhD in game theory at the European University Institute, he worked at Lehman Brothers, the Bank of England, and the Bank for International Settlements on monetary and financial stability. At the European Investment Bank, he focuses on public investment and human capital.

Margit Schratzenstaller has been Senior Economist at the Austrian Institute of Economic Research (WIFO) since 2003; she was Deputy Director of WIFO from 2006 to 2008 and 2015 to 2019. Schratzenstaller-Altzinger is a member of the Austrian Fiscal Council and the board of ÖGfE – the Austrian Society for European Politics. She is alsoa member of the Scientific Advisory Board of the Vienna Climate Council and of the board of trustees of the European Forum Alpbach and the KDZ–Centre for Administrative Research. Her areas of expertise include (European) tax and budget policy, EU budget, green fiscal reform, family policy, and gender budgeting. She has prepared numerous studies for the European Parliament and the European Commission as well as national clients. After studying economics at the University of Gießen (Dipl.-Oec., PhD) and the University of Wisconsin-Milwaukee (MA (Econ)), she was a post-doc at the DFG-funded Research Training Group 'Future of the European Social Model' at the University of Göttingen.

Annamaria Tueske is an Economist in the Economics Department of the EIB. Her current work focuses on public investment, climate and energy economics, and sustainable finance. Prior to joining the EIB, Annamaria worked at the University of Luxembourg, at the OECD, and at the Fiscal Council of Hungary. Her academic training focused on industrial organisation, networks, and transport economics; she graduated from the Toulouse School of Economics.

Andrew Watt is Head of the Unit of European Economic Policy at the Macroeconomic Policy Institute (IMK), part of the Hans-Böckler Foundation. He holds a PhD from the University of Hamburg. His main research fields are European economic and employment policy and comparative political economy, with a particular interest in the interaction between wage-setting and macroeconomic policy. Recent work has focused on reform of the economic governance of the euro area, emphasising the need to coordinate monetary, fiscal, and wage policy in order to achieve balanced growth and favourable employment outcomes. He has served as advisor to numerous European and national institutions, including the European Commission, the European Economic and Social Committee, and Eurofound.

Laurent Zylberberg is General Controller at the French Caisse des Dépôts et Consignations (CDC). He holds PhD in Sociology at Sciences Po (Paris) and a Master's degree in Law from Paris-Sorbonne University. After acting as a political adviser for French Ministers between 1988 and 1993, he was social counsellor at the French Embassy in London. He worked for many years in the telecom sector before joining CDC in 2014; there he oversaw international and public affairs until 2023. He also chaired the European Long-Term Investors Association between 2016 and 2023.

List of Figures

List of Tables

About the Team

Alessandra Tosi was the managing editor for this book.

Jennifer Moriarty proof-read this book.

Cover was designed by Jeevanjot Kaur Nagpal.

Jeremy Bowman typeset the book in InDesign and produced the paperback, hardback and EPUB editions. The text font is Tex Gyre Pagella; the heading font is Californian FB.

Cameron Craig produced the PDF, HTML, and XML editions.

This book has been anonymously peer-reviewed by experts in their field. We thank them for their invaluable help.

This book need not end here...

Share

All our books — including the one you have just read — are free to access online so that students, researchers and members of the public who can't afford a printed edition will have access to the same ideas. This title will be accessed online by hundreds of readers each month across the globe: why not share the link so that someone you know is one of them?

This book and additional content is available at:

https://doi.org/10.11647/OBP.0386

Donate

Open Book Publishers is an award-winning, scholar-led, not-for-profit press making knowledge freely available one book at a time. We don't charge authors to publish with us: instead, our work is supported by our library members and by donations from people who believe that research shouldn't be locked behind paywalls.

Why not join them in freeing knowledge by supporting us:

https://www.openbookpublishers.com/support-us

You may also be interested in:

Greening Europe
2022 European Public Investment Outlook
Floriana Cerniglia and Francesco Saraceno (editors)
https://doi.org/10.11647/OBP.0328

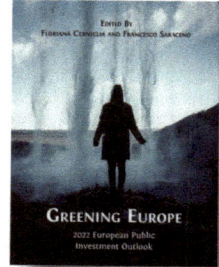

A European Public Investment Outlook
Floriana Cerniglia and Francesco Saraceno (editors)
https://doi.org/10.11647/OBP.0222

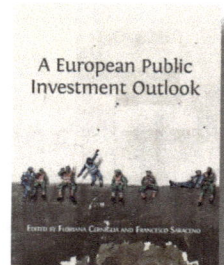

Having Too Much
Philosophical Essays on Limitarianism
Ingrid Robeyns (editor)
https://doi.org/10.11647/OBP.0338

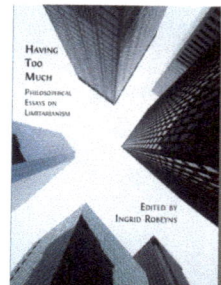

www.ingramcontent.com/pod-product-compliance
Lightning Source LLC
Chambersburg PA
CBHW050236220326
41598CB00044B/7415